"Laurie Kanyer meets you precisely where you are and gently arms you with the skills and knowledge to help you on your journey toward self-acceptance and awareness. She has the voice of an old friend and mentor letting you know a kinder, more generous world awaits you, and opens the windows to your inner world and galvanizes you to visit there more often."

MILLIE BARTLETT
Australia

"This groundbreaking book by Laurie Kanyer practically eliminates creative block. The diverse range of collage exercises will not only open up new creative avenues, but also helps you understand how collaging affects your mood and emotions. Gaining a deeper knowledge of how collage affects your mind and body could lead to more meaningful and powerful approaches to your collage art. If you want to explore the creative and self-development potential of collaging, this book is an invaluable resource."

LES JONES
Publisher, *Contemporary Collage Magazine*
United Kingdom

"As an artist, visual and otherwise, I've come to see collage not just as an art form or technique but as a philosophy and approach to life. We are collages, made of experiences and pieces we keep picking up over the course of our lives, and we have the ability to make and remake ourselves over and over again. Collage is the art of reinvention. This Guidebook looks at collage-making from a mental health standpoint and provides us with the necessary scientific background, explanations but also tools to make this a more conscious process. Her book will surely contribute to a more comprehensive understanding of the possibilities of collage in art therapy."

PETRA ZEHNER
Founder, Paris Collage Collective
France

"Insightful, informative and creative are some of the pillars of the most effective coping skills. This book is an incredible guide and a wonderfully outlined tool that we could all benefit to use, whether it be in conjunction with therapy, or as a standalone tool. A great addition to any coping skill tool box!"

EMILY SHOEMAKER, MA, LMFT, CFLE
United States

"By doing the exercise-experiences in this book you will meet, explore and understand your feelings and emotions better. And that is worth gold. The work one does using this book demonstrates courage and strength. Discoveries await you."

ANGELA GOBBENS, AKA @MISS.PRINTED
founder of The Scandinavian Collage Museum, The Collage Club, and The Collage Garden,
Co-founder of Februllage and the inventor of Locative Collage
Norway

"With decades of applied experience using collage as a tool of healing and transformation in her counseling practice, (Kanyer) presents her findings and wisdom here in self-guided 'collage-making exercise-experiences' that anyone can utilize towards transformation and emotional healing. In a manner that is both personal and engaging, Laurie knowledgeably and gently guides the reader through collage exercises that range from 'Establishing Boundaries', to 'Getting Acquainted with the Parts of Our Emotional Self'. Throughout she encourages the reader to be curious and brave while at the same looking for and expecting miracles. As a collage artist, I found the material thorough, well organized, insightful, and sensitively conveyed. The book is beautifully illustrated with quality collage examples from the Doug + Laurie Kanyer Art Collection to provide inspiration."

SCOTT GORDON, COLLAGIST
United States

"Once again, Laurie Kanyer has drawn on her considerable experience of using collage in classrooms and as part of her counseling practice in order to showcase its transformational power to the reader. Using a series of clear and easy-to-follow 'exercise-experiences', taught as a ritualized, meditative practice, Kanyer demonstrates not only the practical steps of making a collage, but its radical potential in revealing the cognitive functions of the brain."

DR. FREYA GOWRLEY
Art Historian, co-founder, Collage Research Network,
and author, *Collage Before Modernism, Cut and Paste: 400 Years of Collage*
Scotland

"This book has an invitational tone that runs throughout. It encourages the reader to listen to their intuition. So much of collage-making for me is about tuning into one's inner world and I found this to be reflected in the exercise-experiences in this book. I enjoy the balance between skills-based activity and opportunities to develop tools to bolster your emotional well-being. It's a deep and considered book that presents many of the emotional benefits of art making without necessarily being art therapy. An accessible and exciting collage-focused work."

CATHERINE ROGERS
Artist specializing in collage and prison arts programs
United Kingdom

"Laurie's many years of therapeutic practice have given her huge knowledge and experience of peoples' emotional needs. Laurie's genuine, warm, supportive and encouraging presence comes through at every stage to support the user in getting to know themselves better and find better mental harmony and balance. The exercises contained in this Guidebook allow the user to use the collage making process to work on their own emotional journey and find their own truths. This book is thoughtfully written, handsomely designed and is richly illustrated with beautiful collages to inspire the reader."

MIRANDA MILLWARD
Collagist and Museum Learning Specialist
United Kingdom

"If you are wanting to improve your overall quality of life and truly enjoy the art of making collage, then this book is for you. You will learn the art of guided collage, something anyone can learn, and by doing so your mind will change in ways you can't imagine. Laurie has written this guidebook so that the reader moves through each module, learning the exercises at their own pace and choosing ones that are relevant to their needs. As a collagist, I can tell you firsthand that this practice has changed my life. I invite everyone to buy this book and start the journey of finding the real you."

KIM HAMBURG
Collagist
United States

"When life hands you lemons, make a collage! This book helps you to not only understand how your emotions and feelings actually work in your brain, but to understand, process and overcome them as well, using the easy to follow and inventive collage exercises. Laurie Kanyer explains the information and the exercises really well and the gorgeous collages shown in this book are very inspiring. So buy this book, grab your glue, scissors and paper and experience the many benefits of making collages."

JULIETTE PESTEL
Collage Artist, Art Teacher
The Netherlands

"I've long been aware of the meditative and calming effects that come from making collages; it's one of the reasons I love collage so much! So it was very exciting to understand why collage has this effect in Laurie's previous book, Collage Care. In this new Guidebook, she takes these ideas a step further through simple exercises which help the reader be more introspective and intentional, making collage a beautiful tool for self-therapy."

JULIE LIGER-BELAIR
Collagist
Canada

BOOKS BY
Laurie Kanyer, MA

Collage Care: The Method (2023)

*Collage Care: Transforming Emotions and
Life Experiences with Collage (2021)*

*Twenty-Five Things to Do When Grandpa Passes Away,
Mom and Dad Get Divorced or the Dog Dies:
Helping Children Cope with Loss or Change (2004)*

*Parent Connection: Building Attachments
Between Parent and Child (1998)*

*The Journey of Becoming a Mother: Tools for a
New Mother's Emotional Growth and Development (1996)*

Collage Care:
The Method

 Written by Laurie Kanyer, MA

Co-created by CP Harrison
Edited by Doug Kanyer
Designed by JuSt Design - Nela Sheppard
Content curated by Celia Crane and Sarah Best
Proofread by Dawn Kugler
Cover art by Laurie Kanyer

First Edition

Published by Kanyer Publishing
Yakima, Washington, USA

2023

Laurie Kanyer, *Lets Fly for Ten Months* , 2022, Analog Collage, Doug + Laurie Kanyer Art Collection

Dedication

When new members enter into the family constellation, a spirit of change and transformation occurs. The hope is that every addition brings with it a presence that enhances the whole. So it is with the three people to whom this book is dedicated.

We have been blessed by the addition of Andy Dahlhauser and Rishi Mistry to our family. Both of these men have brought a tone of calm, quiet strength. Their intelligence and their commitment to caring for themselves and the family is extraordinary.

During the writing of this book our granddaughter Cecily Ann Kanyer Dahlhauser was born. She absolutely glows. It is our hope that she will live in a world that knows more about emotional well-being and seeing feelings as helpers.

"Putting something over something else."

— Romare Bearden

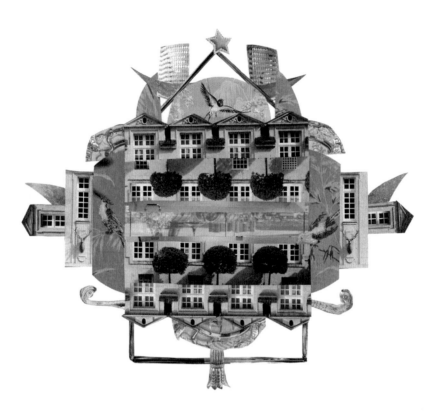

Laurie Kanyer, *Mirror*, 2022, Analog Collage, Doug + Laurie Kanyer Art Collection

CONTENTS

FEATURED ARTISTS

You will find in this book a number of fine art collages made by Collagists from all over the world.
All of the artists featured herein are represented in the Doug + Laurie Kanyer Art Collection.
The Collection is one of very few collections in the world focusing exclusively on collage.
For more on the Collection see: KanyerArtCollection.com.

Agnieszka Zając - United Kingdom - Poland
Anthony Grant - California, United States
Antonio Guerra Álvarez - Spain
Ateljewjlhelm - Germany
Beverly West Leach - Alabama, United States
Carol White - Ireland - United States
Celia Crane - New York, United States
Clive Knights - Oregon, United States - England
CP Harrison - Texas, United States
Daphna Epstein - Florida, United States
Diane L Davis - Alabama, United States
Dorothée Mesander - Greece - The Netherlands
Edina Picco - Italy - Croatia - Germany
Elise Margolis - New York, United States
Emma Anna - Australia
Eve Baldry - United Kingdom
Frances Ryan - Scotland
Fred Free - Massachusetts, United States
Jack Felice - Florida, United States
Jack Ravi - Scotland
Jake Kennedy - United Kingdom
Jennifer Dykeman - Missouri, United States
Kathy Starr - Washington, United States
Lana Turner - Scotland
Laurence Briat - France
Laurie Kanyer - Washington, United States
Lee McKenna - Australia
Les Jones - United Kingdom
Liliana Lalanne - Argentina
Lisa Drake - United Kingdom

Liza Petrides - Cyprus
Luciana Frigerio - Vermont, United States
Liberty Blake - Utah, United States
Lisbeth Søgård-Høyer - Denmark
Marcus Dawson - North Carolina, United States
Mauricio Mo - Mexico
Michael DeSutter - California, United States
Michelle Parchini - Texas, United States
Millie Bartlett - Australia
Miranda Millward - United Kingdom
Molly McCracken - Virginia, United States
Monique Vettraino - Canada
Native - Belgium
Nick Baccari aka Mr. Babies - Arizona, United States
Niko Vartiainen - Finland
Oliver Lunn - United Kingdom
Petra Zehner - France
Riikka Fransila - Finland
Rocio Romero - Spain
Sarah Best - Oregon, United States
Sarah Perkins - United Kingdom
Scott Gordon - California, United States
Sonia Boué - United Kingdom
Susan Lerner - New York, United States
Susan Ringer - United States
Torea Frey - Oregon, USA
Twiggy Boyer - North Carolina, United States
Zoë Heath - United Kingdom
Zohra Hussain - England

Scott Gordon, *Birdsong*, 2021, Analog Collage, Doug + Laurie Kanyer Art Collection

PROLOGUE

by Scott Gordon, MA, Collagist and Writer *aka scottgordonpaperman*

Paper is the most compelling of cultural artifacts. It is at once fragile and delicate yet also strong and resilient (a mirror perhaps of our own condition?). It is forgiving in nature, warm and receptive. It is inexpensive, easy to store, easy to mark, and easy to crumble, rip, shred, cut, fold, and tear. It can be glossy and crisp or faded and worn. It endures and it disintegrates.

And it is everywhere. It is an indispensable part of everyday life. It is so common and utilitarian in fact, that we have become desensitized to it and have taken it for granted. It can even be seen as a nuisance.

Ultimately though, it provides a glimpse into the sum of our past and of our current condition. It is a record of our need for reckoning while at the same time providing an accounting of those lives that have faded from view.

Whether it be declarations of love or articulations of business transactions or scientific theories, paper announces that "we were here, and this is how we figured our place in the world."

As such, it is never silent. It is always communicating. It is "stained with our humanity."

Even so, the discarded fragments are the most compelling. They speak of ruin and decay while at the same time speaking of nobility because they have withstood the ravages of time to arrive here in their tattered state of mystery. While most of them have long since lost the context of their making and meaning, there remains an inherent beauty in their quiet un-wholeness.

Working with paper thus becomes a form of remembrance, not of a specific memory per se, but of memory in general – of the fragmented stories that have long since settled in the dust. It is a testimony to our hope and assertion that our being here may have yet mattered, or at the very least sparkled briefly in the vast shimmering of the stars.

FOREWORD

by Sonia Boué, Artist-Activist and Writer with a background in Art Therapy and Art History

"…to hold as 'twere the mirror up to nature…" — William Shakespeare, *Hamlet*

Collage Care: The Method—a book for our times. This book is a rare gem. As we turn the pages we find stunningly beautiful collage works and "exercise-experiences" in which the art of *Collage Care: The Method* holds a mirror to human nature. Laurie Kanyer demonstrates exceptional care for her readers in this highly original publication which outlines a meticulously researched self-care methodology par excellence.

Therapeutic expertise underpins her step-by-step approach to creative self-discovery using the Collage Care model. The writing is intimate and we find ourselves peering into the consulting rooms in which the "exercise-experiences" have been honed. It is truly humbling to imagine the very many transformative encounters facilitated in these spaces. This book is thus a testimony to Laurie's extensive therapeutic practice, securing it for generations to come. It is an extraordinary legacy and a labour of love.

Therapeutic spaces act as sanctuaries for the soul. The hurly burly of the everyday is paused and the complexities of our emotional lives can be met with unaccustomed attention. This book allows for such reflection, while also providing guide rails in the form of detailed prompts for self-care along the way. It is a timely publication for our angst-ridden and uncertain world.

Laurie provides the means to conjure spaces for healing and transformation at home or in the studio. It is telling that many (myself included) turned to collage during the global pandemic, as the world around us closed down and we sought sanctuary within our own walls. Indeed, Collage Care proved synergistic with my Arts Council England funded project, Neurophototherapy (2021), prompting me to research the model and cite Laurie's first volume *Collage Care: Transforming Emotions and Life Experiences with Collage* in my project evaluations.

I have also drawn deeply on a Collage Care practice in my own life and work as an artist-activist. It now forms a vital daily self-care ritual, and I have used it to soothe visceral anxiety and bouts of grief. It has also brought insight, joy and connection. I have learned that there need be no separation between art and life, and that emotional transformations can be enacted wherever a table top is at hand.

Collage Care: The Method offers a way through. This is because Laurie is gifted with an uncanny ability to deconstruct emotional processes in ways which are clear and enabling. She therefore decodes the emotional world in the exact manner many people may require (and indeed long for). *Collage Care: The Method* is both a pragmatic support and a philosophy, in the sense that it offers a way of processing and understanding the world. Inclusion is all about the right kind of welcome. Laurie understands this perfectly, welcoming all comers to draw up a chair, set up a simple worktop, and get making. *Collage Care: The Method* can offer blissful doses of downtime, becoming a go-to ritual for decompression. Practiced over time, I have found it can also become a radical act of self-love.

This book helps all kinds of brains. It takes all kinds of brains to make a world, and there's an in-built flex to Laurie's method which welcomes all. As a neurodivergent creative and consultant, I can attest to some of the particular benefits of *Collage Care: The Method* from a neurodivergent perspective. Laurie's crystalline clarity has enabled my 'wayward' brain to follow step-by-step instructions, while also granting the freedom to interpret the exercises in my own way.

In my experience neurodivergence is not at all uncommon. We now also include many allied conditions under this umbrella term. In truth, we may all at some point in our lives struggle cognitively, be it as a result of emotional trauma, or through an acquired injury or illness. Neurodivergence can be understood as comprising multiple variations and challenges in our neurological functioning, which may also cause difficulty in the area of emotional regulation. I see great potential for neurodivergent people to benefit from *Collage Care: The Method*, particularly when it comes to processing. For example, events and emotions can feel disconnected, and it can be challenging to locate what "a something" is (as Laurie puts it). We may feel overwhelmed and unable to untangle our emotions when faced with the infinite complexity of human interactions. Laurie Kanyer's brilliance is to lay it out so completely for those who need structure. Those who don't can freestyle it and play. *Collage Care: The Method* arrives as a blessing in turbulent times and forms an essential companion to Laurie's first *Collage Care* publication.

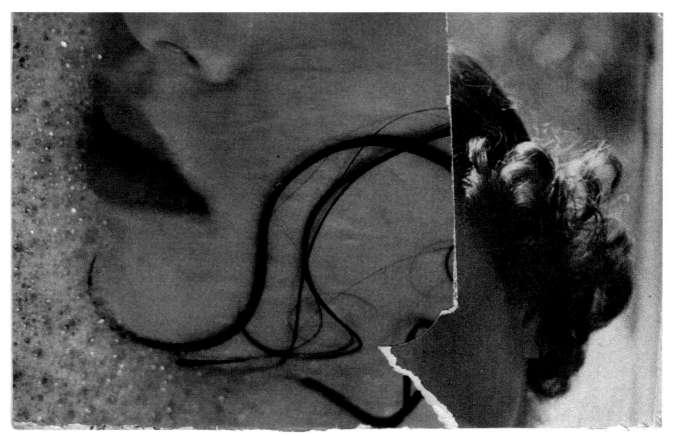

Sonia Boué, *Situation update*, 2022, Analog Collage, Courtesy of the Artist

Laurie Kanyer, collage-making process

PREFACE

Welcome! We are glad you are here.

Are you curious about your emotions and feelings? Have you occasionally wondered about why you feel the way you do? Are you looking for ways to solve challenging "somethings" that pop up, or to get along better with others? You are not alone. Now, like never before, people are exploring their emotional selves and seeking ways to be emotionally healthy.

You should know that this is not a surprising development. Emotions and feelings play such a large role in the quality of one's life. Allow me to extend my thanks and congratulations, as you have come to the right place to learn more about your emotional self and to gain a deeper knowledge about your emotions, feelings and life experiences.

How It Began - Using Collage-Making in a High School Class Out of Necessity

In the mid-1980s, while on staff at a community college, my department chair asked if I would be willing to teach a high school course in child psychology. The college had a partnership with the local school district and they needed an expert to fill in a few sections. It happened to be at the high school from which I had graduated and so I jumped at the opportunity.

My enthusiasm for the opportunity waned a bit when I discovered the class had no textbook or curriculum. Class was to begin in five days. With no time to spare, I formed a syllabus and gathered all of the magazines I could find. My thought was the students could use collage-making to further their learnings on the topics I planned to teach.

The Method was Developed by Accident

I developed a preset daily class format knowing the material we would cover would touch on sensitive topics. I decided to use a predictable format as a foundation to explore potent and tender materials. My suspicion was that those who took this class were curious on a personal level as well as academic about the emotional, psychological world of humans, namely children. I knew that if they experienced a predictable routine in the class it would ease their spirits, allowing them to explore and consider the lessons. This predictable format is the exact model you will experience in this book.

Following this preset pattern, I would ask my students at the end of every class period to reflect on the lesson of the day. What did they learn? How did they feel? What did they think about the topic? For their answer, they could choose to either use collage-making or write a brief reflection paper. Most did both, but collage-making was preferred by the majority. The course was an elective and many of the teens had learning hardships, some were in chemical dependency recovery, and others were overachievers who needed less school work. Because of this mix, I wanted to avoid assigning out-of-class homework.

One thing all of these students had in common was they had too much on their plate, with extra-curricular activities, part-time jobs, or difficulties at home. I simply devised a quick and effective method for them to document their learnings in class and to get their thoughts and feelings out as it related to the daily lessons. I wanted to decrease their load. I was just nine years out of high school myself, so I could remember, and empathized.

Surprising results and outcomes emerged. There were impressive transformations.

When it came time for tests a majority of the students achieved above a B, and no one failed. All of the students passed the course with the lowest grade of a C. Compliance with the daily reflection activity was one-hundred percent. Everyone took part. Students began to bring magazines to contribute to the source material pile. Attendance at the class, which was held early in the day, was high. Their grades in my class were higher than in other courses they took part in.

The difference? The use of collage-making to mark their learnings, process their ideas, and express their emotions and feelings. Some years later, I learned many of those students would become therapists, medical professionals, educators and school principals. Some became parents in short order.

Using Collage-Making with Adults

Later, I worked with pregnant and parenting adults who were experiencing poverty and other associated hardships. They were receiving government-backed financial aid grants. They attended my groups three times a week, two hours each session, and took part in individual counseling sessions with me outside of the group setting. I also offered case management, which allowed me to go with them to appointments and teach them skills to access the things they needed. It was an intense program.

Much like the high school class, each of the in-group sessions followed a preset format consisting of the exact same components each time we met. These sessions were two hours long so I was able to expand the model. The format for the first hour consisted of an opening welcome, reviewing of set ground rules, a thought-provoking introductory question, and then a time of them sharing their individual celebrations and concerns. We tapped into the wisdom of the group using Suggestion Circle to help resolve their concerns (see page 199 for how to do Suggestion Circle).

In the second hour, I made a short presentation, just as I did in the high school classroom. This presentation consisted of an opening quote, a mini-lesson, and a content roundup of the major points of the lesson. They then used collage-making as a way to reflect, contemplate, and document their learnings. We finished each session with a closing quote.

I rotated between having the parents make a collage in response to the lesson (as my high school students did) or more often I provided a step-by-step, guided collage-making exercise-experience related to the topic (like those featured in this book). There was a time for sharing their collage if they were comfortable. We ended with them expressing any resentment or appreciations they had of our time together. I frequently added other tools aimed to assist them. The Takeaway Action Tools on page 226 are the exact tools I used.

Collage-making in this setting was instrumental, as many of the women had learning challenges and most of their responses needed to be kept confidential. I had written a book on childhood grief and loss, where I documented the value of modulating and pacing the hormonal energy of the brain connected to grief. I knew collage-making would help them. With collage-making they could communicate their ideas and reduce their energetic/emotional stress.

The Outcome was Remarkable

The state of Washington does an annual review of their goals and intended outcomes for the programs they funded, with the overarching goal of parents securing employment. Their statewide study of like-programs aimed to gauge the effectiveness of these programs. The study showed my program had a 19% success rate, compared to 2% for other programs. While these numbers are shockingly low, as there are many barriers for this demographic to obtain employment, it is clear my program was more effective.

Surprising results and outcomes once again emerged. There were impressive transformations.

The difference? Once more, the answer was the use of collage-making to mark their learnings and process their ideas, to express their emotions and feelings. Years later, many of the women have on-going employment, many went on to complete high school, some went on to college. Their interpersonal skills improved and their self-efficacy was enhanced.

Collage-Making, as Opposed to Making a Fine Art Collage

It is important to mention that I used the process of collage-making in my instructional and therapeutic background. And by collage-making, I mean cutting, pasting, and tearing paper and then gluing it to another piece of paper. We were not making "fine art" collages. My theory was that the act and process of collage-making offered unique benefits that would help, heal and transform many emotional, cognitive, communication and behavioral aspects for my clients. I was not having them make fine art collages, which could elicit comparison and critique, or harken back to earlier life experiences of making art. And while likely connected in both form and function, this was not intentional, traditional, art therapy.

Decades of Using Collage-Making with Amazing Results

I spent decades facilitating the use of collage-making as a tool to explore tender and potent topics related to being a human. In every case it provided a way to ease the magnitude of those tender topics, which include emotions, feelings, communication hardships, gaining cooperation with kids and adults and more. The students and clients did not have to worry about spelling and penmanship. They could express their thoughts, document their learnings, and mark their feelings on a topic with an image, rather than in writing. Often what they made was beautiful, eloquent and authentic.

Due to the limited time in the classroom or group counseling session, the resulting collages often had an immediate, focused feel and look to them. The elements were chosen with thought and intention. They had a visual tone of force, power and resolute knowing. The idea was to get their point across directly within the time restraints. Many had a visual feel similar to the art of noted collagist Fred Free (see a Fred Free collage on page 27).

Using Collage-Making Myself

I later took up collage-making when a sudden emotional jolt occurred in my own life. I had made collage most of my life, in the form of scrapbooks, however making a fully-formed collage in response to a "small t" trauma was a new application for me. I have made hundreds of them since that time. I use collage-making now as an intentional self-care tool to help, heal and transform my life. Eventually, I reached out to the international collage world to collaborate and look for ways to amplify and magnify collage in art history.

Collage Collection Amplifying Fine Art Collage

My husband Doug and I have been art collectors since the late 1970's. For a majority of that time we collected the works of artists from our local area (see KanyerArtCollection.com). That shifted gears in 2016. Having fallen in love with the medium of collage, we committed to collecting collage exclusively. The goal was to uplift the medium from a fine art perspective and expand it in art history. We began to buy collages internationally. I had many conversations with collagists from all over the world. I began to share what I knew about collage-making as a helping, healing and transformational tool.

Conversations with Collagists Internationally

Perhaps because they learned I was a counselor and educator, collagists have quite naturally shared with me how and when they came to make collage. Almost to a person, it appeared they came to make collages after or during a time of great life strain. A measurable, challenging "something" had taken place in their life and they spontaneously seemed to take to cutting or tearing magazines, and then gluing paper-to-paper.

Some were established fine artists, who had attended art school. Others were serious hobbyists, who found they had some talent and ended up making collage as a vocation, rather than simply for fun. What they had in common was turning to collage-making during a measurable crisis or serious life event.

To confirm this observation I conducted a study. I asked participants this question: "Was there a "something", a person, place, event, circumstance or situation that caused you to begin to collage?" Of the 80 people who took part in the study, 78 reported that a significant life event, a "something", ignited them to begin to use collage-making.

Curiosity About How Collage-Making Helps, Heals and Transforms

Eventually the artists in the Collection were very curious about what I knew about how collage-making helps, heals and transforms lives. One artist in-particular, Andrea Burgay, urged me to write a book. Having written books in the past I was very hesitant, as book-writing is laborious and is complicated by my being dyslexic.

She suggested I start by making a simple list. I did so, and by the end of the day I had 55 ways collage-making helps, heals and transforms. Later another 70 ways came forth. That list became the Gems featured in the book *Collage Care, Transforming Emotions, Feelings and Life Experiences with Collage* (2021). Essentially it documented, with empirical evidence, that my theory that collage-making when used as an intervention helps, heals and transforms. Indeed, many of the people in my study said "Collage saved my life."

A Book was Born

During the COVID-19 pandemic I set out to actually write this book. It was to consist of a collection of exercise-experiences that were based on the exact format and model from my classes, individual counseling sessions and groups. The collagist and painter CP Harrison joined this project and tested all the exercise-experiences I wrote. Harrison is not only an artist, but a counselor for the American Cancer Society. Many of his fine art collages are featured in this book.

That plan got side-tracked due to the pandemic. I knew collage helps, heals and transforms. I decided that I would first publish the evidence, the Gems, on how collage helped (see a brief summary in the Appendix on page 231). The exercise-experiences would have to wait.

My hope was that collagists, in reading the Gems, would continue to keep using collage-making during this world-wide crisis. I believed if they kept using collage-making they would be well, or better off, than if they did not make collages. And I hoped to convince other people who found themselves in crisis due to COVID to start to use collage-making.

This Book

Once the evidence (the 125 Gems) of how collage helps was published, I returned to editing the exercise-experiences that are featured here, specifically in this book. In all, I have written over 100 exercise-experiences that have followed the same method and model I used for decades. This book features the basic 30. My husband Doug joined in this book project as the editor, and we continued with the design team of JuSt Designs which is headed by Nela Sheppard.

Where We Are Now - Collage Care: The Method

My son Wyatt Kanyer is also a therapist. After he helped to edit *Collage Care*, he pointed out that I had created a model-method using a specific intervention, collage-making. This had not occurred to me, but it was true.

Out of necessity I had accidentally developed a theory. I had tested and practiced the theory. I developed and proved the model. I had studied the impact of the theory and used the model for decades. And in 2021, I published the findings of decades of study in *Collage Care, Transforming Emotions, Feelings and Life Experiences with Collage (2021).*

He encouraged me to document the theory and model, which I did, and I now call it *Collage Care: The Method.*

Collage Care: The Method in Action

This book is *Collage Care: The Method* in action for your personal use. It is offered here in an educational format presented in self-guided, collage-making, exercise-experiences. They are presented in separate, educational, self-care modules. As you do the exercise-experiences in this book you are using the same format and with the same care others have received for decades.

Using these patterned exercise-experiences, which incorporate collage-making, you, like those I worked with for decades, will experience healing, help and transformation. *Collage Care: The Method* does so with ease, safety and confidentiality. Using these exercise-experiences offers you greater perspective and keen insight on the trials of life. You will be gaining insight and information, in addition to life skills and deeper wisdom.

Professional Applications

Much like any known counseling model, method or educational curriculum you might use in your practice, you can use these guided collage-making exercise-experiences with those you serve. Like many of the models you already use, they can be delivered individually or in groups.

No Panacea

Having worked with people who have experienced difficult and challenging "somethings" in their life, I have found collage-making to be of great help. I have personally witnessed remarkable transformations and experienced it myself.

We live in a time of great enthusiasm and excitement about wellness and self-healing. There seem to be answers everywhere and professionals seem to have an "answer for everything". I feel it is important and moral to mention that while I know the value of this material, I also know that each one brings unique and special circumstances to this work.

Let this material be a compliment to what you are already finding helpful in your life and a tool in your tool box to move forward in life. As with any tool, it has applications for one situation and likely not another. You pick tools up and use them for a specific application, and then use others.

What is my point? It is to be humble in my claims and practical in my evangelism about this model. Be comforted to know that if you find one item here that helps, that is a success. If you find yourself using these exercise-experiences for a month, and then move to something else, that too is a success. If you adopt this as a primary mode to address life, wonderful. If you find after exploring this material that it does not resonate, keep looking. Avoid being lulled into some false sense of security that one idea, one place, one person, one model, will be the fix.

Saying that, do give this a try. Many others have gone before you and have found some special transformation.

Lisa Drake, *I am, I am (Taken from "I took a deep breath and listened to the old brag of my heart. I am, I am, I am," Sylvia Plath)*, 2022, Analog Collage in Vintage book, Doug + Laurie Kanyer Art Collection

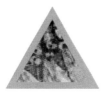

An Orientation to
Collage Care: The Method

THE LANDSCAPE OF THIS BOOK

This Guidebook contains numerous self-guided, collage-making exercise-experiences. They are translated from my in-person classroom and counseling work. For decades I used the collage-making process with students and clients. Now you can have a similar experience of your very own.

GOALS AND HOPES

The overarching hope of this material is for one to build skills, gain tools and acquire knowledge on the topics of emotions, feelings and life experiences. The ultimate goal is to transform and get to know one's True Self better.

The hope in using these collage-making exercise-experiences is to find harmony and balance in your life. Collage-making is the tool used to accomplish the goals. You will be able to improve your relationships and expand your choices about how you react to situations. The exercise-experiences are designed to fortify skills you already have, and to increase them with information and tools.

YOU ARE THE GUIDE - YOU KNOW WHAT YOU KNOW!

Before we dive into this Guidebook, I want to say with all my heart and with deep conviction that you have inside of you an inner knowing that is profound and significant. It is waiting for further discovery, fortification and honor. It is true that we all benefit from mentors, teachers and guides; their job is to offer support, information and encouragement for you to find your very path and direction. This book is one such guide, a humble one, and all of the contents are merely suggestions and ideas for you to discover.

As you explore the bits, bobbles and mechanisms of this book, please consider the following. You know, and hold it to be true, that this is your journey and the self-guided exercises are roadmaps. As with any roadmap, those on the journey make their own choices and discoveries. Even if you are on the same trip with another, their experience will be different, yet, oh so precious, from yours.

NO RIGHT OR WRONG

As you do the self-guided exercises, release yourself from any burden to do it "right" or "get it right". What is offered here is information and a thoughtful process for you to use and consider. What I have seen is how people use information and experiences to build their own understanding. You are the one who will know what is best for you. Since there has never been, nor will there ever be another one like you, what you know is right for you!

One of my great influences was author Jean Illsley Clarke. She guided, trained and mentored me, and once told me that "You are in charge of setting up a helpful process for those you serve. They are in charge of the results, their own learnings and conclusions." One of the most cherished affirmations she wrote was, "You know what you know." As you explore the Guidebook, "know what you know" and come to your own conclusions. What you come up with will be just right for you, and honored by this author.

INFORMATION IS DELIVERED IN MODULES

The exercise-experiences are offered in a modular format. By definition a module is a single bit of information designed to teach skills or offer knowledge. In some ways, this book is like a collage itself. Organized modules make it easier to locate so you can think, choose and use what you need.

Each module contains vital materials, packed with complex information presented in a simple manner, offering quick access to valuable ideas. The individual exercise-experiences are part of the modules and are like the singular elements of a collage; the end result of all the exercise-experiences is like a finished collage.

Most people need all this information and readers will benefit from taking part in them all.

KNOWLEDGE, TOOLS, SKILLS AND EXPERIENCES - PROCESS AND PRODUCT ORIENTED

This book is about transformation and change as it connects to emotions, feelings and life experiences. It is also about validating, accepting and honoring you. It is a journey. We offer you both knowledge and experiences.

This guidebook is both process - and product-oriented, for the purpose of helping you to investigate, research, and transform your emotions, feelings and life experiences. This process is designed to unfold informational insights and to create a product, a collage to document what you know and learned.

By product-oriented, I mean that once you complete an exercise-experience you will have made a tangible, physical collage on each topic. The resulting end-product is a collage that holds all your learnings, skills and experiences.

Your ending collage, in which you took part, will be the visible proof of the experience leading to transformation. The goal of each exercise-experience is to use collage to help you consider new information about your feelings, emotions and life experiences. You will be reading, cutting, pasting, arranging, creating, changing and transforming.

OVERALL BOOK ORGANIZATION
The book is divided into Five Parts:

- **Part One - Beginning - Introductory Exercise-Experiences**

- **Part Two - Exercise-Experiences on Emotions, Feelings, Moods and Memories**

- **Part Three - Exercise-Experiences on Caring for Emotions and Feelings**

- **Part Four - Exercise-Experiences to Resolve Challenges**

- **Part Five - Exercise-Experiences to Assist Interpersonal Challenges**

THE TERM "EXERCISE-EXPERIENCES"

When I talk about the exercises, I may also refer to them as an experience. Notice, as you read, the use of the term "exercise-experience". I combine the two, and here is why. All those who read and use the book exercises will receive the same exercise instructions, yet each person will have their own unique experiences. You are offered a structured exercise, with specific instructions, and you will be having an experience.

By referring to them as "exercise-experiences" I am leaving room for the outcome for each reader to be special, unique and nuanced. It is a signal to you that I am honoring how the material will unfold and unlock key life experiences for you and by you.

This Guidebook offers a thoughtful and researched process. The exercise-experiences are designed for you to have an experience to transform your life. All of the exercise-experiences are offered to improve the relationship you have with yourself and with others. They are offered to help you get through difficult circumstances by giving you skills to help you transform and change, so that you can be your True Self.

TONE

As you read these self-guided, collage-making exercise-experiences notice they are written in a friendly but succinct tone. They are similar to the recipe instructions in a cookbook. The goal is to give clear guidelines, information, and steps to accomplish a specific outcome. They are designed this way to make the process of the exercise-experience easy to follow and to achieve clarity, rather than being clinical, overbearing or dictatorial.

TWO TYPES OF MODULES

You will find herein two types of exercise-experience modules. They are designed to help you by offering skill-based tools, information and practice so you can be most effective in your life. Some of the exercise-experiences are skill-based and others more informational in nature.

SKILL-BASED MODULES

The skill-based modules offer an explanation of the skills considered most helpful to emotions, feelings and life experiences. An example is "Asking for Help or Assistance". In these modules you will get an explanation of the importance of the skill, what the skill is, and how collage-making will support the skill. You will then be presented with an exercise-experience pertaining to the skill. They are designed for you to try, return to over time, practice to gain effectiveness, and to then use the skills in your life.

KEY FOUNDATIONAL INFORMATION MODULES

Information supports people's transformation and unlocks profound opportunities. Most people did not receive formal education on the topics of emotions and feelings in school; accordingly, one can benefit from this information now. This means one's knowledge base on the core ideas about emotions and feelings could improve.

Key Foundational Information Modules provide foundational knowledge on emotions, feelings and life experience based on what we know in the present. This is a primer on these topics. You will be reading and then using collage-making to deepen your learning.

TOPICAL CONNECTION - SEQUENCE - CROSS REFERENCE

While the exercise-experiences are written as separate topical modules, many relate to one another. In some cases the exercise-experiences produce the most positive results when done in sequence. As often as possible the exercises that have a strong relationship to one another are adjacent to one another, in a specific part of the book.

For those exercise-experiences that need to be done in sequence, there will be a reminder and an explanation at the introduction of the Part. A good example of this is Part Four - Exercise-Experiences to Resolve a Challenge. However, once you have done them all in their intended sequence, feel free to return to them individually and use them on their own.

Some of the exercise-experiences make reference to content that is discussed in a deeper fashion in another exercise. To accommodate for the interconnection of some of the topics you will find easy-to-access cross reference notes. They will appear as (see page #). This will give you a chance, if you choose, to read more deeply on the topic that is cross referenced.

TAKEAWAY ACTION TOOLS

When you complete each of the exercise-experiences you will then be asked to turn to the back of the book on page 225 and find the concluding activities called Takeaway Action Tools. Contained there you will find a list of proven tools, from many traditions, known to transform and enhance the quality of life. I used them as tools with my clients for decades. All are generalized tools that will help you in most life circumstances beyond their connection to an exercise.

PREDICTABLE RITUAL-LIKE LAYOUT

Each of the modules containing the exercise-experiences follow a patterned and predictable format. They each have the exact same layout, components and design. It is vital when exploring emotions, feelings and life experiences to have a predictable and set pattern. In the in-person work I did with clients, each time we gathered, the exercises-experiences followed a set and known ritual and routine. This offered my clients and participants comfort and familiarity as they took part in exploring tender topics.

Each time you use one of the modules you will have no surprises as to how the material will be presented. Take a moment right now and scan the Contents at the beginning. Choose two chapters to compare. Notice and observe the thoughtful, predictable design.

For each exercise-experience you will be exploring unique topics. Each time you complete an exercise-experience you will then turn to the back of the book and use the Takeaway Action Tools. The Tools use ancient, proven techniques such as reflection, meditation, and contemplation to complete each exercise-experience.

INFORMATION IS REPEATED THROUGHOUT

Hermann Ebbinghaus, a pioneering psychologist, proved that for information to be remembered and used one must hear it seven times. Accordingly, key information will be repeated. It is understood that some of the content herein will be new; the value of repetition in this circumstance cannot be overstated. To help one recall and use the material, you will find repetition.

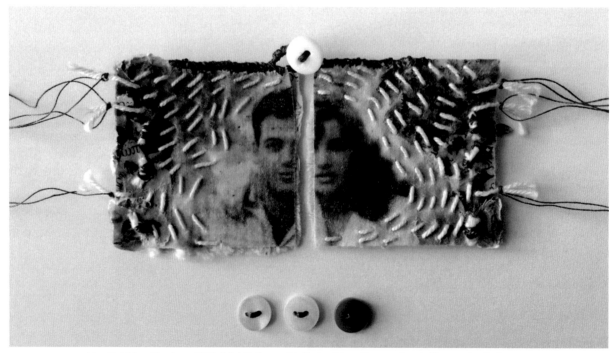

Liza Petrides, *Precious*, 2021, Mini Collage with Embroidery, Doug + Laurie Kanyer Art Collection

4

Layout of each of the
GUIDEBOOK EXERCISE-EXPERIENCE Modules

Each exercise-experience focuses on a topic related to emotions, feelings and life experiences delivered as a module. Like a collage, the exercise-experiences have multiple elements and components. The content is concise, yet in-depth. There is an exact, predetermined pattern and rhythm designed to offer a predictable ritual to aid transformation. This pattern is defined below:

OPENING QUOTE

The OPENING QUOTE is offered to connect you with thoughts from wise sages from across time to provide you with encouragement and deep wisdom as you begin each exercise-experience.

FOCAL COLLAGE IMAGE

Each chapter features a FOCAL POINT to rest your eyes upon and to inspire you.

INFORMATION TO THINK ABOUT AND CONSIDER

This material is full of information to set the stage for you to do further study on each topic. The topic will be the focus of each guided exercise-experience. Each topic is related to INFORMATION TO THINK ABOUT AND CONSIDER, in the context of emotions, feelings or life experiences. Occasionally, the INFORMATION TO THINK ABOUT AND CONSIDER will continue over a number of pages.

CONTENT ROUND UP TO REVIEW–RECALL–REMEMBER

Here you will find a brief summary of what you just read, in a few short sentences. This will assist you in recalling and remembering the key points. Later, when you return to repeat an exercise-experience, you will be able to read this information for a swift refresher.

GUIDED COLLAGE EXPERIENCE–MAKE A COLLAGE

Here you will find instructions on how to do the collage-making exercise-experience on the topic. Each step of the exercise-experience is written in a simple, terse, and direct format. The steps are designed to expand your personal growth and transformation using collage-making, while considering the topic

TRIANGLE

You will be asked to make a TRIANGLE-SHAPE from your source material as the first and last step of every GUIDED COLLAGE EXPERIENCE—MAKE A COLLAGE. Humans thrive in a pattern of predictability. Using the triangle each time you start and end an GUIDED COLLAGE EXPERIENCE—MAKE A COLLAGE will help you feel more present and increase your comfort as you explore new ideas. As Journalist Nick Kosir says, "Actions speak louder than words, but consistency speaks louder than both."

ENDING QUOTE

The ENDING QUOTE is offered to connect you with thoughts from wise sages from across time to provide you with encouragement and deep wisdom as you end each exercise-experience.

Jennifer Dykeman, *A Beautiful Broken Heart*, 2020, Collage on Board, Doug + Laurie Kanyer Art Collection

Layout of the
TAKEAWAY ACTION TOOLS

To conclude your experience, you will be asked to turn to page 225 in the back of the book. There you will find a series of key TAKEAWAY ACTION TOOLS. The TOOLS are all immensely helpful in expanding the experience. You can use them all or choose only the ones that appeal to you.

The TOOLS are:

REFLECT AND PONDER

It is important to reflect rather than ruminate (worry). Educator and Mental Health Advocate Jordan Burnham puts it this way: "Reflection gives us access to the very best of our minds, from remarkable (our unique genius) to meaningful (compassion, empathy, and the capacity for joy). It may be hard work but reflection enables all the rewards and stuff in life worth living."

Reflection is like looking in a mirror and seeing your strengths and areas of growth. Reflection offers you the chance to witness your beauty and seize new opportunities. Reflection is a way to offer you a chance to engage in some deep thought and make decisions.

This time of intentional pondering and reflection gives your brain the chance to integrate the experience. To make new memories and decisions, your brain needs time to weigh the new experiences. It needs to make connections, comparisons and then to contrast the new information to older information.

The process of integration is like locating a new file of awareness to insert into the file drawers of your mind. This time of reflection will allow you to pull out archaic, unneeded files, such as memories, beliefs, decisions, conclusions and ideas that no longer serve you. You will be able to discard old material that no longer fits having done the exercise-experience. By reflecting and pondering you will be able to insert the new material.

According to Burnham, "Rumination worrying eats up mental energy that could have otherwise been spent on something worthwhile or nourishing to oneself and provides nothing but suffering. It eats up our cognitive budget as it replays events in our lives without gaining insight or progressing (transforming)."

INQUIRE - ASK OF YOURSELF

This tool contains questions that give you a way to have a deeper conversation with yourself about what you are feeling, thinking, learning and deciding after the exercise-experience.

MEDITATION AND SOMATIC POSTURES

This tool offers you a self-guided meditation with some calming somatic body postures, to engage your mind, body and heart. This tool is offered so you can absorb the exercise-experience mentally and physically, to transform and know yourself deeper.

VISUALIZE AND SEE

This tool offers you an opportunity to use the proven power of positive visualization to claim the transformation of the experience. Think of positive visualization as a "mental rehearsal" that one carries out in one's mind.

READ SUPPORTIVE THOUGHT

This tool asks you to read aloud the supportive thought, which activates your auditory learning capability and magnifies this affirmative message.

CONTEMPLATE

This tool offers a time and an opportunity to tap into one's expansive awareness. It offers time spent in wonder, while focusing on a particular aspect of the exercise-experience. It is different from reflection where you are seeing the collage as a mirror. Contemplation invites focus and crystallization of your experience.

THANK YOURSELF

This tool invites you to show deep personal appreciation to yourself for the time, energy and consideration you extended to take part in the experience. It also offers you a chance to accept yourself as whole before you took part in the exercise-experience, as well as after.

MAKE A PERSONAL PROMISE TO YOURSELF

This tool invites you to make a promise and a vow to yourself to continue to invest in and use self-care techniques. Do this to the level in which you are presently able. As best as you possibly can, continue with your on-going self-care.

COMMIT TO GROWTH

This tool invites you to use a collage element as a signal and an invitation to yourself to continue to transform over time, and to notice your interpersonal growth.

LABEL AND NAME

This tool asks you to denote a label or a name for the entire experience. Such labeling provides order and builds a cognizant, intentional memory marker of the experience in which you took part.

SHARE WITH OTHERS

This tool invites you to find others to share this exercise-experience with, in the future and in your own time and space. This will not only expand your learning and increase intimacy with others, but you will also use your auditory learning to expand your own experience.

RETURN TO THE CHAPTER AND READ ENDING QUOTE

Coming full circle, this tool shows you the path to complete the entire experience, connecting all the pieces by reading the ending quote. This quote offers a bookend used to frame and ground the experience as you finish.

About a "Something"

THE VALUE OF THE COLLAGE-MAKING PROCESS AND "SOMETHINGS"

For decades I applied the collage-making process as a tool with my students and clients. This use of collage-making was always done in an organized and systematic format, for the purpose of considering and then transforming a "something" in their lives. This format is exactly what you will find herein.

For all those years my students and clients would come to class or session and say, "I have to tell you about "something", or "I need help with "something", or "Can you coach, teach or tell me about "something". A "something", by definition, is a person, place, event, circumstance, or situation that is currently taking place, or took place at some time in the past. The "something" causes one's Emotional Response System (ERS) to be activated and calls for resolution. To resolve a "something" one will need information, skills and tools to resolve.

In the exercise-experiences in this book I apply the same collage-making process to give you access to skills, tools and information to solve or transform a "something" in your life. The collage-making process may sound simple, but many of life's most important truths are.

THE COLLAGE-MAKING PROCESS IS SPECIAL

The collage-making process is special, as it unlocks mechanisms in the brain to bring forth remarkable opportunities to transform. In the exercise-experiences, collage-making becomes a form of visual journaling. The exercise-experiences utilize all learning styles. Upon completing your collage-making you will be able to run your fingers across the substrate surface and actually "feel your feelings"!

THE SUBSTRATE CAN HOLD AND CONTAIN "SOMETHINGS" AND SHOW YOUR EFFORTS

It is remarkable that the substrate, the sturdy paper upon which one places collage elements, becomes a safe container to hold and carry the burden of the "something". The benefit of the substrate as a safe container, holding the potency of a "something," is extraordinary. The substrate is the place where it can reside, significantly decreasing distress. Collage-making also documents the "something" and your efforts. You can see your work as the collage emerges. It does so in a confidential way. Only you know what the symbolic collage-making elements mean.

COLLAGE-MAKING IS MINDFUL AND GROUNDING

Using collage-making invites one to be in the present moment, grounded in the here-and-now. It prevents rumination and anxious worry. Collage-making can be a conscious, mindful practice. With its studied searching, cutting and pasting of paper elements, collage-making is a form of contemplation. Because one needs to be fully present and intentionally focused when making a collage, one has to be deeply aware. You have to be attentive when searching for elements, cutting with scissors and deciding where to glue items down. This attention to detail offers the mind space, reduces emotional distress, and unlocks new possibilities.

COLLAGE-MAKING MAY OFFER THE BEST AVAILABLE COUNSEL

This book is not therapy, but you will find that it is therapeutic. The intention is to complement your wellness plan and not to replace getting professional help. The information and experiences provided herein will support your emotional well-being. You are likely to find, as so many have, that using the collage-making process will offer you some of the best counsel you have ever received. If you are wondering why this is the case, the answer is that you are the author of your own transformation and well-being. Your dedicated, focused energy in using the collage-making process and contemplating the tools and topics will be reassuring and supportive.

USE COLLAGE-MAKING WHEN TALKING SEEMS TO NOT FIT

Talking a "something" out is highly encouraged and celebrated. While there are great benefits to sharing one's emotions and feelings with others verbally, there are situations or circumstances where talking it out may not fit. When one has had a death in a group or a profound trauma, or it is not in one's temperament, such is the case for some introverts, talking may not fit.

Collage-making is a fantastic way for one experiencing a vast array of "somethings" to communicate and honor feelings. While talking has noted benefits, the use of collage-making has equally powerful benefits when talking does not fit. It can be a way to show what took place, and eventually, to possibly be a conversation starter.

The respect of one who might need to not speak for a time should be respected and alternatives like collage-making and quietly being present can be extremely helpful.

125 WAYS DOCUMENTING HOW COLLAGE-MAKING IS SPECIAL

In my book *Collage Care: Transforming Emotions and Life Experiences with Collage* (2021), I document 125 ways how collage-making helps to produce significant life changes. These 125 ways were discovered following decades of study, and I refer to them as Gems (so named by collagist Andrea Burgay). You can see a complete list of the Gems in the Appendix on page 231. I highly recommend you get a copy of this book (see the Appendix on page 242 for where to acquire it in soft cover or to download it as an eBook).

COLLAGE-MAKING PROCESS CORRELATED TO EMOTIONS

- Using curiosity, wonder, and appreciation is an initial step. Fine art collagists, those who make collage with serious, professional intentions, have a long-held tradition of being deeply curious and full of wonder related to the paper material that they use to make their art. Before they cut and paste symbolic elements from magazines and books to make collage, they often spend time examining and honoring them with wonder and appreciation. They have a reverent curiosity about the origin, history and information of the paper source material. In a very real way this is how one might approach emotions, feelings, and life experiences. Whether old or new, deep or lightly felt, such emotional and life experiences are to be considered with curiosity, wonder, and appreciation.

- Searching, seeking and locating the symbolic paper elements, from printed, often discarded source material, exemplify the aspects of a "something". This searching process is like one's journey to understand emotions, feelings and life experiences. It is also similar to the work one does to find, define and understand oneself. It is very much like the experience of searching for belonging in life.

- Cutting or tearing the paper elements that are used from found or discarded printed source material are symbols to show the aspects of a "something". This part of collage-making could be a metaphor for the experiences of joy, hardship, or loss. The cutting in collage-making replicates life, ultimate change, and the challenges of transformation. It shows loss and change, no matter if the "something" is exciting like a new baby, or heavy like a death. It can also be reflective of the various aspects of the hardship itself.

- Gluing or pasting is the permanent placement of the elements onto a foundation consisting of sturdy paper. This sturdy foundation is referred to as a substrate. This aspect of the collage-making process could symbolize the act of belonging, cleaving, bonding or finding a place of love, protection, support and help. A place where one ultimately belongs. It also is a metaphor for wholeness after any experience. It is similar to having been on a journey, brought home some souvenirs, and then found exactly where they will remain in your life.

WHAT IF YOU ARE A FINE ARTIST?

I recommend a two-part process if you are a fine artist.

When originally approaching each exercise-experience, try to suspend your usual and familiar intention of making fine art or precious arts and crafts. Try to adopt the notion that one is using an artistic process (collage-making) to address topics on emotions and social interactions. The goal is not to make fine art. Try to follow the exercise-experience as it is written, to get the experience of the comforting ritual. Later, if you choose, add your own flare using your skills.

All of the research participants who tested this book were artists. Some of them followed the exercise-experience exactly and then later, when they repeated the exercise-experience for on-going skill practice, they made it their own way. Others finished the exercise-experience as it was written and then, when they were done, proceeded to add their artistic look.

The research conducted on these collage-making exercise-experiences netted some interesting results. All participants in the study were given the same materials and exercise-experiences. Some followed the exercise-experience step-by-step. Others felt compelled to interpret the exercise-experience in their own manner. Miraculously, the outcome was the same. People were transformed.

In conclusion, the power of the content written in the exercise, coupled with collage-making, brought forth profound results. This, my friends, is the mystery and miracle of having access to quality information with the added benefit of the collage-making process. This is a self-guided format and thus you can be your own guide. Tap into your intrinsic wisdom, as you know what works best for you.

DIGITAL COLLAGE

These exercise-experiences have not been trialled with digital collage artists. If you are a digital collage artist, feel free to follow the exercise-experience prompts and then adapt it to fit your own needs.

Lana Turner, *I need to know*, 2020, Analog Collage, Doug + Laurie Kanyer Art Collection

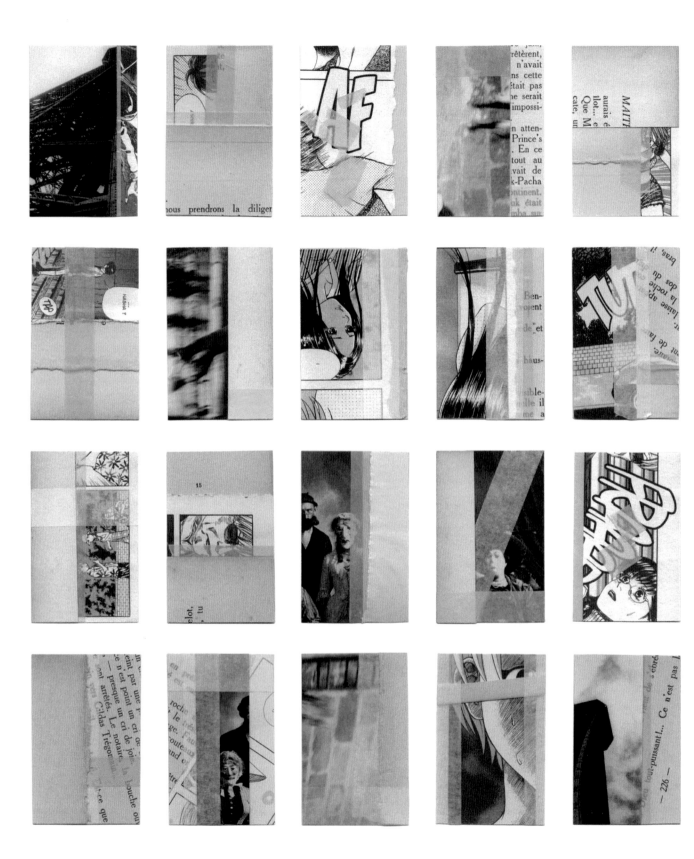

Petra Zehner, *Finding Joy in the Smallest of Things*, 2020, Mini Collages, Doug + Kanyer Art Collection

Collage Care Values, Tenets and Assumptions

When one engages in material that investigates sensitive topics like emotions, feelings and life experience, it is vital for you to know what the originator believes. It is ethically responsible to share these beliefs so you know if they coincide with some of your own values and beliefs. Accordingly, you will find below a summary of these values and beliefs.

People are whole, growing and transforming throughout their lives.

People have strengths that can be built upon.

People can find or develop solutions to their struggles.

The collage-making process is a miraculous tool that opens up channels in the brain to support and transform one's life.

The collage-making process serves as a bridge from earlier or current life struggles towards help, healing and transformation.

People do the very best they can with the information and tools they have, and can benefit from additional information and tools.

Self-care is a way to tend to oneself in the present, and in doing so it helps to heal wounds from earlier.

Self-care is a profound example of self-love.

People can recognize and accept the things that can't be changed, and change the things that can.

People need support, tools, skills and information to manage life processes and the emotions and feelings that result.

Experiences people have in their life, or the things they inherited from others, do not necessarily dictate the path and course of their life.

People can change their Early Life Impressions, Beliefs and Values to better fit in their lives in the here-and-now.

When people have developed skills and tools and have information, they will be better equipped to think, choose and use what is best for themselves and tap into their own wisdom.

There is more than can be seen on the surface. There are things going on behind the scenes that are advocating for good in a person's life.

Life experiences can block one's gifts and True Self, and people can use skills, tools, information and new helpful experiences to remove blocks.

Julie Liger-Belair, *island house 8*, 2023, Analog Collage, Doug + Laurie Kanyer Art Collection

The Importance of Self-Care

One of our overarching beliefs is that the act of caring for one's self is not only practical, but healing and restorative. It is also an act of prevention. Investing in self-care helps decrease the chance of illness. Brushing your teeth is an act of self-care. Going for a walk is an act of self-care. Processing challenging "somethings" using collage-making is an act of self-care. Self-care is not selfish or self-indulgent, it is essential to good health and overall well-being.

There is a sizable market in the promotion of certain products, especially beauty products, under the guise of self-care. These marketing schemes have to some degree exploited the notion of self-care to make a sale. Tending to oneself with necessary products is needed, but self-care is very often affordable and not over-indulgent.

Self-care includes activities that care for your body, mind and soul. It enhances one's relationship with oneself and others. Self-care is an umbrella term which includes self-love, self-awareness and self-respect. Self-care is an act of tending to oneself today, rather than neglecting oneself. The notion of self-care is not a concept promoting the elevation of self over others. Rather, it is to intentionally care for yourself for the purpose of experiencing a full, satisfying life, and to be able to actively participate in community and the care of others.

We believe the tender and thoughtful care of one's emotions heals past and current wounds, provides new insights, and can fill the holes of neglect from years gone by. In doing so one can imagine a sort of reparenting, or parenting in the here-and-now. Our caregivers offered what they could, with what they knew, influenced by the complexity of their lives. Hopefully, they offered quality care. However, due to the intricacies of life, almost everyone has some holes or wounds in the care they received. Accordingly, when you take care of yourself today you can imagine yourself as a helpful caregiver to your very own self.

When you are living a life where you are investing in your self-care by addressing and transforming stressful emotions and experiences, rather than stuffing them or indulging in hurtful distractions (see page 149 on STERBs), you will be able to flourish and contribute to other's welfare. In addition, you need tools to help reduce any stressful or taxing emotional events today. The uncomfortable residue from a potent emotional or stressful experience can cause you to be less fruitful and can affect your perception of the world.

Collage-making can help you help yourself when faced with challenging "somethings". In this way making a collage is an act of self-care, leading to self-awareness, and demonstrates the self-love that one needs to function fully.

One way to look at it is to imagine yourself on an airplane. Suddenly, there is enough turbulence that the emergency air bags are released. It is vital for you to first tend to your own oxygen needs (self-care) and then to assist others. If you are breathing and functioning (tending to your self-care) you will live, and therefore be able to help others survive.

When you make collages to address potent emotions and weighty life experiences as an act of self-care, it is as if you are on the plane with sudden, unexpected disturbances. As you make the collage, it is as if you are taking in clean-flowing-air during an in-flight incident. By making a collage to address stressors you will then be well enough—having the strength to move forward—to be able to help others who need assistance. The alternative could be devastating.

Collage-making is a useful tool to consider your emotions and life events. It will help you understand them, minimize the effect of negative circumstances on your system, and then assist you in moving on, avoiding the taxing effects of hardships. This is far from being selfish and self-absorbed. It is practical and wise to invest in self-care, self-awareness, and self-love. Collage-making has the healing capacity to bring forth protection, strength, insight, and health for you that naturally pours over to others.

Agnieszka Zając, *Dreams Never Ends*, 2023, Analog Collage, Courtesy of the Artist

To Receive the Best Experience

In order to get the closest to in-person exercise-experience try the following suggestions:

REGULAR TIME OF MEDITATION FOR TRANSFORMATION AND LEARNING

Consider using *Collage Care: The Method* as a way to experience a regular time of meditation, contemplation and intentional learning. For some it can become part of your spiritual practice or regular self-care practice.

SET ASIDE SOME SPECIAL TIME

Discover a significant special time to use the exercise-experiences. Take your time to begin to read. Cut and paste only when you are ready. Plan to take enough quiet, private time to allow yourself to do each exercise-experience. Many who took part in the research found it was best to do an exercise-experience over a number of days. Feel free to space them out over days and come back to them later. Consider that skill-building and transformation takes time. Time in practice offers ways to get familiar with tools. You are worth your own precious investment of energy to make internal shifts.

EXPECT THE EXERCISE-EXPERIENCE TO TAKE TIME

While we would like to give one an estimate of how long each exercise-experience will take, we have come to realize that this is impossible. For any given journey there are multiple variables that would influence the time requirement. In my work with clients, we found that a single exercise-experience could take just an hour, or it could take several days or even weeks. So please know this will take time. Also, when time expectations are imposed there arises the risk of "perfectionism" or "right and wrong" interference to the process. You can find ways to be calm, curious and confident without placing any pre-determined time allotment.

THE DEPTH AND BREADTH OF THE EXERCISE-EXPERIENCES

Many of the exercise-experiences will offer you an opportunity to reflect and contemplate on deep topics. You are invited here to monitor how deep and far you go in your exploration. The beauty of a self-guided process is to offer the chance to step away when needed and to engage deeply when the opportunity arises.

NEW EXPERIENCES WILL HAVE A POSITIVE CUMULATIVE EFFECT

To some degree, you will be examining past events in your life, but the only reason to do so is to see how they contribute to the here and now, not to allow them to shape your current existence. The feelings you have about your past can be turned into the fuel that ignites a passion toward discovering new truths and a reacquaintance with your original True Self.

One of the reasons collage-making is so valuable is it is SYMBOLIC of the power to take the old, discarded past, and create something new and true in the present. With this book you will do this a lot. The making of something new has a cumulative positive effect on your life and the finished collage is the evidence of it all!

As the completed collages begin to pile up, their energy will resonate and reflect back to you your own wonder and majesty. Every time you take this journey it will help you to shed the past and claim the now. It will help you to accept the past and step fuller into the present.

Michelle Parchini, *Nature Abides*, 2020, Digital Collage, Doug + Laurie Kanyer Art Collection

REPEAT THE EXERCISE-EXPERIENCES

Insofar as many modules concern skills that can be applied to address and transform "somethings" that you encounter over time, you may want to repeat them. The exercises are designed to be used over and over, to be applied to transform new "somethings" in your life. I will also share here that, in the event you find yourself not choosing to use an exercise, I highly encourage you to just cut and paste. This action itself will help you to regulate and improve your emotional state.

USE A TRIANGLE OR ANOTHER POWER SYMBOL

Predictable rituals are vital to emotional well-being. When you take predictable, anticipated steps you know where you are, what you are doing, and why. This is why we encourage you to start each exercise-experience with the ritual of making a small triangle shape from source material and placing that as the first element you glue down on the substrate. Additionally, when you come to the ending spot in the exercise-experience, to then finish the collage-making by adding another triangle shape. Using the triangle at the beginning and the ending of your collage will offer a familiar and comforting rhythm.

When you make a triangle shape and place it on the substrate at the beginning and ending of the exercise, it offers grounding and strength to the task ahead of you. This predictable ritual will also help to set forth a unifying pattern on all the exercise-experiences you do. It will be a signal that you are engaging in a special time of transformational collage-making. Placing a triangle on your substrate as you begin to make a collage will signal to you that you are doing important work—making it with consideration, reverence, honor, and deep respect.

Additionally, people need signals to designate beginnings and endings of experiences. To say to oneself in effect "I have started, and I now have ended." You might look up the famed TV children's television show Mr. Rogers. Watch and see how he uses a regular, predictable ritual pattern to open and close the show.

What we know is some days are unpredictable. Small ritual-like patterns, such as using the triangle, help one emotionally to cope with the unknown. The information in the exercises is likely to be unknown to you. In using the triangle each time, you will have a grounding tool to explore the information.

I happen to like and have used the triangle for a very long time. In Exercise-Experience One you will learn more about the triangle. It is known to be very powerful. If you have another power symbol you like better, use it to accomplish the same goal.

MAKE A SMALL, YET SIGNIFICANT TRIANGLE

When you use the triangle or other symbol, make it small in size, perhaps no bigger than a couple of inches. You can leave it to be seen on your substrate or cover it up. Also, you do not need to labor on the design or look of the triangle. Merely make a triangle shape and glue it anywhere on the substrate. It is the act of doing, more than the look of it, that matters.

TAP INTO YOUR HELPFUL CHARACTER TRAITS

One of the overarching hopes of this book is to become familiar with your emotions and feelings AND your True Self. Your True Self is the first being, your original soul. Richard Schwartz, PhD, founder of Internal Family Systems, found in his work that each person has in their True Self eight (8) innate helpful character traits (Schwartz, n.d.). They all begin with the letter C. He found time-and-time again that, no matter what a person had been through, they could bring forth these quality character traits.

You too have the capacity to bring the 8c's to these exercise-experiences. The 8c's are as follows: compassion, curiosity, calm, clarity, creativity, courage, confidence and connectedness. You are invited to embrace and bring forth these qualities in yourself.

Whenever you find that you do not have the energy to access your innate ability to bring forth the 8c's, take some time away and rest. The 8c's are necessary to optimize the experiences in this book. Imagine going on a dream trip and finding you are filled with angst. Is it not better to slow down, rest and inquire of yourself as to what you need rather than just pushing through?

BE GENTLE WITH YOURSELF AND APPROACH WITH CURIOSITY

As you go through the exercise-experiences, which in some cases are about heavy, deep topics, pace yourself like you would in a physical exercise class. Pause and gather yourself as needed. Pushing and pressure can ignite resistance. Coach yourself to be reasonable and kind to yourself.

It is kind, when you are doing something new, to be curious about your responses. Offer yourself room to adjust and get accustomed to the landscape. If you find you are becoming critical or judgmental try to be curious about your reactions in order to get to know yourself better. There is likely a reason you may resist or halt a bit. Take the time with the curiosity you would extend to a new friend about their life as you work on this material.

SEE YOURSELF AS WHOLE AND AMAZING - NOT BROKEN

You are whole and full of abundant possibilities. I believe all people have strengths and are whole. People sometimes refer to others as dysfunctional or broken. This could not be further from the truth. Consider, is a seed that is open and cracked to let sprouts out into the earth less whole than the mature plant?

I do believe, and have experienced it myself, that events and hardships can wear on a person, causing pain that leads to the development of defensive, protective parts of you. The injuries of life can cause one to have worn places, and also to have parts of oneself develop into sections to function. This does not mean you are not whole! This book offers tools to recover and heal from hardships in which you remain whole and capable.

ASK YOURSELF FOR PERMISSION

Imagine sitting down for a meal at a new restaurant and the server asks, "May I pour you some water?" It may sound unusual, but asking yourself permission to proceed is a kind, respectful act. Asking permission of yourself gives you a chance to pause and consider the time and investment. It offers you a chance to show yourself you are in charge of this exercise-experience. It will reassure you that you are making decisions related to the pace and the flow of the experience. The act of asking yourself for permission demonstrates a willingness to care, honor and respect yourself.

THANK YOURSELF

This material is inspiring and important. It can also be quite emotionally charged. As you move through it and have new learning and experiences, take time to sincerely thank yourself for your efforts and work. You are the guide and the director of your experience and self-appreciation builds confidence and self-care.

OFFER YOURSELF CHOICES

All of the exercise-experiences are important and the beauty of a self-guided method is you get to choose. There are so many places in life where one might find few choices. However, here you are invited to think, choose and use what works best for you.

YOU HAVE DONE BRAVE THINGS BEFORE

Remember you have done new, brave things in your life. As you begin to explore these modules, bring forth the courage it took to enter a new classroom each year as a child, or to show up for the first day of a new job as an adult. Use these past successes, learnings and the skills you acquired to encourage you as you begin. Reassure yourself it is natural to have starts and pauses. Take them as they come. Also remind yourself that you are going to be there for yourself to offer support and care. You are not alone on this journey.

EMBRACE TRANSFORMATION

Whether one embraces change and invites transformation or not, it will happen in life. It is a fact of life that can easily be observed in children. Without their actual permission, transformation happens; they grow and change. Since you are going to change just with the passing of time, why not enhance it by actively accepting it and leaning into it to produce the most optimal experience?

This is a book about change. Another word for change is transformation. Change in this book is the act of learning skills to help increase comfort in life. Change in examining Earlier Life Impressions and revising them to be more fitting for today. Change in applying collage-making, a possible new experience, as a tool and mechanism to unfold new awareness.

I am not saying you need to change. I am saying you will age and change over time and that one can embrace a fuller life by bringing forth newer viewpoints and experiences. Additionally, most people have a need for quality information and skills pertaining to their emotional and social functions. You, like most of us, may need to update what you know, thereby changing to match the natural change that happens throughout life.

ENGAGE IN DEEP BREATHING

You take an average of 16 breaths a minute, 960 breaths an hour, 23,000 breaths a day (Nestor, 2020). As you work through this book, you are literally one breath away from bringing enhanced emotional well-being into a new existence. Breathing more slowly helps to increase calmness and elicit relaxation in the mood and body. It will improve your mental processing and concentration.

Pause regularly to take a number of deep, slow breaths, in through your nose and out through your nose. A good goal is to take six deep breaths a minute to relax and reduce any strain. Engage your diaphragm and fill your abdomen. To have a measure on how deeply you breathe, place one hand on your chest, and another on the lower part of your abdomen, right at your waistline. Feel the air come in and out of your body. Anytime you feel tension, stop and breathe. Notice if your breathing changes. Should your breathing speed up, pause wherever you are in the exercise-experience and come back later.

USE ALL YOUR SENSES

Expand the depth of the exercise-experiences by tapping into all your senses. Feel free to light a candle or burn incense to amplify your experience. Pour a nice cup of tea, coffee or your favorite beverage. Using all of your senses—sight, sound, touch, smell, and taste—will magnify the experience.

PLAY MUSIC

Music is known to activate and impress upon every known part of the brain. When coupled with collage-making, one can imagine the benefits. Music is known to improve your mood. It improves blood flow and lowers your levels of stress-related hormones. It increases happy hormones, like dopamine, known to ease emotional pain.

Choose gentle, calming music. Choose tracks with a slow tempo, gentle chord shifts, and notes that are held for a period of time. Essentially calm, soothing music. Avoid heavy music with a chaotic tempo, as it can have the opposite effect.

TOPICS CAN BE ACTIVATING

The process of considering your emotions, feelings and life experiences is a relatively potent and tender thing to do. You may occasionally experience topics in this book that are heavy, deep or emotionally activating. Monitor your pace to avoid feeling overwhelmed by too much information. Let the ideas in this book marinate. Sit with them a bit, offer yourself time to ponder and consider. You may find you need to read a bit one day, and return the following day. You decide. Avoid pressure and perfection. You have time—there is no rush.

NO RIGHT OR WRONG, BETTER OR WORSE - BEWARE OF PERFECTIONISM

There is no right or wrong, good or bad, up or down with this work. It is uniquely just for you. This is your journey. While in these chapters you will be asked to put elements in a certain way or place them in a certain spot. This is simply like a guide telling you where to put your foot on a rock climb. This climb is yours and you are also choosing which climb experience to take.

I share this here to challenge any notion you have held from an earlier life impression that things need to be perfect. Perfectionism is a crushing by-product of a number of beliefs, ranging from thinking one's worth is connected to what they do on the one hand, to re-living harsh criticism from others on the other. It can also be shaped by earlier life impressions to please others. You are under no obligation to be pleasing here. Collage-making at its core is imperfect, messy. This is a journey and most journeys have detours. With this work you are invited to transform away from any effects of past perfectionism or desire to get it right.

PAUSE TO USE A SOMATIC POSTURE

If you get overwhelmed, use a Somatic Posture. Peter A Levine, Ph.D has developed, studied and tested Somatic Experiencing®. His discoveries are naturalistic and neurobiological body postures that have been proven to release strain and to comfort the nervous system. These postures bring forth calm and ease stress in the body.

In considering the information in this book, you will benefit from an intermittent pause. When you find you need a pause, try the following somatic postures discovered by Levine:

- **PLACE** your right hand on your left shoulder and your left hand on your right shoulder. Gently tap your shoulders with your fingertips. If you wish, close your eyes. Breathe and notice your energy shifting.

- **PLACE** your right hand in the middle of your left armpit. Place your left hand on your right shoulder. If you wish, close your eyes. Breathe normally. Breathe and notice your energy shifting.

Collage-making is also a somatic practice that uses your small muscles to counteract the strain and effect of heavy hormones to bring forth comfort in the body, enhancing transformation.

FOCUS ON THE SUBSTRATE AS A SAFE BOUNDARY

The value of emotional safety cannot be overstated. When learning about emotions one must have a safe space to explore and learn. I suggest that you view your substrate, the paper you build your collage upon, as your safe protective harbor. Imagine the boundaries of the paper being like a comforting container to offer a place for shelter and security. Put as much as you need on the substrate and leave it all there. Let it carry the "something".

STORAGE AND CARE OF THE COLLAGES

Knowing that the substrates are like safe boundaries and containers for tender and sensitive topics, one then would want to plan for where to store them over time. Collagist and art therapist Sonia Boué, who has studied this material, suggests one find a special box or drawer to place the collages. This will offer your mind a sense of ease as you know where they are safely stored.

As Sonia says, "You can return to them or never revisit them again. Knowing where they are will be a great relief and comfort." Placing them in a dedicated spot will serve as a place of honor. Sonia goes on to say, "You can review your collages at a later date or defer a decision to discard them altogether. "

REFRAME BELIEFS ABOUT YOUR ARTIST SKILLS

Using an artistic process might be a sensitive topic for you. This is understandable, as you may have had your creativity judged or criticized in the past. These self-guided collage-making exercise-experiences are not about making a masterpiece. While you might love what you make, it is not really about making art at all. You are simply using the actions of cutting and gluing paper to examine concepts and expand your knowledge.

You do not have to show your collage to anyone. You are simply using paper glued to paper as a learning tool. Use the exercise-experiences in a spirit of investigation about becoming a healthier person. Do so in a tender and kind spirit towards yourself.

KEEP OR DISCARD

You can keep what you make or choose to discard it. Regardless of whether you keep or dispose of the collage, the overarching goal is to support your emotional well-being. Discarding a collage about a heavy situation can be very cathartic. Conversely, you may love your collage and what it represents to you. Keep the collage in that case, even frame it. Whether you keep or throw it away, it is your decision.

LOOK FOR AND EXPECT MIRACLES

It is hard to explain, but when using the collage-making process miracles appear. This is due to the unique combination of components used in the collage-making coupled with the exercise-experiences. As you search for just the right elements and you're thinking about what it is you want to find, an element seems to miraculously appear. It is as though that particular element was waiting for you. This sweet surprise supports one's emotional well-being and brings forth joy. Some might call this coincidence. Others might call it luck. When this happenstance of attraction occurs it can feel as though the universe is listening in on your very thoughts. It is as if there are forces beyond what you can see advocating for goodness in your life to ignite hope and joy.

EMBRACE PERCEIVED MISTAKES AS OPPORTUNITIES

Earlier in your life you may have experienced criticism from others. As a result, you may find that you criticize yourself for small and inconsequential hiccups. Or maybe you had intended for a plan or project to go a certain way and you find yourself berating yourself when it does not turn out as imagined.

You are formally invited here in *Collage Care: The Method* to embrace real or perceive errors as opportunities and surprises. You are in charge and guiding the process, not words from the past or even your harsh self-talk. Challenge yourself to move beyond harsh criticism from the past, and open your eyes to the surprises that can be adjusted and transformed to work especially for you.

A WORD TO THE WISE ABOUT ADVERTISING

Many of the magazines you will use as your source material are filled with advertisements. They are designed with the specific goal of getting you to buy something. Advertising is designed to make you believe you need something, that your life will be better if you buy their product. Even worse, they are designed as an appeal to emotion, to make you feel that you are not OK, or don't fit in unless you have their product. This is hurtful. This is not true. Do not be fooled.

Advertising is a form of social conditioning designed to get you to buy things. Use the images or pictures displayed in advertising for your collage, but rely on your own personal smart thinking and deep wisdom as you use them. This awareness will allow you to make collages that support your emotional wellness.

Note: If your source material is vintage, from many decades back, you will also be exposed to racism and sexism prevalent in older magazines. For women, people of color, queer people, or other groups that have survived historical oppression, this may be an opportunity to pause and choose another source material for the sake of self-protection.

Laurence Briat, *Dove of Hope*, 2022, Analog Collage on Book Page, Doug + Laurie Kanyer Art Collection

Key Information About the Brain

Your brain is a very complicated and wonderful organ. It is by orders of magnitude the most complex entity in all of creation. There are said to be 100 billion neurons in the brain, with 100 trillion associated connections! It is made of multiple parts or sections that are unified and work together. Each part has a role in processing certain types of information and doing certain functions. Your brain is where your emotions and feelings originate in cooperation with your senses and whole-body system.

THE BRAIN KNOWS IT EXISTS

The brain is where emotions and feelings are initiated, where memories and earlier life impressions are stored. It is the only organ that is aware of its own existence! Unlike other organs that do not know they exist, the brain knows of itself.

The brain has the ability to analyze some of its functions, providing information about itself to itself. It will have an emotional experience and later follow up with feedback, insight and critiques. It can also plan and imagine the future, setting expectations of itself and its performance.

THE BRAIN CAN SELF CORRECT TO IMPROVE WELL-BEING

The brain literally talks to itself! Accordingly, it has the tendency to correct itself via self-diagnosis and self-treatment. It has the capacity to make significant improvements to its health and well-being.

When one's brain is under duress, or has an absence of quality information about itself, it may not give the best feedback to itself. In the absence of quality information it might not know how to help itself. Additionally, it may rely on old, archaic information or social myths. With quality information it can track itself, appreciate its efforts, encourage itself, and make adjustments.

You don't have to rely on old standards or earlier impressions from decades past, those archaic social beliefs about mental health. With the material in this book you can gain foundational information so you can have a deeper appreciation of your emotional world.

THE BRAIN CAN SHIFT AND CHANGE

Despite its complexity, the brain is malleable. It can be changed. Expert Neuroscientist David Eagleman, author of *Livewire: The Inside Story of the Ever-Changing Brain*, looks at the brain as if it is an electrical mesh-like fabric that is vitally flexible and changes shape with each new experience and subsequent learnings (Eagleman, 2020). "The brain is literally live-wired, not hard-wired," reports Eagleman.

For years people associated the brain with a computer system's hard-wiring. Today we know there are better comparisons, as the hardwiring of a computer is not flexible nor moldable on its own. The brain, on the other hand, is changeable. Computers are programmed by humans and those processes are static, while the brain is constantly evolving. Eagleman maintains that the brain has the ability to shift and change in response to new experiences.

Indeed, that is the purpose of this book...to offer hope that no matter what you are faced with or have felt, no matter what you may have decided in the past, there are tools that can help. Tools, such as the exercise-experiences in this book, can offer you a new construct, a new frame, to help your amazing brain feel and think in new ways. You are offered herein the chance to shift and pivot with new valuable life experiences.

Reading this book and doing the exercise-experiences help motivate the pleasure centers of the brain, thus releasing happy hormone chemicals. Such chemicals are identified as dopamine, oxytocin, serotonin, and endorphins, otherwise known as the "Feeling Good Hormones".

- Dopamine is often associated with the anticipation of happiness or pleasure and achieving a goal.

- Oxytocin is often associated with a person's ability to make social connections, to bond and become empathetic to self and others.

- Serotonin is the mood-regulating hormone. When serotonin is in balance, one feels good, less irritable and more socially connected.

- Endorphins are associated with the reduction or masking of the sensation of pain, allowing one to persevere in trying circumstances.

The excretion of these brain hormones and chemicals while collage-making will rejuvenate the body and brain. The brain and body are inextricably connected. These happy hormones flow through your entire system—all organs—to sweep the body and brain into a feel-good state. In exploring this book you have the opportunity to change your brain and body and experience the benefits of life-giving pleasureful hormones.

HOW THE EXERCISE-EXPERIENCES ENGAGE PARTS OF THE BRAIN TO SUPPORT WELLNESS

Your brain is a very complicated and wonderful organ. It coordinates and manages many of the functions of the body. It is made of multiple parts or sections that are unified and work together, but each part has a role in processing certain types of information. The exercise-experiences in the book engage many of the different sections to support the overall health of your brain. The list below outlines how certain themes and topics featured in the exercise-experiences interact with particular parts of your brain, leading to transformation:

- **Emotions:** Exercise-experiences aimed to consider emotions will engage the limbic system. The limbic system processes feelings and emotions, as well as the behaviors connected to those emotions.

- **Communication:** Exercise-experiences related to communicating with others will engage the use of the cerebrum. It is divided into two parts, called hemispheres, which are joined by nerve fibers called the corpus callosum. The speech part of communication is controlled by the left side of your cerebrum.

- **Memories:** Exercise-experiences related to memories will engage the hippocampus, a part of the limbic system, the place memories are stored and retrieved.

- **Resolving Challenges:** Exercise-experiences aimed at resolving challenges will engage the frontal lobe, which is responsible for problem-solving, thinking, planning and organizing.

- **Decision Making:** Exercises aimed to consider making decisions will engage the frontal lobe, known to support the ability to think and make choices.

- **Goal Setting:** Exercise-experiences related to goal setting will engage the amygdala as it relates to the emotions connected to making a plan. The frontal lobe will be involved in defining the specific steps to accomplish the goal. The two will work together to manage the steps, keep you engaged, and modulate the emotions of each step.

- **Joy:** Exercise-experiences related to joy and happiness will engage the right frontal lobe, the right frontal cortex, the precuneus, the left amygdala and the left insula. It is the connection in the brain among cognitive processing, the frontal cortex, the insula, and the amygdala.

- **Beliefs:** Exercise-experiences related to beliefs will engage the frontal lobe with an integration of subcortical information by the prefrontal cortex. The amygdala and hippocampus, which are part of the limbic system affecting emotions, are also involved.

As you work through the exercise-experiences you'll begin to improve your emotional well-being by utilizing various parts of your brain.

Fred Free, *irresponsible frivolity*, 2019, Analog Collage, Doug + Laurie Kanyer Art Collection

Scott Gordon, *a treachery of images*, 2022, Analog Collage, Doug + Laurie Kanyer Art Collection

PREPARING TO BEGIN

YOUR WORKSPACE

You will need to decide where to set up your collage-making workspace. There's no need to be elaborate. It merely needs to be a comfortable spot to sit and make your collages; a table and a chair. If you like to move around to a variety of places to collage, simply find a box large enough to hold a stack of magazines, scissors, glue, and some substrates. I use my dining room table from time to time. You can find underneath the tablecloth, hidden from view, numerous collages in process.

BASIC COLLAGE CONSTRUCTION

Adhering paper-to-paper is a simple way to define how to make collage. Collage-making is simply gluing unrelated found paper elements together on the same substrate or paper foundation. Having experience and practice in collage-making is not needed to do the exercise-experiences.

EQUIPMENT AND MATERIALS

Substrate is the sturdy, foundational base or paper upon which you make your collage.

To enable you to choose a substrate that fits the exercise-experience, read all the instructions in the exercise-experiences all the way through before you begin. You will then be able to select an appropriate substrate size. Because each person will have a different response to the collage-making instructions, it is impossible to make a recommendation on the standard size to use. By reading the instructions you will be able to then make your selections. If you find you run out of room, feel free to use the back of the substrate.

Source Material is the paper you will use to cut out elements to add to your substrate to make the collage. Examples of source material are magazines (current or decades old), books, letters, postcards, mail, bills, photographs, parchment paper, foil, decks of cards, or greeting cards. Any discarded paper material is just fine.

Elements are the items you cut out of source material to symbolically show aspects of each exercise-experience. There are typically many elements in each collage. In the instructions you will be prompted to locate elements and to place and glue them on the substrate. It is important to know these elements need to be a size that will fit on the substrate. In many cases smaller elements will work the best.

Glue can be whatever you want to use to adhere elements of your collage to the substrate. This may be tape or any glue you like (acid free preferred). If you want, look up how to make a homemade glue called Wheat Paste.

Pens, pencils, markers, crayons, paint and paint brushes can be used to make marks on your collage as well.

Scissors that you already have are just fine. **Note:** Some of the material you use may be potent and even bleak. You may find that using scissors might not be the best choice when interacting with these materials, and manually tearing paper would be a safer option.

Note: If you want to archive or keep your collage(s), please consider using acid free paper, glue, or tape.

REPRESENTATIONAL OR SYMBOLIC ELEMENTS

Depending on your preference and circumstances you may want to use either symbolic or representational elements to show the "something" you are addressing. You will notice that all the exercise-experiences ask for "symbolic" elements. I do this to increase confidentiality, as I did with my clients and students. A symbolic element would be one that does not look exactly like the thing you are addressing, and the meaning is only understood by you.

On the other hand you may want to use representational elements. A representational element would be one that looks similar or exactly like the "thing". Say the "something" is about a car; a representational element would look exactly like a car. This is really for you to decide, and may vary from one exercise-experience to another.

ON-LINE DIGITAL ELEMENTS

There are great benefits in the turning of pages in books and magazines as you search for elements. Conversely, if you want to find just the right representational element to express yourself, finding one online and printing it off makes sense as well. In some instances, going online may shorten the time in searching for a specific element.

ABOUT FINE ART COLLAGE

If you are interested in learning more about the art-form of collage there are many examples in this book created by artist and co-creator CP Harrison. You will also find herein examples from a multitude of artists from The Doug + Laurie Kanyer Collection.

If you become curious about collage as an art form and want more technical instruction on collage itself, consider getting a copy of any of these books:

- Project Collage: 50 Projects to Spark Your Creativity by Bev Speight

- If You Can Cut You Can Collage by Hollie Chastain

- Artful Memories by Jane Chipp and Jack Ravi

Onward to Start Your Collage Experience on page 33.

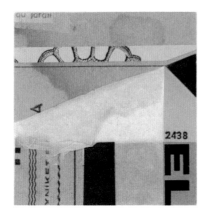 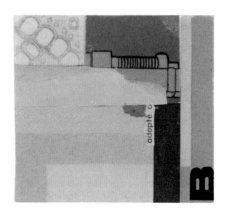

Dorothée Mesander, *Abstraction of House and Garden (I grew up in)*, 2020, Mini Collage, Doug + Laurie Kanyer Art Collection

Antonio Guerra Álvarez, *Essence of home*, 2019, Digital Collage, Doug + Laurie Kanyer Art Collection

Niko Vartiainen, *Midsommar*, 2022, Analog Collage, Doug + Laurie Kanyer Art Collection

PART 1
Beginning: Introductory Exercise-Experiences

"What can we gain by sailing to the moon if
we are not able to cross the abyss that
separates us from ourselves?"

— Thomas Merton

CP Harrison, *Magic Number*, 2020, Analog Collage, Courtesy of the Artist

EXPLORING THE POWER OF THE TRIANGLE SHAPE

**A collage-making exercise-experience to learn about the triangle
as an emblem of power and transformation.**

"The stars are the apexes of what wonderful triangles!" — Henry David Thoreau

INFORMATION TO THINK ABOUT AND CONSIDER

You are about to embark on an adventure, a journey of exploration using collage-making to transform feelings and learn about emotions. To accomplish your goals you can use an inspirational symbol or emblem to inspire you. Something to gaze upon to engage your will and deepen your commitment toward realizing your goals.

For centuries humans have used symbols to ignite and inspire higher truths and values. These symbols are like personal shields, touchstones of strength and inspiration. Symbols have also been used to represent people in groups with similar values, as a unifying emblem. Most important human endeavors seem to have a symbol of representation, such as Scottish clan tartans, family crests, flags of the nations and sports team logos. They are icons which inspire and remind people of higher principles and goals in life. Symbols are usually simple in presentation and easy to discern, recall and remember.

The triangle is one such symbol. It has deep historical significance in many cultures and is often seen as representing the intersection and connection of the "threes". Each side of the triangle represents one of three connected and interdependent tenets. The triangle is also the strongest of shapes, withstanding almost any pressure, nearly impossible to break; much like your True Self. Well known architect R. Buckminster Fuller proved that the triangle could withstand twice as much pressure as the rectangle. He based his famous geodesic shelters on triangles, giving the structures unprecedented strength.

The triangle in mathematics and physics is also the symbol for change. It is the symbol that represents what takes place when there is a shift, essentially symbolizing transformation. The collage-making process we use in the exercise-experiences is about supporting changes in life. Using the exercise-experiences you will be taking discarded, printed materials, and then changing and altering them into something new. In the exercise-experiences you will be changing as you practice skills, experiment with new tools, and gain key knowledge.

For these reasons, the triangle is an excellent shape for you to consider using as you begin to explore the exercise-experiences. Think of it as a grounding beacon toward deeper self-awareness. As you use the exercise-experiences in the book the triangle will be the unifying symbol in the collages you make. You will start each collage-making with a triangle and you will end each collage-making with a triangle. Similar to the sun, the moon and the stars, the triangle will be your grounding symbol. The use of this powerful symbol each time you start and end an exercise-experience will offer you a familiar and comforting ritual.

It will also be your personal symbol and emblem of strength and perseverance for this journey. In some ways this triangle collage will be like a lighthouse, a power beacon and emblem showing you the way.

HISTORICAL MEANINGS OF THE TRIANGLE

Beginning, middle and ending	Life, death, rebirth
Past, present, future	Create, revise, sustain
Phases of the moon; waxing, waning and full	Earth, air, sky
Body, mind, spirit	Serenity, courage, wisdom
Acceptance, understanding, appreciation	Head, heart, gut (intuition)
Mother, maiden, crone	Earth, wind, fire
Divine ideas, new ideas, higher awareness	Father, Son, Holy Ghost
Thoughts, feelings, emotions	Physical, mental, spiritual
Love, truth, wisdom	Unity, service, recovery (*Via Alcoholics Anonymous*)
Woman, man, child	Thoughts, feelings and behaviors (In Cognitive
Strength, care, courage	Behavioral Therapy, the counseling model)
Sun, moon and stars	Three choices or wishes in traditional fairy tales
Left, right, center	Symbolism of a three-strand braid
Morality, concentration and insight	Symbolism of the strength of a three-strand cord

---

CONTENT ROUND UP to REVIEW—RECALL—REMEMBER

- Symbols like the triangle have been used for centuries to ignite and inspire higher truths and values.

- The triangle is known to be the strongest of all shapes nearly impossible to break, like your True Self.

- You can adopt a symbol like the triangle as your emblem of personal strength as you use collage-making to transform your emotions and life experiences.

- The triangle will be your grounding symbol, a beacon to help show the way, like a lighthouse of inspiration.

- Using a triangle as you make your collages will unify your work and provide a needed ritual to add predictability for this time of exploration.

GUIDED COLLAGE EXPERIENCE—MAKE A COLLAGE

1. **GATHER** the materials, glue, magazines, books and a substrate (the paper you make your collage upon).

2. **DRAW** a large triangle shape on your substrate.

3. **CUT** out elements from your source material to symbolically show the meanings of the triangle you chose from page 36. Glue the elements on top of the triangle shape you just drew, filling it completely.

4. **VISUALIZE** this triangle collage as a pillar of strength, a grounding, balancing and foundational symbol for you as you take part in the exercise-experience to come later in the book.

5. **MOVING FORWARD,** in each exercise-experience you will begin and end your collages with a triangle shape, for the purpose of reinforcing the principles you selected here. Doing this will be a comforting ritual each time you make a collage.

6. **WRITE** or use collage elements to create a supportive thought to encapsulate this experience. Put this anywhere on your collage. An example: "I can choose a personal emblem of strength and inspiration to create a framework of security and grounding for my life."

7. **PLACE** a triangle-shaped element anywhere on the substrate to symbolize your personal strength and to offer a comforting and familiar ritual.

8. **EXTEND** your transformation by completing the TAKEAWAY ACTION TOOLS (page 225).

9. **RETURN** here after completing the Takeaway Action Tools to read the ending quote below.

"Almost any group of three is going to form a triangle
with two points closer to one another."

— Amy Dickinson

Diane Davis, *Abdicated Twilight*, 2020, Mini Collages, Doug + Laurie Kanyer Art Collection

Frances Ryan, *The Laughing Cavalier*, 2020, Analog Collage, Doug + Laurie Kanyer Art Collection

GETTING TO KNOW YOUR TRUE SELF

A collage-making exercise-experience to know yourself better.

"When we feel life escapes us and we don't recognize ourselves anymore, we do well to build a safe haven in our frame of mind before the essence of our being evaporates and the keystones of our mental structure disintegrate." — Erik Pevernagie

INFORMATION TO THINK ABOUT AND CONSIDER

The process of living can be both heavy and light. Events, places, roles, people—the chosen or unchosen, imposed or selected—can be smooth and life giving. Conversely, these things may be clunky and burdensome. Such experiences naturally cause a layer of understanding, contributing to your awareness of oneself and the world. This layer of understanding shapes how you view the world, yourself, and others. It becomes a kind of protective coating. This coating is an evolving operating system directing you how to think, feel and behave. It is often called the 'personality' (Hudson, R., Riso D.,1999).

Protective Personality Coating

As noted by famed authors Russ Hudson and Don Riso in their epic book, *The Wisdom of the Enneagram: The Complete Guide to Psychological and Spiritual Growth for the Nine Personality Types*, this "personality coating" is used as a tool to predict and maneuver your way through life. The personality coating forms a pattern of behaving, steering your thinking, problem solving and decisions.

Your personality coating is designed to protect your True Self, your essence. This process of forming a coating starts from the very beginning of your life (Hudson, R., Riso D., 1999). The personality coating is like a sheet of plastic wrap placed over a container to preserve the precious morsels of food inside. Hudson and Riso point out that this can be good. However, it may also be too heavy or dramatic. Such personality coating can keep you from knowing and accessing your True Self (Hudson, R., Riso D. 1999).

Your True Self

Your True Self is present at the very beginning of your life, before the events of life occur, before you may have had to defend yourself by forming your personality coating. I believe, as shared by the authors, that the original True Self never leaves; it cannot be harmed, no matter what happens in life. It is always there to be known, seen and discovered.

However, your personality coating can become impenetrable and can hide, separate, or cut off channels to your True Self. This can limit important information, knowledge, and insight of your True Self. The wisdom of the True Self can be buried outside of conscious awareness, and you may feel as though you don't really know yourself.

Revising Earlier Impressions - Softening the Personality Coating

Collage-making is a tool that can assist in releasing the power of a 'heavy' personality. It can offer a type of miraculous revision of the earlier impressions and conclusions that lead to a thicker personality coating. With collage-making you can have new experiences, in the present, leading to self-reflection and knowledge, connecting you to your True Self. You may be able to say to yourself, "Do I need to act, think, or feel that way any longer?" This may lead to a softening or loosening of the coating of personality, allowing you to be more authentic to yourself and others. By softening the personality coating with the use of collage-making, you will be able to let your real True Self shine through.

Revealing Feelings With Collage-Making

Collage-making may reveal that your feelings are reactions to the personality coating you have designed to cope with what was in front of you. It can help you to understand how and why your personality coating developed certain notions about life. It will offer you a chance to see if you really feel that way at present. This awareness may lead to seeing, understanding, and knowing more. Once aware, one can then begin to "let go of" or change the way one reacts to situations. We hope you will be able to simply say to yourself, "I see, and now that I know more, I can move into a fuller life. I can pivot and transform."

With collage-making your True Self may be able to show you how to get through a situation, to know the elements of the situation better, and to then gently walk onward, letting each person, place or event have its place in your history. This will allow you the chance to observe your memories and feelings, and then with a clearer view, to move on to a revised pattern. It will be as if you already knew but had yet to discover key, hidden, information due to the overly protected personality coating.

Compassion for One's Self

Collage-making can lead to compassion that can come from seeing your story from a new perspective. In collage-making you engage in the physical creative process of the telling of your story. This invites you to suspend judgement of yourself; to not be a jury of the harsh shame, often sought by the personality.

Collage-making offers you a way to quiet the mind, to use your body to unearth and observe bits of life not yet unfolded. In doing so you move from the fixed ideals and beliefs of the personality coating to the fluid recognition of your original, True Self. It helps to install people, places and things from your life experiences in a more appropriate spot, to not let them be heavy and restrictive.

A Collage-Making Discovery

In his practice, acclaimed collagist and Professor of Architecture Clive Knights expands upon the subject of using collage-making in the recognition of True Self. Professor Knights not only uses paper but also light when making collages. He discovered this process in late 2018. He calls this collage-making technique Light-Ray Excavations.

Let's use his method to illustrate the concept of how the personality coating covers and protects your original, True Self, and to further define how a too-thick coating will prevent access to it. Your True Self is always there to be discovered, known and explored.

Says Professor Knights, "Like most compelling experiences, they emerge when one least expects it. My first encounter with Light-Ray Excavation came on a wintry afternoon in my studio while experimenting with a new light table. As I unthinkingly laid old *LIFE* magazine pages over the bright, white screen, it became apparent that a surreptitious dialogue had been waiting to take place between the content on each side of the page, silently, unnoticed for decades and illuminated for the first time by the merger of back-to-back images. I fantasized that a typographer, decades ago, had secretly but deliberately brought the images together, unbeknownst to readers, forming intimate invisible communities amongst the pages, pressed against each other, blind to their unique proximity, but content in their umbral existence. Now brought to light by sheer accident, it is as if they had waited patiently to perform one final unanticipated task: by means of the projection of light the images could at last conspire, like metaphor, to reveal in their fusion a deeper identity that transcended them both (Knights, 2020)."

We will use Professor Knights' collage-making technique discovery to consider how your True Self is there waiting to be seen and known. Your True Self has always been there! Come back to this tool anytime you need to be reminded of this truth.

CONTENT ROUND UP to REVIEW—RECALL—REMEMBER

- People develop a coating called personality to protect and defend their True Self from pain.

- The protective coating of the personality can keep you from knowing your True Self.

- Using collage-making will offer you access to your True Self, helping you think and revise Early Life Impressions about an event or an experience.

- The True Self is waiting to be known, and using collage-making can help to soften the coating of the personality.

- Light Ray Excavation is a way to comprehend the presence of the True Self.

Clive Knights, *Apparition*, 2019, Light-Ray Excavation, Doug + Laurie Kanyer Art Collection

Rocio Romero, *Bonny Baby*, 2019, Analog Collage, Doug + Laurie Kanyer Art Collection

GUIDED COLLAGE EXPERIENCE—MAKE A COLLAGE

1. **GATHER** a brightly colored magazine page, tape, phone with a camera, or an actual camera. Tear the page out of the magazine and photograph both sides of the page. These photos will symbolically show your adapted personality coating that you developed to protect your True Self.

2. **LOCATE** a sunny window or use a light table. Tape the page onto the window or to the light table, and observe it closely. As you view the light coming through you will notice there is a collage that is hidden inside the page! This hidden collage symbolizes your original True Self that is hidden by your personality coating. Knights calls this a Light Ray Excavation Collage (LREC). For our use here see it as a symbol of your True Self, such that it has always been there for you to discover.

3. **TAKE** a photo of the Light Ray Excavation Collage taped to the window. Study the three photos you took. Look at the photos of each page before you tape it up to the window. These symbolize the adapted coating personality. Look at the Light-Ray Excavation Collage photo, which symbolically shows your True Self. See your True Self is that always with you ready to be known. It was merely 'hidden' due to the thickness of your personality coating.

4. **SPEND** some time honoring your personality coating as it is represented by the first two images. Honor it for protecting you and your original True Self. Look at the third image and consider what your True Self knows. What do you really think about issues, events, and situations? How can deeper knowledge of your True Self help to support and guide you? As you move through the exercise-experiences in this book, your True Self is invited to move forward. In the process, your personality coating will be offered a chance to release a bit so that the two can come together to offer you a fuller life.

5. **CONSIDER** as you interact with others that they too have developed a personality coating, and may not know their True Self well, if at all. Imagine what things cause them to develop a thick coating and what their True Self might really be like.

6. **PLACE** a triangle-shaped element anywhere on the substrate to symbolize your personal strength and to offer a comforting and familiar ritual.

7. **EXTEND** your transformation by completing the TAKEAWAY ACTION TOOLS (page 225).

8. **RETURN** here after completing the Takeaway Action Tools to read the ending quotes below.

"You'll never know who you are unless you shed who you pretend to be."

— Vironika Tugaleva

*"The freedom to be yourself is a gift only you can give yourself.
But once you do, no one can take it away."*

— Doe Zantamata

Laurie Kanyer, *Spiral Star*, 2021, Analog Collage, Doug + Laurie Kanyer Art Collection

PART 2
Exercise-Experiences on Emotions, Feelings, Moods, and Memories

"Emotional intelligence is the ability to sense, understand,
and effectively apply the power and acumen of
emotions as a source of human energy,
information, connection,
and influence."

— Robert K. Cooper, PhD

CP Harrison, *Everybody Can't Be Born at the Same the Same Time*, 2020, Courtesy of the Artist

MECHANISMS OF THE EMOTIONAL RESPONSE SYSTEM

A collage-making exercise-experience on the basics of the Emotional Response System.

"Emotions are neither right or wrong, they just are." — Wyatt Kanyer

INFORMATION TO THINK ABOUT AND CONSIDER

Why does one get scared, or mad, or sad? Why does seeing a certain person unsettle, while with another there is no reaction? Why are some people more emotional than others?

A Brief Explanation of Emotions and the Mechanisms of the Emotional Response System

One's Emotional Response System consists of a number of mechanisms that work together. The mechanisms are emotions, feelings, memories and Early Life Impressions. The Emotional Response System contributes to how one acts, behaves, and thinks related to a "something". A "something", by definition, is a person, place, event, circumstance, or situation that is currently taking place, or took place at some time in the past. The "something" causes one's Emotional Response System (ERS) to be activated and calls for resolution. To resolve a "something" one will need information, skills and tools.

Emotions

Many people use the terms emotions and feelings synonymously. Although you can experience them at nearly the same time, they are not interchangeable. Emotions are physical, bodily, sensory reactions to a "something". Emotions are registered and felt in the body. They are connected to the release of hormone chemicals into the body called neurotransmitters (oxytocin, epinephrine, adrenaline, cortisol, dopamine, norepinephrine, serotonin, GABA). These neurotransmitters are released into the body, alerting you to pay attention to a "something". They are physical, bodily responses that occur just before feelings. Emotions are automatic and do not have cognitive thinking features attached to them. They are nearly immediate when activated and are designed to help.

Feelings

Feelings are different from emotions. Feelings, however, are responses generated in connection to an emotional event. Emotions happen first in connection to a "something" and then feelings happen in swift order thereafter. Feelings feature more of a cognitive thought process related to an event that ignited an emotion.

Feelings, as well as emotions, are associated and connected to the other mechanisms of the Emotional Response System, such as memories and Early Life Impressions. A feeling begins the complicated process of consideration and decision-making related to the "something" that activates the emotions. It should be noted that an individual can experience more than one emotion and feeling at the same time.

Memories

Memories are snippets of information stored in one's memory bank based on experiences from earlier in life. They are fragments of encoded material designed to be utilized over time. Memories shape the quality and tone of the emotional response. These fragments are coded in the memory bank in short- and long-term retrieval files. When a new emotional "something" happens, a memory of a similar event from before can be attached. It is then used to shape and inform the emotional response. Note, this process of attaching a memory is likely not conscious.

Memories are fluid and flexible. They can change over time. They can merge together with new experiences to form new memories. There are memories you are consciously aware of and also those that are subconscious. Memories are accessed and activated not only in the brain's storage system, but also based on an abundance of exterior sensory input related to an experience in the present. See the exercise-experience titled Exploring Memories on page 93 for more.

Early Life Impressions

Humans create Early Life Impressions. These impressions inform and contribute to foundational conclusions, decisions and beliefs that support how one maneuvers and sees the world. Early Life Impressions consist of one's decisions and beliefs about themselves, others, and the world in general. They are built from experience and are a component of our self-talk. They are used over time, to help one know how to be and predict what the world is about.

When a new "something" happens that causes an emotional arousal, one's Early Life Impressions are used to navigate and make decisions on how to react. "I am strong and unflappable", "I am sensitive and weak" are examples of Early Life Impressions.

Early Life Impressions are used in the present but were created in your earlier childhood years. From your very earliest days you received information and made conclusions and decisions about the world, and you in the world. These conclusions and decisions were developed by a very young and inexperienced child without the benefit of adult-like thinking. When an experience happens to the "younger you" it creates a conclusion about things that are used in your life over time.

Early Life Impressions are formed by what one experiences, what others do and say in relation to you. They are composed from both verbal and nonverbal bits of information collected, organized and stored. Along with feelings and memories they assist and inform one's patterned, Emotional Response System. They are used to predict what might take place in any given circumstance and how we might handle a new "something".

Early Life Impressions are part of a response coding system used to alert us to information we have gathered from familiar experiences from our past. When something happens one might access some Early Life Impressions which offer an established pattern of conclusions, ideas, and beliefs.

Self-Talk

Early Life Impressions contribute to the things you say to yourself. They are part of one's self-talk. The many parts of yourself will have a variety of Early Life Impressions to reinforce their beliefs.

One's self-talk can take lines from Early Life Impressions to direct one's functioning in the present. Self-talk is influenced by Early Life Impressions that will in turn shape how one will behave, either to maintain safety and security, or in contrast, proceed with excitement or another feeling. During an emotional event they will offer quick evaluations and judgements of the situation. They will make a nearly immediate plan for what to do. You can literally hear yourself access an Early Life Impression and say it to yourself (see the exercise-experience titled Self-Talk on page 83).

Early Life Impressions Can be Refined and Revised

It is valuable to clarify that your emotions, feelings, memories and Early Life Impressions are uniquely created and curated for you, by you. They are part of your coping and functioning system. One's Early Life Impressions can contribute to thoughts, feelings, self-image, self-esteem and behavioral patterns in the present.

Similarly, it is valuable to remember that they were formed and developed in an earlier place and time, likely when you were much younger. The question of "are they 100% accurate and fitting for today?" is a valuable one to ask. Remember that the situation of today is not exactly like the past.

The good news is that those earlier impressions and decisions can be amended. They can be refined, re-defined, dissected, investigated and changed to assure they are helpful for today. The example from above, "I am sensitive and weak," can be re-considered and investigated in the present time to determine if this statement is really true now. People can, and do, revise the Early Life Impressions created by their younger selves. This may in fact be necessary, as a child may have built impressions that are too generalized and possibly not logical. You can shift your understanding and use of your earlier impressions over time. They are there to be adjusted, if you choose.

There are many factors that contribute to the way a person responds emotionally. In addition to one's Early Life Impressions and memories, gender, temperament, decade-of-birth, and many other factors affect the Emotional Response System (see the exercise-experience on page 55 for a comprehensive list of the many things that shape how an individual expresses emotions).

More About Emotions

Emotions are initiated by a complex sensory "interpretation-and-action" process in the brain designed to attune to and decipher a "something". The "something" is perceived by one's sensory system to be important or critical enough to require a response. In most cases this happens because the sensory arousal to a "something" is potent enough to alert the emotional system. The "something" can be either negative or positive, scary or exciting, along a broad range on the individual spectrum. Depending upon the situation, the use of one's basic emotions may be life savers.

It is believed that emotions can be ignited in an instant to address a "something" in preparation to react. Emotions occur to prepare oneself and to then move forward, stay alert, observe or dismiss one's attention. They are designed to be time-limited. The original design was for an emotion to take place in the present to signal an alert for you to take notice of a "something". From there you determine if it needs to be addressed or not. Depending on the situation you can move forward to address the "something," or dismiss it and go forth. Emotions happen like breathing, often in an automatic way, giving you information to assist you to function in life.

Primal Origins

Emotions are connected to primal systems from earlier in human evolution. Such systems were designed to address a "something", and were usually to maintain safety. To put a more serious spin on it, humans are calibrated to stay alive and functioning. Emotions play a huge role.

Emotions are part of an elaborate primal system designed to work cooperatively to prepare and activate the body to react. This Emotional Response System is called Fight, Flight, Freeze or Fawn Response. In some ways one's emotional profile and responses have an evolutionary or DNA-genetic link. They are stored in cellular memory coding files with origins from earlier in human existence. Emotions and feelings are part of the autonomic nervous system that resides in the brain. Accordingly, your Emotional Response System carries legacy information from earlier in human history, as well as your own personal history.

Emotions are Sensory

Emotions are part of a sophisticated system that relies upon and utilizes your senses. One's senses (sight, sound, smell, touch, and taste) provide the brain information that may elicit an emotion. Emotions are calibrated by the intensity of what the body senses, both internally and externally. When you perceive, through your complex sensory system, a "something" that is "interesting and new," or "dangerous and scary" you are designed to react and to prepare to address the situation emotionally. Through this system of miraculous awareness one is programmed to pay attention to sensations which might indicate harm, shatter one's security, affect safety or simply put us off our course.

Emotions Just Are - No Bad Emotions or Feelings

When I say that emotions "just are" I am meaning that they are neither good nor bad. They are automatic bursts of energy. They are simply basic and valuable signals that have complex and nuanced meanings connected to a situation in the present.

Emotional Responses are Connected to the Whole Body

Emotional responses take place in the brain AND the entire body (Kanyer, L., 2004). Emotions are connected to and work with the rest of the body. As mentioned earlier, the brain in response to an emotional reaction excretes or pours out powerful hormones (oxytocin, epinephrine/adrenaline, cortisol, dopamine, norepinephrine, serotonin, GABA), flooding the entire body. The hormones tell the body that something is happening and is signaling it to possibly respond.

In a situation where safety is a concern, the hormones are epinephrine, adrenaline and cortisol. These powerful hormones provide potent energy to the body, including one's muscle system, to move or to do something else. They will for instance send a message to the heart, causing an increased heart rate, which will prepare you to move swiftly. You might feel the hormone of adrenaline hitting the nerves in your hands and discover yourself wringing your hands.

Emotions May Not Initially be Cognitive

The initial emotional process is not a cognitive experience or something that you can process with your thinking or reasoning. Social Worker Wyatt Kanyer says, "Words come after the emotions (Kanyer, W., 2022)." The emotional centers are not the thinking centers of your brain. Your brain, like your heart, has sections that are connected to perform tasks but used at different times for different functions. Thoughts follow down the line after the initial sensory emotional reaction. It can take time for the thinking and processing to kick in, usually with the expression of feelings. "In most cases you will be thinking about what you experienced after you felt it," reports Kanyer (Kanyer, W., 2022).

Emotions and Memories

To maneuver a new "something" in the present, your emotions and feelings are connected to and coupled with your memories. Once again, this happens very swiftly and often outside of one's awareness.

When a new situation emerges and your body registers a sensory input to pay attention to a "something," it accesses its memory bank. The memory bank contains past experiences and stored information. These memory snippets, ignited by the emotional sensory input, are attached which then contribute to the emotional response. The entire process is about quickly tapping into the past knowledge you stored to assist in addressing the new "something".

Feelings Are More Cognitive

Feelings are attached to an emotional experience. However, feelings also have a connection to thinking, cognition, and verbal expression with words. The value of studying feelings is to be able to decrease one's reactivity and to best choose how to respond (see the exercise-experience on page 79 which offers an in-depth look on expanding one's vocabulary of feeling words).

Once the emotional reaction takes place, feelings are then formed. There are two types of feelings: Primary and Secondary. A Primary Feeling is the first to emerge. They are basic feelings of mad, sad, happy, scared and love. From there Secondary Feelings emerge. Secondary Feelings are more refined and nuanced.

You can have a multitude of feelings related to an emotional reaction (see exercise-experience Feelings Stepping Stones Pathway on page 61). It is a tool for how to understand the expression of feelings. Many chapters in this guidebook focus on the various aspects of feelings.

Putting It All Together

The following is a simplified overview of how the system works. It is offered as a way to summarize the mechanisms, in a list format, to offer greater clarity. Accordingly, here is an example of how the Emotional Response System typically works:

A "Something" Happens - For example; you were at a park in your teenage years. You remove your shoes to run in the grass. You are stung by a bee and your leg swells up. You are in pain.

An Emotional, Physical, Sensory Reaction Takes Place - You yell out and fall down in the grass, holding your foot.

Hormones are Secreted into the Whole Body - To address the bee's sting your whole body is flooded by hormones sent from the brain, preparing you to address the concern. You quickly look up to see how far it is to your car.

Primary Feelings are Registered - Related to the painful bee sting, you feel scared (a Primary Feeling).

Memories are Accessed - Once the emotion and Primary Feelings are expressed, you are then able to further use memory to support the work of addressing the concern. You might say to yourself, "I remember that when I got stung by a bee as a child, my mom put mud on the affected area. I'll try that." You then might cry out to someone "make some mud for my foot," or quickly make the mud yourself.

Early Life Impressions are Accessed - You might say to yourself, "Why did I not think to keep my shoes on?"

Secondary Feelings as Accessed - Once things have settled a bit you are able to ponder your feelings and identify deeper, more nuanced, feelings like frustration, bitterness, or puzzlement (Secondary Feelings).

Cognition Flows - After the initial shock of the concern and an assessment about your safety has been made, you may be able to access further knowledge and cognition. This will allow you to begin to think and generate ideas about what to do to further relieve and tend to the pain.

Evaluate and Expand Feeling Patterns - Once some additional time has passed, you then add and expand to your emotions-feelings patterns, memories and Early Life Impressions. You form new memories, develop new beliefs about parks, bare feet, green grass and the potential for injury from a bee. You may also evaluate the solution you choose and its effectiveness.

Sharing and Telling the Story - Part of the ongoing process of an emotional experience with "something" is to talk about it with yourself and others. This is also a sophisticated process of acknowledging the experience, fortifying your thoughts, and more.

Moving Forward - In the future, each time you consider going to the park or see green grass, or even see a shoe that looks like those you wore that day, your Emotional Response System with all its mechanisms can be accessed. The memory of this "something" may help to predict the likelihood of a similar circumstance taking place. You may choose a variety of actions, which may include avoiding parks altogether. Remember, this pattern is varied for each person and is affected by a bundle of other aspects.

Collage Can Help the Emotional Reaction Systems

This is why we need tools like collage-making. Collage-making provides us a tangible way to consider current and past situations, in the interest of creating a response to an emotional circumstance. Collage-making further helps to heal those hurts, misunderstandings, and traumas from the past.

Feelings, memories, Early Life Impressions, thoughts, and beliefs are complex and nuanced. Having a tool like collage-making to excavate, till and plant more contemporary conclusions is life-giving. It is readily available, non-judgmental and helpful.

Collage-making also uses a body movement process. It is helpful to release stored-up sensory input and any residual hormone deposits that can get stuck in the body. To support well-being after an emotional experience, one needs to have tools that use body movement to release and regulate the weight of the experience. By using collage-making when an emotional experience happens, one is then able to release the effect on the whole body (mind and body). Collage-making thus is able to help rejuvenate, renew, and recoup one's balance and function.

CONTENT ROUND UP to REVIEW—RECALL—REMEMBER

- One's Emotional Response System consists of a number of mechanisms that work together. The mechanisms are emotions, feelings, memories and earlier life impressions.

- Humans create Early Life Impressions that can contribute to and form foundational conclusions, decisions and beliefs that support how one maneuvers and sees the world.

- Memories are snippets of information stored in one's memory bank based on experiences from earlier in life. They are fragments of encoded material designed to be utilized over time.

- Emotions are connected to primal systems from earlier in human evolution, designed to address a "something" and usually to maintain safety. They are helpers.

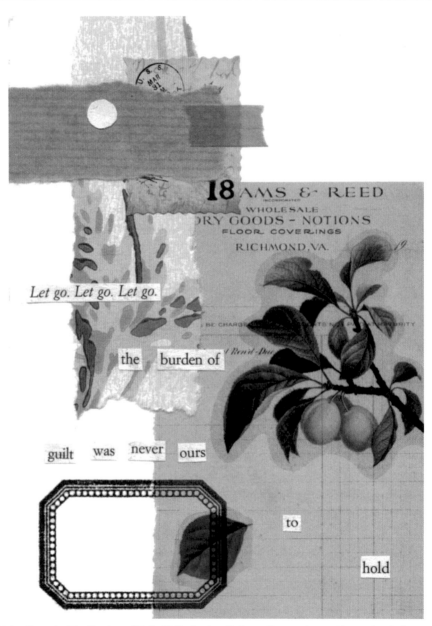

Zohra Hussain, *The Burden of Guilt*, 2021, Analog Collage, Doug + Laurie Kanyer Art Collection

GUIDED COLLAGE EXPERIENCE—MAKE A COLLAGE

1. **GATHER** materials (glue, magazines, books and a substrate to make your collage on). Cut a small, triangle-shaped element from your source material. Place it anywhere on the substrate to provide a personal symbol of power and strength and to offer a comforting, familiar ritual to begin.

2. **DRAW** a large circle on your substrate. Find elements to symbolize the various mechanisms of emotions and feelings (listed below). Cut them out and place them, in no particular order, inside the circle on the substrate.

   The Elements of the Emotional Response System:
   A "something" happens.
   An emotional, physical, sensory reaction takes place in the body.
   Hormones are secreted into the whole body.
   Primary Feelings are registered.
   Memories are accessed.
   Early life Impressions are accessed.
   Secondary Feelings are accessed.
   Cognition Flows; once things have settled a bit one's ability to think and process may begin to take place.
   The process repeats as needed.

3. **TAKE** some time to ponder the mechanisms of emotions and feelings. This system is a process designed to help you function in the world related to a variety of "somethings" you may encounter. Take time to appreciate your feelings and the emotional process as "helpers" to maintain balance and well-being. Locate, cut out, and glue symbolic elements on the substrate about what you are deciding related to your emotions and feelings after reading this material.

4. **WRITE** or use collage elements to create a supportive thought to encapsulate this experience. Put this anywhere on your collage. Example: "I can begin to understand that feelings are helpers. They are neither good or bad, positive or negative, but rather tools to support life."

5. **PLACE** a triangle-shaped element anywhere on the substrate to symbolize your personal strength and to offer a comforting and familiar ritual.

6. **EXTEND** your transformation by completing the TAKEAWAY ACTION TOOLS (page 225).

7. **RETURN** here after completing the Takeaway Action Tools to read the ending quote below.

"Sometimes I feel I need a spare heart to feel all the things I feel."

— Sanober Khan

Twiggy Boyer, *All of Us Together*, 2018, Analog Collage, Doug + Laurie Kanyer Art Collection

FACTORS THAT SHAPE HOW FEELINGS ARE EXPRESSED

A collage-making exercise-experience to understand what influences how you express emotions.

"In order to move on, you must understand why you felt what you did and why you no longer need to feel it." — Mitch Albom

INFORMATION TO THINK ABOUT AND CONSIDER

A curious aspect about feelings, and it is truly remarkable, is there is a marked variance in how each individual feels and expresses their feelings. Even in response to the very same event, people will conjure up in their brain their own emotional-feeling responses. Some people, for example, will be frightened by an experience and others not, depending on what is taking place in their unique brain (Dahl, 2020).

Each person's feeling response can be shaped by a number of factors, as outlined in the following list. These factors can contribute to why people may have a difficult time understanding one another when experiencing the same event, or just attempting to understand reports of other experiences. You can revise how you express feelings by choosing to move beyond any restrictions you may have experienced.

As you look at this list, recognize that it is offered so you can have a baseline to confront and understand where your feeling patterns originated. The list will provide information about why you may "feel the way you feel about feelings". The list is about understanding what contributes to your beliefs about feelings and to see what, if any, adjustment or revision is indicated. It will also help you to appreciate how and why others express, or don't express, their own feelings.

Factors that Shape the Expression of Feelings

Each of us have beliefs or rules—patterns or pathways—either inside or outside of our awareness, that affect how we express feelings. The following list comprises the items that contribute and shape how people express feelings. Any combination of them could contribute to your style of feeling expression.

Temperament

There are two known temperament types: Introverts and Extroverts. Each has a typical way of functioning in the world that can affect how they share their feelings.

Introverts

Introverts tend to be more reserved, keeping their feelings to themselves. They feel most comfortable and draw life energy by being in smaller groups of people.

Extroverts

Extroverts tend to be verbally expressive, sharing openly about their feelings. They feel most comfortable drawing life energy by being in larger groups of people.

Past Experiences

Your beliefs about how to share your feelings can be shaped by your past experience and the impressions you developed. Your beliefs may be impacted by how you shared a certain type of feeling with others. You may have had pleasurable experiences with sharing and some discouraging ones too. These experiences could determine your willingness to take risks and express certain feelings.

One great aspect of using the tool of collage-making is you can first share the feeling with yourself on the collage. Such practice will help increase your comfort with sharing certain feelings. You can then make plans to share your collage and your feelings with others as you feel comfortable.

Family Rules

Each family has their own unique feeling "code system". This code system consists of the ways they are open to hear and support the expression of certain feelings. The code also gives cues as to those feelings that are not accepted or tolerated at all by the group. Each family is different, and the expression of the "OK family code" of emotions is an example of unique features in families. The "code system" is typical and normal for that family group, and is learned either through observation, trial-and-error in expressing feelings (and getting feedback), or direct instruction from the adults and elders in the family.

Age

Like many things in life, one shapes beliefs about feelings as a youngster or adolescent. Your thoughts on many things in life were created as a child, and in many cases those childlike notions, called Early Life Impressions, follow you into adulthood and could need revising. As an example, you learned about certain holidays and the corresponding mythology (Santa Claus is an illustration) as a child. As an adult you revised your notion of Santa and now know more about the myths of his existence. The same can be said about feelings. The age you learned about certain feelings contributes to how you view them and use them today.

Gender

Most people will experience, from the time of their birth, some acculturation as to how to behave or express oneself in the context of their gender. Gender role stereotypes shape hairstyle, clothing, feeling expressions and more. Parents are increasingly understanding the value of emotional intelligence and not cutting off the expression of emotions based on gender, but there is room for improvement. Expecting male children to not cry, to be emotionally restrictive, or to be stoic would be examples of classic male gender roles. Expecting female children to be more expressive and open emotionally is another.

Birth Order

The order children come into a family oftentimes holds particular expectations and roles. These roles imposed by birth order have certain social biases and assumptions as to how a person expresses oneself emotionally.

Cumulative Strains

New stressors you may be experiencing, coupled with cumulative strains from the past, can cause the brain to focus on thoughts and perceptions (sometimes very inaccurate) that impact how you express feelings. This is similar to heart arteries getting clogged with cholesterol and thereby impairing the heart's natural function.

Cultural and Social Rules

The rules of your social groups, beyond your family, can have some influence on your expression of certain feelings and can keep you from saying how you feel. This means a certain type of feelings may or may not be permitted to be expressed within certain groups or contexts. Such social rules may cause one to adhere to cultural or social norms of how to express feelings. Certain social beliefs and their accompanying language ("just pull yourself up by your bootstraps" or "it's all in your head" or "you are just imagining it") can confuse the brain and keep you from feeling better or getting the help you need. The groups we are talking about could be a club, sports team, your workplace, your school, a religious organization, or others. Since humans are created to be with others you may tend to avoid expressing a feeling contrary to the group in order to belong in the group. Over time this can wear on your understanding of self and others. It is like using a compass where someone has told you to never go NORTH.

Even though the feeling is unacceptable to the group, it does not mean it doesn't exist. Not being able to express your true feelings can result in you not feeling heard, or understood, within the group. You may doubt yourself or feel unsettled. It may lead to you feeling resentful toward the group or being too hard on yourself as you attempt to meet their standards of behavior.

Your Personality

According to renowned Enneagram experts Hudson and Riso, authors of *The Wisdom of the Enneagram: The Complete Guide to Psychological and Spiritual Growth for the Nine Types*, humans create a personality pattern to cope with the uncertainties of the world and connected unmet needs (Hudson, Riso, 1999). In order to protect what they call one's Essence, and what I call one's True Self, people develop a personality type to get our needs met. This essentially means to be bonded, connected and cherished by others (Hudson, Riso, 1999). In the Enneagram model there are nine distinct personality types and each have patterns of how they express feelings (Hudson, Riso, 1999).

Each personality has a series of connected operating behaviors typically used to get needs met. The personality type is chosen early in childhood to decrease the chance of pain and suffering to the True Self. Sadly, for each type there are behavioral limitations imposed, and this can affect the expression and even awareness of one's feelings. The personality is like an actor moving in the world with a series of script directives. The personality actor operates initially to offer help, but in the end can affect well-being and restrict from knowing one's True Self (Hudson, Riso, 1999).

Awareness of this information can help you to address your adapted personality traits. Such awareness can shift your behavior patterns to be more present to yourself and express feelings more freely.

Decade of Birth

The era in which you grew up can also shape how you express feelings. Depending upon your decade of birth, your pattern of feelings expression is impacted by the traditions of that period of time. Additionally, the major global events taking place in the era you were born will have an impact on your feelings. For example, if you grew up during a war, famine, or economic depression you will likely have a different feeling expression pattern than a person who did not have those traumas.

Trauma Wounds

The effects of a trauma—as understood and defined by each person—can also impact the way feelings are shared and explored. A trauma event can be experienced by a group and understood as emotionally heavy. Each individual, however, will register the event in their brain in their own nuanced way. The trauma will have differing effects on each person and their ability to feel and maneuver beyond the event. As Dr. Bruce Perry explains, "When considering trauma one needs to consider the event itself; how did the person register the experience and what lingering or long term effect did it have on the person's functioning. A trauma is any pattern of activation of your stress response system that leads to an alteration in how that systemic functioning leads to an overactivity or over reactivity" (Perry, 2021).

It is vital to note that there are 'Big T' and 'Little t' traumas. Furthermore, even though one might never experience a massive Big T trauma, cumulative exposure or micro aggressions (Little t) can have the same impact as a massive trauma (Perry, 2021).

Trust Wounds

If you have told another how you feel, and then the other person breaks confidentiality and tells others about your feelings, you may feel cautious in sharing feelings. This is a violation of trust and healthy boundaries. Such interactions can hinder and impact the way you share and express feelings in the future.

Cross Pollination

Insofar as humans are relational and built for connectedness, it is not surprising that feelings between people could be shared, or pollinated, from one person to another (Bourg, S. 2012). There is an energy field between people related to feelings. One person in a group could feel a feeling and because of close proximity to others, their feelings can affect the feelings of others around them. It is much like a bee gathering pollen from a certain feeling flower, and then being in community with other bees, the entire hive of bees experiences the same.

This process is formally referred to as Feeling Contagion. Humans have empathic features and tend to mirror each other's feelings. A complicated physiological emotional tone is set by one member within a group. Through observing the person's feelings and the associated non-verbal feeling expressions, others begin to mirror the feeling cues (Carter, 2012). The challenge with Feeling Contagion is that individuals may discount their own feelings and desires based on the potency of the group feelings. They may experience pressure to match the feeling of the group and discount or ignore their own feelings. In some ways this is "feeling-peer-pressure" and can be disabling to the individual.

Similarly, Feeling Contagion could also lift the spirits of a group (think of a coach of a competitive sports team). Conversely, imagine you not actually being in a depressed mood but being around someone who is depressively moody; you may become depressed. This could affect your entire well-being.

Physical Ailments - Chronic Illnesses - Injuries

Illness, injury, ailments and various disorders such as a Thyroid condition can affect how you express your feelings. The mind and the rest of the body are connected, and if something is not functioning properly or you have been hurt and are healing your feelings may vary.

Environmental Factors

The safety of your home, neighborhood and who you live with can affect your expression of feelings. When you are not feeling comfortable, uplifted, or safe your emotional tone can shift.

Neuro-Diversity

Each person's system of nerves in the brain is unique to the individual. The vast complicated map of how the nervous system is constructed and how it displays itself can affect how one expresses their feelings. Neuro-Diversity (ND) is an umbrella term to define a number of conditions, which may include Autism, Dyslexia, ADHD, ADD and other brain nervous systems. Such conditions may contribute to what is typical functioning for that unique individual and their expression of feelings. Thankfully, professionals and the general public are now recognizing and respecting that what is typical for the individual need not be the same for everyone. Neuro-Diverse individuals may display feelings differently than people without these conditions.

What Have We Missed? The Good News

There is good news! You can add new skills to manage and transform feelings. Tools like collage-making help one process and understand feelings at any time in your life. You can challenge all of the things that affect your patterns of how you express emotions, and grow to heal beyond your previous experiences.

CONTENT ROUND UP to REVIEW—RECALL—REMEMBER

- There are many factors that affect how one expresses feelings.

- One's personal makeup shaped by your personality or life experiences can affect how you express your feelings and you can learn ways to adapt and heal to better express your feelings.

- A majority of the factors that affect how you express your feelings come from the ideas of others, and you can challenge those social pressures.

GUIDED COLLAGE EXPERIENCE—MAKE A COLLAGE

1. **GATHER** materials (glue, magazines, books and a substrate to make your collage on). Cut a small, triangle-shaped element from your source material. Place it anywhere on the substrate to provide a personal symbol of power and strength and to offer a comforting, familiar ritual to begin.

2. **READ** the list of factors that can affect the expression of your emotions and feelings that was provided earlier. Locate and cut out elements that symbolize items from the list that apply to how you express your own emotions and feelings. Glue them anywhere on your substrate.

3. **LOOK** at the elements you placed and glued on the substrate. Ask yourself what factors you appreciate, and the factors you think need to be challenged, changed and or confronted. Locate and cut out elements to symbolize the factors you appreciate, and those you want to challenge, change and or confront. Glue them near the elements you placed in Step 2.

4. **WRITE** or use collage elements to create a supportive thought to encapsulate this experience. Put this anywhere on your collage. Example: "I can evaluate those things that influence how I express my feelings."

5. **PLACE** a triangle-shaped element anywhere on the substrate to symbolize your personal strength and to offer a comforting and familiar ritual.

6. **EXTEND** your transformation by completing the TAKEAWAY ACTION TOOLS (page 225).

7. **RETURN** here after completing the Takeaway Action Tools to read the ending quote below.

"Whatever makes you feel the sun from the inside out, chase that."

— Gemma Troy

Laurie Kanyer, *There May Be a Problem*, 2018 , Analog Collage, Doug + Laurie Kanyer Art Collection

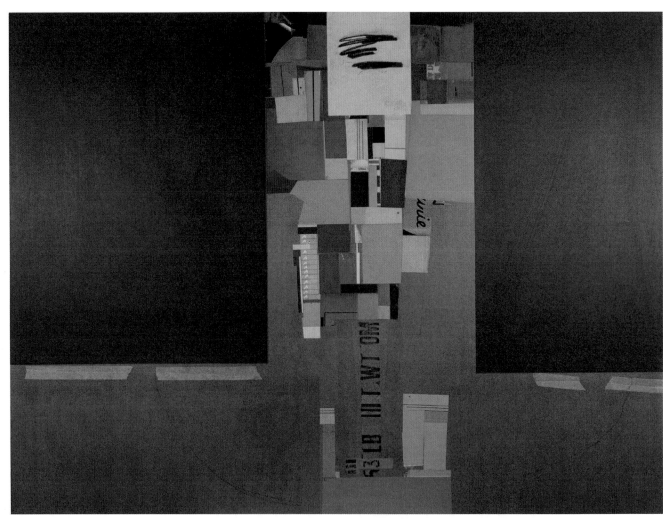

Liberty Blake, *Self Portrait, Meditations on a Yellow Rug*, 2021, Analog Collage, Private Collection

THE FEELINGS STEPPING STONES PATHWAY

A collage-making tool to practice exploring the steps of expressing feelings.

"The best and most beautiful things in the world cannot be seen or even touched.
They must be felt with the heart" — Helen Keller

Special note: In the book *Collage Care: Transforming Emotions and Life Experiences with Collage* (Laurie Kanyer, 2021) this model was described as a staircase. It has now been renamed The Feelings Stepping Stones Pathway for clarity and accuracy.

INFORMATION TO THINK ABOUT AND CONSIDER

The Feelings Stepping Stones Pathway is a tool to help explain the process of how feelings can be expressed in healthy, helpful ways. It is a diagram, using the metaphor of a journey, where one takes a walk along a pathway. During this walk one can then learn to process and express emotions and feelings. The Feelings Stepping Stones Pathway breaks down in detail the specific steps of expressing feelings. It is an analytical model developed to increase your emotional intelligence and expand your overall knowledge of feelings. It will provide insight toward helpful ways to regulate, pace, guide and direct your feelings.

The Brain is Where Emotions and Feelings Originate

The brain, like any other organ, is connected to the whole body, analogous to the heart pumping blood and the lungs processing air. The brain not only creates emotions and feelings but it learns, decides, plans, remembers and implements things. It also talks to itself, giving directions and reinforcing character traits and beliefs.

The Brain Knows It Exists

Unlike other organs, the brain knows it exists, which is remarkable. This is impressive, yet it at times can be a challenge. The brain will note an issue of concern. It can actually talk to itself when feeling off-kilter or unwell. It can go on to diagnose the concern, form a treatment plan and move to implement the plan to make a correction in what it detects. Your self-talk is one element of this phenomenon.

The challenge comes when the brain has a lack of accurate information, limited options, or has developed unhelpful patterns to address concerns. This could be related to how it has learned to express emotions and feelings. The brain uses the patterns and traditions that it has from earlier in life to manage the issue at hand. When an emotional experience is occurring, the brain uses the patterns it is familiar with to express the feelings. As noted on page 55, there are many things that contribute to your feeling-expression patterns.

The Feelings Stepping Stones Pathway offers an updated way for you to understand these patterns and recognize helpful steps. Knowing the pathway allows one to revise old ways of processing feelings, thereby modulating and expressing them in healthy ways. Be reassured you can learn more about your emotions and feelings at any time in your life.

About Emotions

Emotions are created in the brain and are the reactions developed in response to a "something" in life. They are helpers, designed to communicate something to you that is important. Initially, you experience your emotions as a series of physical sensations in the body as a result of chemicals (called hormones) being poured into your system.

These chemicals communicate something important to your entire body, causing you to activate or react. A feeling is then formulated. It all works together to form a particular coded "feeling language" to help you to respond if you need to address a situation. For example, you may need to solve a challenge, seek safety, get some help, or may even indicate you are falling in love!

This is a physiological process, ignited by an emotion, to prepare you to respond or react. Let us say, by way of further example, that you are interviewing for a new job. This is an event that will naturally produce some emotions. In response to the event you may find that your heart rate increases, you may begin to wring your hands, you begin to bounce your knees, or you find yourself clenching your jaw.

Feelings

Feelings are the next layer in the process, stimulated by the emotional-physical experience taking place. You can have more than one feeling at the same time. For example, you may feel both excited and concerned about a new job possibility. When you get to the job interview you experience an emotional reaction as hormones pour through the body, alerting you that something important is taking place. Feelings are then formulated. You may experience feelings of strain, stress, nervousness, or excitement.

Feelings are signals, helping to direct and influence your behaviors and thought processes. For feelings to be useful, you need to process them for the purpose of putting them into an action plan. Knowing the Feelings Stepping Stones Pathway will help you express feelings effectively. Keep in mind that beneficial Steps may be missed due to lack of knowledge of the process or past unhelpful patterns. Both can impact how the feeling is used. This can be confusing.

Having a working knowledge of the Steps will help you to transform your feelings and use them in a productive way. Knowing the Steps will transform how you use emotions and feelings, rather than using archaic or unhelpful methods that could cause harm to you or others. It bears repeating that you can learn more about your emotions and feelings any time in your life, and in the process transform them into a positive life force. One of the most significant Steps is giving yourself the encouragement and permission to feel your feelings.

Feeling Words

Being able to tell others about your feelings is vital. In order to accurately describe what you are feeling, it is necessary to have a rich and deep vocabulary of words. Your vocabulary of feeling words is often derived from the labels or words for feelings used by your social group or family. As you grew up, you adopted the cues for the words your group used to attach to what you were feeling. This can be limiting, and it is important to expand your vocabulary of feeling words to be able to express yourself well. Your dictionary or collection of feeling words can be expanded and fortified all throughout your life.

A point of emphasis in the Feelings Stepping Stones Pathway, as earlier stated, is to be able to share your feelings with others. In order to accurately share what you feel, you may need to build a deeper, fuller dictionary of feeling words. Finding just the right word to express your feelings is critical in the transformation of emotions and expression of feelings (see the exercise-experience titled Expanding Your Vocabulary of Feeling Words on page 79 and see page 230 for examples of feeling words). You will recognize that some of the feeling words are closely related to one another, but slightly different. Others may be vastly different from one another. Identifying just the right word to label your feelings will help you to feel understood by yourself and others.

Remember You Are Not Your Feelings

How you describe your feelings to yourself and others counts. How you choose to phrase or describe things reinforces thoughts and beliefs about them. Feelings are things unto themselves and not descriptive labels about who you are. You are not your feelings! Rather, your feelings are simply the part of an Emotional Response System in connection to a "something".

When describing your feelings, rather than saying, I am mad" or "I am bitter" which would describe you, choose to say, "I am feeling mad" or "I am feeling bitter." This will prevent the chance of you and others labeling you as your feelings.

Feelings Stepping Stones Pathway—
A Model to Look at Healthy Ways People Process Feelings

How Does the Model Work?

On any given day you will experience emotions and feelings connected to a "something". Sometimes when you experience a "something", you then register a strong emotional response in your brain and body. Other times an event will take place, and the emotional response is barely noticeable; it just rolls off your shoulders, and you move on.

When you have a significant emotional response, one that is registered and noticed in your body and awareness, you will then formulate feelings. The model below articulates in detail the steps one takes when having a feeling.

Not a Measuring Stick, Nor a Judge

As you examine the Steps, it will be important to remember that this is an illustration to help one understand the process. It is not a measuring stick, nor is it a rigid tracking system. It is a simplistic way to show a very complicated process and to support you in gaining a clearer view of what you might be experiencing.

As you read these Steps, know that they are offered to increase your awareness and expand your knowledge, not to be a judge or a jury. As you deepen your awareness and knowledge of the feeling expression system, you can improve and transform the quality of your life and your emotional well-being. The model gives you clues to consider and steps to add to your pattern of how you express yourself.

Entering the Feelings Stepping Stones Pathway

Stepping Stone One: A "something" takes place and you have an emotional response that registers in your body. You become aware of what is happening in your body, signaling you to pay attention. For example; you might be grinding your teeth, clenching your jaw, wringing your hands, feeling pressure in your neck, feeling hot. You might observe that your verbal expression has also shifted. The speed of your speech and your tone, both in your head and to others, may change and speed up.

Stepping Stone Two: You have a chat with yourself (self-talk) using an internal dialog about what is taking place. You give yourself permission and encouragement to feel and express your feeling(s) to yourself or someone else, instead of ignoring, stuffing or discounting them (Brackett, M. 2019). In doing this you are able to use the feeling to respond to the situation. You might say, "I am feeling frightened and can figure this out. I am giving myself encouragement and permission to sort it out and move to get help by telling someone."

Stepping Stone Three: You begin actively looking into yourself to access, grasp, and decipher the feeling in order to label your feeling(s) with word(s) or phrase(s). It is vital to accurately identify your feelings with precise feeling words to use them effectively and to experience acceptance.

> **Important Note:** There are two types of feeling words: Primary and Secondary. Examples of Primary Feeling words: mad, sad, happy, scared and love. Secondary Feelings words are infinite and nuanced. They are more refined and they provide a more definitive label to describe the feeling. Examples would include words like frightened, bewildered, aghast, exuberant, surprised, or blissful (see Primary and Secondary Feelings on page 67 for more and see page 230 for an expansive list of feeling words). Notice the variety and intensity of many of the words and how each possesses a nuanced and specific meaning.

Stepping Stone Four: You express your feeling(s) to yourself first. "I am feeling mad (Primary Feeling) and bitter, broken and betrayed (Secondary Feeling). In making a collage you can show these feelings and then choose to talk to someone, including yourself, about it.

Stepping Stone Five: You witness and observe yourself expressing the feeling(s). For example, let's say you are talking to someone about how you are feeling. As they listen to you and respond, they quietly witness you express your feelings, and you are seeing them seeing you. This is deeply restorative.

In this book, you use collage-making to express and witness your feelings. When you create a collage you are actually seeing, witnessing and observing yourself sharing your feelings. You are the one expressing the feeling and you are also the viewer who is witnessing and listening. The feeling is therefore not stuck and hidden within. It is being seen by you! In the process of witnessing, it is exceedingly important to do so without judgement. This too is restorative.

Stepping Stone Six: You accept, acknowledge and validate your feelings, having expressed them. This is remarkable, because having done the other steps, you are now able to see your feelings as important and valuable. You are not denying or apologizing for the feeling(s). You are practicing acceptance, validating the feeling(s) as true, and seeing them as gifts and signals to solve a problem, get help, or reflect on a situation.

Stepping Stone Seven: You pace, modulate and regulate the emotions and associated hormones. This is accomplished via the process of having expressed, witnessed and accepted the feelings. This allows for release of the hormones and the feelings now flowing through your system. The physical movement and activity in collage-making, the cutting, pasting and turning of the pages, helps to move the hormones in the body and directs the feeling to a productive outcome. This then allows for the feeling to become a helpful signal to address a "something", rather than denying or discounting them, which would further upset your system.

Stepping Stone Eight: You use the feeling as a signal to inform decision-making and problem solving. Yes, you can think and feel at the same time! You begin to gather information and suggestions to solve the concern that caused the initial emotional reaction.

Stepping Stone Nine: You consider your choices. Such choices include but are certainly not limited to; gathering more information, asking for suggestions from others, or pausing for a time to ponder, reflect and contemplate the situation.

Stepping Stone Ten: You move forward by either activating a choice (or choices) or letting the situation melt away. Since you've expressed your feelings, you now have the option, if necessary, of pausing until a better time to move forward. In making a Feelings Stepping Stones Pathway collage, you identify what you are experiencing, label with words what you see on the forthcoming collage, and in the process transform your emotions and improve the quality of your life and relationships.

CONTENT ROUND UP to REVIEW—RECALL—REMEMBER

- You can utilize the model called the Feelings Stepping Stones Pathway to analyze and become more familiar with the steps of expressing feelings.

- Your vocabulary of words to express feelings can be expanded and revised at any time.

- Collage-making can help you to regulate the emotion hormones coming from your brain, which pour into your body to alert you to pay attention to something.

- Collage-making gives you a visual format to see and witness your feelings and to be better understood by you and others.

GUIDED COLLAGE EXPERIENCE—MAKE A COLLAGE

1. **GATHER** materials (glue, magazines, books and a substrate to make your collage on). Cut a small, triangle-shaped element from your source material. Place it anywhere on the substrate to provide a personal symbol of power and strength and to offer a comforting, familiar ritual to begin.

2. **ORIENT** the substrate horizontally. Draw a diagonal line from the top left-hand corner to the bottom right-hand corner.

3. **REVIEW** the steps of the Feelings Stepping Stones Pathway. Start at the top left corner and paste an element from your source material to symbolize each of the steps. Place each next to the previous one, working down the line. Locate element(s) that exemplify:

   - A "something" that caused an emotional response that registered in your body.

   - Noticing your self-talk. Giving yourself encouragement and permission to feel your feelings.

   - Accessing and deciphering the feeling and searching for a precise word to describe the feeling.

   - Expressing your feelings to yourself first and then others.

   - Observing and witnessing yourself expressing the feelings.

   - Validating, accepting, and acknowledging your feelings.

   - Modulating and pacing the emotional hormone response.

   - Using your feelings to inform decisions and resolve challenges.

   - Moving on to resolve the "something" or letting it melt away.

   - Use The Feelings Stepping Stones Pathway any time to accurately analyze a "something" and its related feelings. You can also use it to consider feelings from the past.

4. **WRITE** or use collage elements to create a supportive thought to encapsulate this experience. Put this anywhere on your collages. Example: "I can give myself encouragement to feel my feelings, and I can use the Feelings Stepping Stones Pathway to process my emotions and feelings."

5. **PLACE** a triangle-shaped element anywhere on the substrate to symbolize your personal strength and to offer a comforting and familiar ritual.

6. **EXTEND** your transformation by completing the TAKEAWAY ACTION TOOLS (page 225).

7. **RETURN** here after completing the Takeaway Action Tools to read the ending quote below.

> *"Never apologize for showing your feelings. When you do,*
> *you are apologizing for the truth."*
>
> — José N. Harris

Sonia Boué, *Hand on Heart (let the healing begin)*, 2022, Analog Collage, Doug + Laurie Kanyer Art Collection

PRIMARY AND SECONDARY FEELINGS

A collage-making exercise-experience to learn about the layers of feelings.

"You can feel all your feelings." — Jean Illsley Clarke

INFORMATION TO THINK ABOUT AND CONSIDER

When you have an experience and register an emotional reaction, you then formulate a series of feelings that follow. These feelings are "attached" to the emotion. Feelings essentially have two layers: Primary and Secondary. The Primary Feeling is the first feeling layer to show itself. The Secondary Feeling is the next layer connected to and following the Primary Feeling. Secondary Feelings are more nuanced and refined, and are the more accurate and true feelings you have about a "something". You can have many feelings at once.

The Five Primary Feelings are:

Happy - often expressed in connection to an intimate experience, good fortune, or success.

Mad - often expressed when someone crosses your boundary.

Sad - often expressed when you are dealing with loss, disappointment, or unachieved expectation.

Afraid - otherwise called fear, "afraid" is expressed in response to a threat or danger.

Love - often expressed when you feel particularly attached or enthralled with someone or something.

Primary Feelings may be easy to see on a person's face and in their body language. Your body has an emotional-physical reaction connected to a "something". As an example, when someone experiences sadness you notice that an individual's face, and especially their eyes, may be drawn downward. Or you are in love with the food at a restaurant…you can almost see the anticipation in your physical demeanor.

Primary Feelings Are The First Layer

People very often believe that a Primary Feeling is the entirety of an experience. Primary Feelings, however, are simply the first layer of feelings. There is much more that is going on when you experience a feeling.

Primary Feelings are like the curtain on a stage that you see at the beginning of a play. Hiding behind the curtain is the next layer, the Secondary Feelings, which are the more true and accurate feelings. Secondary Feelings are like the real characters and the story in a play. Primary Feelings are the first initial jolt of feeling(s) that take place, but the Secondary Feelings are more accurate. They describe what you are truly thinking and feeling about the event.

Secondary Feelings Are Nuanced

For example; you may at the beginning of an upsetting emotional experience feel the Primary Feeling of MAD. But if you explore it more deeply and look beyond MAD, you will have the opportunity to reveal the true, precise, or deeper feelings connected to the event. The deeper emotions are the Secondary Feelings. These Secondary Feelings may actually be BETRAYAL or BEWILDERMENT, and are much more refined, nuanced feelings connected to the situation.

Secondary Feelings Offer Deeper Information

Moving beyond MAD and unpacking BETRAYED and BEWILDERED will help you to then discern and discover what to do about the situation. If you discover your feelings are BETRAYAL, you may be motivated to determine who you can really trust. You may choose to shift connections with those who betrayed you, and revise your beliefs about them and their behavior. If you express the feeling of BEWILDERED, you will find yourself possibly asking for more information, seeking more input to decrease confusion.

In determining your Secondary Feelings you will make more sophisticated decisions and appropriate plans to address the event or situation. Had you stayed at the MAD feeling layer and not considered the Secondary Feelings layer you may have missed an opportunity to know more. If you are aware that you were feeling betrayed and bewildered, coupled with MAD, you will have the chance to access more sophisticated and accurate information. You can think and feel at the same time when accessing both layers of feelings.

Pause Here and Let This Soak In. FEELINGS are HELPERS!

In the example cited above, if you stay stuck in only identifying the Primary Feeling of MAD you might, in fact, be limiting in your ability to function or solve problems. Instead, MAD could lead to hurting oneself or others. When you exert the energy to inquire of yourself what you feel beyond MAD, and delve into BETRAYED and BEWILDERED, an entirely different set of possibilities become available. Most of all, you are affirmed that what you feel about an experience is important and you are important. Your feelings are helpers.

An Illustration

Observing Primary and Secondary Feelings could be compared to looking at a tree. You can notice there are the parts of a tree that are easy to see and to observe, and other parts that are buried and can't be seen without some digging into the earth.

Imagine you are going for a walk and see a tree swaying in the wind. The wind is like a "something" that causes an emotional reaction leading to feelings. The tree, as it sways and bends, is responding to the event of the wind blowing. It is having a reaction to the wind, like your feelings of Sad or Mad when you have a disagreement with someone. You can see the branches bending, leaves falling, and hear the noise of the wind whistling. This is like a human having an emotional reaction to a "something". The Primary Feeling is the initial response, the first feeling layer, to a situation, like the tree in the wind.

What you can't easily observe when the tree is reacting to the force of the wind are the other things going on, beneath the earth in the root system. This is true with human emotions too. The feeling that is below the surface, underneath the first, Primary Feeling, is the Secondary Feeling. The Secondary Feeling is like all the activity taking place in the earth affecting the roots of the tree in the dirt in reaction to the powerful wind event. Secondary Feelings symbolize an abundance of other feelings connected in the first reaction to the situation.

Some More Examples

If SAD is the Primary Feeling, equivalent to the tree branches cracking a bit as the wind blows, then Secondary Feelings, such as HELPLESS, INSECURE, ANXIOUS, OVERWHELMED, or PERSISTENT may equate to the tree roots digging deeper to secure the tree.

If HAPPY is the Primary Feeling, in reaction to the event, like the noise of the wind dancing in the branches and the leaves joyously drifting away, then some Secondary Feelings, like the roots finding a new source of water, could be EXCITED, ENERGETIC, OPTIMISTIC, or THRILLED.

Another way to illustrate Primary and Secondary Feelings is to think of an iceberg (Johnston, 1984). What can be observed from a boat is the large massive chunk of ice rising above the surface of the water. This is like the Primary Feeling. Below the water, what you cannot see but is very real and important, is the rest of the iceberg which is like your Secondary Feelings. Exploring the layers of your feelings helps you to get to the root of your authentic feelings! In doing so you become a more authentic, productive, and capable human!

How People Describe Emotions and Feelings

Depending on what country you come from there are different ways of talking about how you feel. In the United States it is common to say I am (fill in the blank, mad, sad, bitter, surprised, so forth). The problem with this way of describing a feeling is it accidentally labels you with the feeling. The down side of saying "I am bitter" in this way is that others could describe you like this. "Paul is a bitter person."

In Ireland the way one describes experiencing a feeling is by saying, "Sadness has come upon me." They describe it this way because of how the words in their language are arranged in a sentence. In truth, saying that a feeling comes upon one is a more accurate way to talk about what experiencing a feeling is really like. Feelings do "come upon" a person. You experience a feeling connected to a "something" that is laid upon your being. You are not your feelings, and really should not be described as such.

Whether you are in Jamaica or Washington State, USA try describing your feelings by saying, "I am feeling (fill in the feeling word). This tells a more accurate story. Something happens and a feeling arises that you actually experience in your body. Or adopt the Irish sentence structure of describing this phenomena of experiencing a feeling and say, "The feeling of disappointment has come upon me."

CONTENT ROUND UP to REVIEW—RECALL—REMEMBER

- Feelings have layers called Primary and Secondary Feelings.

- There are five Primary Feelings, and hundreds, if not thousands, of Secondary Feelings. The Primary Feeling is what is shown at first when a situation arises and the Secondary Feeling follows.

- Your truest and authentic feelings are your Secondary Feelings.

- Secondary Feelings have infinite and nuanced qualities to them. They are distinct and precise relating to a situation.

- Taking time to discover, accept and express your Secondary Feelings will help you to know yourself better. It allows you to describe to others what is taking place for you in any given situation.

Emma Anna, *Imagine*, 2021, Analog Collage, Doug + Laurie Kanyer Art Collection

Daphna Epstein, *June Bells*, 2022, Digital Collage, Doug + Laurie Kanyer Art Collection

GUIDED COLLAGE EXPERIENCE–MAKE A COLLAGE

1. **GATHER** materials (glue, magazines, books and a substrate to make your collage on). Cut a small, triangle-shaped element from your source material. Place it anywhere on the substrate to provide a personal symbol of power and strength and to offer a comforting, familiar ritual to begin.

2. **LOCATE** a tree element or make a symbolic tree-like structure using elements. Cut it out and glue it down on your substrate. Think of a time you felt strongly about something. Ask yourself, did you feel happy, mad, sad, scared or in love? Find an element(s) to symbolize your Primary Feeling. Glue the element near the branches and leaves of the trees.

3. **CONSIDER** what other emotions accompany what you felt. What were any Secondary Feelings you experienced about the "something"? Refer to the list of Feeling Words on page 230 for suggestions or look in a dictionary. Find elements to symbolize words to describe all of your Secondary Feeling to identify and describe how you felt. Take your time and find as many words as possible to show how you really felt. Cut them out and glue them near the trunk or near where the roots of the tree would be. If you later think of another word to add, do so. Use this guided collage-making experience to help you in the future to get to the ROOT of how you really feel!

4. **WRITE** or use collage elements to create a supportive thought to encapsulate this experience. Put this anywhere on your collage. An example: "I can become familiar with my feelings and take time to discover them."

5. **PLACE** a triangle-shaped element anywhere on the substrate to symbolize your personal strength and to offer a comforting and familiar ritual.

6. **EXTEND** your transformation by completing the TAKEAWAY ACTION TOOLS (page 225).

7. **RETURN** here after completing the Takeaway Action Tools to read the ending quote below.

"Feelings or emotions are a universal language and are to be honored. They are the authentic expression of who you are at your deepest place."

— Judith Wright

Lana Turner, *What We've Never Had We Don't Miss*, 2020, Collage in Vintage Book, Doug + Laurie Kanyer Art Collection

Miranda Millward, *Lavender Finch*, 2022, Analog Collage, Doug + Laurie Kanyer Art Collection

THE WIDE SPECTRUM OF EMOTIONS AND FEELINGS

A collage-making exercise-experience to explore the value of the wide spectrum of feelings.

"Your emotions make you human. Even the unpleasant ones have a purpose." — Sabaa Tahir

INFORMATION TO THINK ABOUT AND CONSIDER

Emotions and feelings occur across a broad spectrum. There are no bad emotions and feelings, as they are merely helpers to support one's well-being. That being said, emotions and feelings will be activated in response to a "something", and the "something" can be on a spectrum from hard and negative, to neutral and commonplace, all the way to joyful and positive. The resulting emotions and feelings will therefore also be on a spectrum from hard and negative, to neutral and commonplace, to joyful and positive.

There are No Bad or Good Emotions and Feelings

For the purpose of our discussion here we will attempt to help you to understand how emotions and feelings on the more intense ends of the spectrum are helpers, rather than good or bad, negative or positive. While they are potent and strongly felt when activated, they are needed to ensure well-being. Emotions and feelings on the outer range of the spectrum serve unique and important functions and purposes. Each person will distinctly interpret these emotions and feelings on their own personal spectrum. This is why talking to one another about one's feelings is so important. In doing so one can come to understand what happens for others when a "something" provokes a strong response.

For example, the emotions and feelings that are activated when one experiences the "something" of a near car accident could be interpreted as strongly negative. These emotions and feelings could be labeled as negative since the "something" itself, the near car accident, is clearly a negative, bad "something". Examples of the resultant emotions and feelings could be mad, scared, devastated, or outraged. They could be labeled by someone as negative or bad since the "something" that stirred them is negative. The feelings themselves are not negative, they simply match the negative event.

Conversely, the emotions and feelings that are activated when seeing a person at the grocery store whom you love, when you were not expecting to do so, could be interpreted as strongly positive or good. These emotions and feelings are labeled as positive since the "something" itself, the surprise of a loved one at the store, could be experienced as clearly positive or good. Examples of the resultant emotions and feelings could be love, joy, delight, or excitement. They are labeled by some as positive or good, as the "something" that stirred them is positive. The feelings themselves are not positive, they simply match the positive event.

On the other hand, there are many mid-range emotions and feelings that are everyday and commonplace. They are rather neutral in their tone. They occur when no "something" is in play or the "something" is perceived as neither strongly negative or positive. Emotions and feelings like settled, calm, or peaceful are examples of neutral. An example of a neutral "something" might be emotions and feelings connected to the daily watching of a favorite television show or going to the grocery store.

All Feelings Have Purpose - Feelings are Helpers

As author Tracy Kennedy (Kennedy, n.d) points out, there are valid purposes for emotions and feelings all across the spectrum. For example:

- Anger - to fight against threats.
- Fear - to protect us from danger.
- Anticipation - to look forward and plan.
- Surprise - to focus on new situations.
- Joy - to remind us what's important.
- Sadness - to connect us with those we love.
- Trust - to connect with people who help.
- Disgust - to reject what is unhealthy.

Courtney E. Ackerman, MA, points out, "Without disgust, for example, would you be moved to do something when you observe something vile? Without joy, one might overlook what is important to them. Without fear, what would move you to protect yourself from danger? (Ackerman, 2021)." Ackerman goes on to say that even during seemingly positive events there are negative feelings, and vice versa. Consider the strain during the holidays with all of the extra work and activities, or the joy at funerals when seeing people you have not seen for a long time and reminiscing with them.

Avoid Judging Emotions and Feelings

When one adopts the attitude that emotions and feelings are designed to help, then one can also adopt the notion that they are neither good, bad, positive or negative. You can begin to see them as tools designed for a helpful purpose.

When you see feelings this way you also enjoy the further benefit of not judging feelings that you have, or judging feelings that others have. You instead become curious as to what the emotions and feelings are signaling one to do and discover how to use them to support your well-being.

Why People Focus on Perceived Negative Feelings

Note that the brain is wired to attend to and focus on negative feelings far more than positive or neutral feelings. This is referred to as Negative Bias (Rozin & Royzman, E. 2001). Negative Bias is an evolutionary phenomenon that leads to safety, alerts one to potential threats and promotes overall survival by noticing things that seem to be negative. A small impulse of negativity will register in your brain to keep you alert to a hazard, be that a person, situation or event. Past negative experiences with a person, place or situation can produce a continued negative feeling tone or an alert system to protect you. This is why first impressions that are negative take time to overcome.

In an interesting twist, a new negative event with something previously neutral or positive may lead to a negative response. This can affect the way you make decisions, as you will find you give more weight to negative aspects or feelings to prevent future challenges. Some say it takes seven positive feelings to douse the potency of negative impressions and emotions.

Strong Emotions and Feelings Produce Potent Hormones

Both negative and positive feelings tend to elicit a more powerful chemical reaction pouring from the brain to the whole body. Anger and fear will cause a flood of adrenaline and cortisol, while anticipation will send a jolt of dopamine. In both cases one can feel a sense of being more alive or aware as these hormones activate in the system.

These feelings of being alive or aware have an addictive quality to them. People may be tempted to look for drama or take risks in their life to get a dose of adrenaline or cortisol, or be tempted to seek pleasureful, exciting experiences to get a sharp jolt of dopamine. In both cases, a belief may have been formed that neutral feelings lead to boredom, and that the notion of living in a place of neutrality is not really living. Be aware of this tendency.

Over-exposure to too much negativity or positivity can lead to exhaustion, burnout and other problems. This over-exposure may lead to high input levels of adrenaline, cortisol or dopamine, which can be hard on the system. Acknowledging this information is helpful, as it offers you a chance to consider your lifestyle, your associates, your job and other contributors (see the exercise-experience titled Avoiding Drama featured on page 213 for more). One can make helpful adjustments and move to experience more neutral feelings in life. People who experience more neutral feelings seem to have better health and less illness.

Collage-Making Can Help

You can use collage-making to modulate, regulate, and express your potent and strong feelings to release them from your system (Kanyer, 2018, 2021). Collage-making can reduce the chance of such negative feelings expanding and diluting the quality of your life. You can use collage-making to consider the negative, potent, and strong feelings you experience, and therefore dissipate the possibility of harmful chemicals polluting your system.

Collage-making will help you to document times of strong, potent positive emotions, but to not see them as the ultimate goal in life. It will help you perceive them as a high point that needs to flow into a more neutral feeling tone, where you can be calm enough to fully express a blessing or the gentle passing of time.

Collage-making, especially when used regularly, can elicit or expand neutral feelings of peace and balance. You can use collage-making to de-escalate the chance of the highs and lows, the hills or the valleys. Collage-making can help you to advance to a higher road of objectivity.

In conclusion, there is a wide spectrum of feelings that are experienced and expressed. Negative feelings will often be given more attention. Both negative and positive emotions can be addictive. It can be helpful to have the goal of working toward the more neutral feelings of resting and calm as a way to avoid the high of euphoric positivity and the dread of profound negativity.

CONTENT ROUND UP to REVIEW—RECALL—REMEMBER

- There is a wide spectrum of feelings. Such feelings range from potent, strong positive feelings, to potent, strong negative feelings, to neutral balanced feelings.

- All feelings are helpers and are designed to assist in life.

- Neutral feelings are those that are connected to a calm state of mind and are associated with increased health and well-being.

- Strong feelings, either positive or negative, carry with them potent brain hormones that can be addictive, and it is wise to be aware of these qualities to avoid extended problems.

GUIDED COLLAGE EXPERIENCE—MAKE A COLLAGE

1. **GATHER** materials (glue, magazines, books and a substrate to make your collage on). Cut a small, triangle-shaped element from your source material. Place it anywhere on the substrate to provide a personal symbol of power and strength and to offer a comforting, familiar ritual to begin.

2. **SEARCH** your source materials for examples of faces, places or things that show negative, positive or neutral feelings. Cut them out and set them aside. As you are cutting, remember times when you've had this range of feelings, and consider the weight or value you connected to the feelings. Which one has the most weight in your memory? Ponder your lifestyle and your past decisions, to discover if you can find events, people or things that led to experiencing these feelings. Choose more elements to show the things that popped into your mind. Cut all the elements out and glue them down on the bottom one-fourth of your collage substrate.

3. **THINK** about a movie or television show where the characters demonstrated the wide range of emotions. Locate an element(s) to show these characters and the effect the wide range of emotions had on them and their life. Cut the elements out and glue them down in the next one-fourth of the substrate. Take time to ponder the lives of these characters and imagine how their lives and the storyline of the show would be different if they had more neutral emotional experiences.

4. **THINK** of a person you know whose life is reflective of a multitude of neutral, calm, balanced feelings, and locate an element to symbolize that person. Cut it out and glue it down in the middle one-fourth of the collage.

5. **NOW** that you know more about the range of positive, negative and neutral emotions, not blaming yourself, but seeking compassion and understanding, ask yourself if you are ready to set a goal to live in a more neutral feeling zone. Look at your source material and find elements to inspire you toward this transformation in life. Cut them out and glue them down on the top one-fourth of the substrate.

6. **WRITE** or use collage elements to create a supportive thought to encapsulate this experience. Put this anywhere on your collage. For example: "I can begin to explore and aspire to live in a more neutral feeling zone."

7. **PLACE** a triangle-shaped element anywhere on the substrate to symbolize your personal strength and to offer a comforting and familiar ritual.

8. **EXTEND** your transformation by completing the TAKEAWAY ACTION TOOLS (page 225).

9. **RETURN** here after completing the Takeaway Action Tools to read the ending quote below.

"The real voyage of discovery consists not in seeking new landscapes,
but in having new eyes."

— Marcel Proust

Miranda Millward, *Watch for the Unexpected*, 2022, Analog Collage, Doug + Laurie Kanyer Art Collection

Les Jones, 56, 2020, Analog Collage, Doug + Laurie Kanyer Art Collection

EXPANDING YOUR VOCABULARY OF FEELING WORDS

A collage-making exercise-experience to increase awareness of possible words to use to express feelings.

"Sometimes I feel I need a spare heart to feel all the things I feel." — Sanober Khan

INFORMATION TO THINK ABOUT AND CONSIDER

When you were born you observed the people in your family and extended social groups and learned how to be a human who fits into the group. You learned from your family the words to express emotions and feelings in the language of your people. As you had experiences, and events took place, you began to express your feelings using the words they either taught you or that you adopted through observation. In doing so they contributed to your personal dictionary of feeling words.

Your Groups Contribute to Feeling Words

Over time, as you were exposed to a larger group of people, you gathered more words to describe your emotions and feelings. Depending on the group and their comfort and traditions with certain words, you discovered ways to communicate about your emotions and feelings. Additionally, the group's acceptance of certain expressions of feelings helped you choose the connected words for those feelings. When you went to school, made friends, played sports or joined clubs you learned even more words, and your vocabulary expanded. You began to develop a personal dictionary of words to use to express various feelings.

Finding the Best Word to Express Feelings

However, in many cases your vocabulary could be limited since it relied primarily on the words used and shared by your social groups. To be able to fully encapsulate what you are feeling, and to be able to accurately express yourself to others, finding just the right word to describe the feeling is key. It is essential to your well-being to make efforts to explore, expand and adopt additional words to express your exact feelings. In doing so, you begin to feel heard and acknowledged by those who care about you. This means actively seeking new and possibly better words than you had learned from others earlier in your life.

Your Vocabulary Can Grow

You can at any time expand and revise your dictionary of feeling words. As you use collage-making in the exercise-experience you have an opportunity to do so. You can transform and elevate your understanding of your feelings by making a concerted attempt to expand your vocabulary of feeling words.

Feeling Words are Nuanced

You will find an extensive list of feelings words on page 230. You will be able to make photocopies of these words for use as elements in your collages. Note, as you read the list, how nuanced the quality of the words to express feelings are. Some are quite similar and some are more diverse. The idea is to build a larger vocabulary so you have words to express, as precisely as possible, what feelings are taking place in your life. For a very simple example, the word "good" is not the same as the word "fine". A more suitable choice for both could be, "I am feeling calm" or "I am feeling balanced." Both words could mean you are feeling good or fine, but they are more refined descriptions that give a fuller understanding of your feelings.

CP Harrison, *For Lost Libras*, 2021, Analog Collage, Doug + Laurie Kanyer Art Collection

GUIDED COLLAGE EXPERIENCE—MAKE A COLLAGE

1. **GATHER** materials (glue, magazines, books and a substrate to make your collage on). Cut a small, triangle-shaped element from your source material. Place it anywhere on the substrate to provide a personal symbol of power and strength and to offer a comforting, familiar ritual to begin.

2. **REVIEW** the steps on the Feelings Stepping Stones Pathway on page 61. Think of a time you felt strongly and find a collage element(s) to symbolize you actively reaching, looking into yourself to access, or grasp and label the feeling as discussed on the Feelings Stepping Stones Pathway.

3. **TURN** to the feeling vocabulary list on page 230. This list is a sample of the variety of feelings, there are many more. Feel free to also search the dictionary for other words. Notice the abundance of words you could use to describe your feeling(s). Find as many collage elements to symbolize words that could be used to label the feeling you experienced. Cut them out and glue them down anywhere on the substrate.

4. **FOCUS** on yourself and search the list of feeling words on page 230 to find one or more that accurately and precisely describes how you are feeling right now. Locate just the right word(s) on the vocabulary list to show your present feeling. You may find there are a number of words to describe your current feelings…this is wonderful. Choose an element(s) to symbolize the word(s), cut them out and glue them on the collage substrate.

5. **LATER,** when you find yourself faced with feelings go to the list of words (or even a dictionary) and once again choose a word(s) to describe how you feel. Find an element, cut it out and glue it to this collage. This collage will document all the words you have found and selected to use. It will serve to show your efforts to continue to expand your vocabulary and dictionary of feeling words. This will affirm the feeling you experienced with the most accurate and precise word, and you will be better equipped to share with others so they can understand your feelings.

6. **WRITE** or use collage elements to create a supportive thought to encapsulate this experience. Put this anywhere on your collage. For example: "I can learn more precise and accurate words to express how I feel".

7. **PLACE** a triangle-shaped element anywhere on the substrate to symbolize your personal strength and to offer a comforting and familiar ritual.

8. **EXTEND** your transformation by completing the TAKEAWAY ACTION TOOLS (page 225).

9. **RETURN** here after completing the Takeaway Action Tools to read the ending quote below.

"In a world full of temporary things you are a perpetual feeling."

— Sanober Khan

Julie Liger-Belair, *Red Thread*, 2020, Analog Collage, Doug + Laurie Kanyer Art Collection

GETTING ACQUAINTED WITH THE PARTS
OF YOUR EMOTIONAL SELF

A collage-making exercise-experience to get to know the parts of yourself better.

"A part is not just a temporary emotional state or habitual thought pattern. Instead, it is a discrete and autonomous mental system that has an idiosyncratic range of emotion, style of expression, set of abilities, desires, and view of the world. In other words, it is as if we each contain a society of people, each of whom is at a different age and has different interests, talents, and temperaments." — Richard Schwartz, PhD

INFORMATION TO THINK ABOUT AND CONSIDER

It might seem surprising to you, but just like the many organs in your body operate in unison to keep you functioning, you have multiple emotional parts. These emotional parts have varied roles and functions, analogous to your physical organs. It is as if you have many people operating in your emotional self all at once.

I first became familiar with this notion in the 1980s. Noted psychiatrist Dr. Eric Berne had observed, in his work with patients, that they seem to have several different emotional states in which they approach life. He labeled the various states as Child, Parent, and Adult. He maintained that each state had positive and negative aspects. The Child contains feelings and needs. The Parent contains rules, beliefs and governing ideals. The Adult contains evaluating, reasoning and thinking (Berne, 1961).

I later became familiar with the work of Richard Schwartz, PhD, founder of Internal Family Systems (IFS). In his work over 40 years, Schwartz discovered that people seemed to have an internal group system of "beings" that he called Parts (Schwartz, 2021). Schwartz's model focuses on the human capacity to develop a number of different "beings" to meet their primary needs, particularly that of safety. In other words humans have a number of personalities to access as needed.

Self-Talk

His discovery helps to explain and understand the running conversation going on in one's mind, often called Self-Talk. Take a moment and ask yourself, have you not had internal conversations trying to figure out what to do? The Parts are developed when a person experiences something, especially some woundedness or a trauma (as defined and experienced by that person). When this happens they will place that hurt part of themselves in what Schwartz calls the Self, in a safe exile. This is done to protect it from further injury. This term is exactly what I mean when I refer to the True Self, i.e. the original being that was present at your birth.

Protection and Saftey - No Bad Parts

When an injury or event occurs that provokes the need to put the Self in an exiled space, a new part will develop to protect and care for the exiled Self. In Schwartz's model there are manager parts, which I like to call helpers or guides. There are also firefighter parts, which protect and address emergencies. They serve to add extra layers of functional support. People create as many parts as needed to survive and move on.

Like Berne, Schwartz acknowledged that there are parts that have a harsh side to them. But he also maintains that there are no bad parts, as all parts provide a service. For example, do you find you have a critical managerial voice in your head that is telling you what to do? Is it trying to keep you in line? It may be harsh for the purpose of keeping you from doing things that could embarrass, cause harm or bring forth trouble in life. This part could be severe and exacting, but aims to protect. The firefighter type might be the one who makes you move swiftly, or even over-act when a perceived dangerous situation arises. They may tell you what to do in an emergency.

The Internal Family System (IFS) also helps us to understand the reactions of others and interpersonal struggles. Have you had a surprising conversation with someone that seemed not consistent with the past? As if their response came out of nowhere? This can be shocking and unsettling. But the IFS parts theory helps us to recognize that there is some need for protection. If approached with compassion and curiosity, with a heart to discover the source of the dissonance, the IFS parts theory helps decrease the upset. You can discover what that particular part of that person is experiencing and aim to understand and speak to the concern.

Working With Parts

What is most amazing is you can learn how to work and converse with the parts of yourself. These conversations can facilitate both deep learning and avenues to revise the role of the parts to better serve you today. I cannot over-emphasize the power of what Richard Schwartz offers. Because the parts were often developed in childhood, when you were still acquiring skills and were still immature, the parts may not know or recognize your abilities to care for yourself in the present. They often benefit from revised information and new jobs.

Collage-Making and Parts

So where does collage-making fit in? Collage-making can help you to become familiar with your parts and to have conversations with them. Collage-making can help you to get to know the parts, understand their job and to appreciate the burden they carry. You can get to know the parts of yourself better and you may be able to release the hardships and responsibilities being carried. Note that many mental health professionals use Schwartz's Internal Family System as a model to help their clients. In addition, Schwartz has a number of wonderful texts on his model that you can read to get a deeper understanding of yourself. You can gather more information on this masterful model.

CONTENT ROUND UP to REVIEW—RECALL—REMEMBER

- People have varied parts of their emotional selves. These parts are defined as Self, Managers and Fire Fighters. The model that discusses this is called Internal Family Systems and was founded and developed by Richard Schwartz PhD.

- A person's parts are developed to facilitate protection and safety for the Self in response to hardship.

- The parts are unique beings that can be communicated with to increase well-being and comfort.

- The parts are able to release the burdens they carry and take on new roles.

GUIDED COLLAGE EXPERIENCE—MAKE A COLLAGE

1. **GATHER** materials (glue, magazines, books and a substrate to make your collage on). Cut a small, triangle-shaped element from your source material. Place it anywhere on the substrate to provide a personal symbol of power and strength and to offer a comforting, familiar ritual to begin.

2. **APPROACH** this collage-making exercise-experience in a spirit of getting to know yourself better and appreciate your ability to care for yourself. With curiosity and compassion ask yourself if there is a part who might be willing to be known. If so, focus on the part and let it reveal itself to you. To get a full appreciation and understanding of the part, find a collage element(s) to symbolize the part. Ask the part to help you find it. Cut the element(s) out and glue them down.

3. **ASK** the part to tell you about itself. How did the part come to be, what is it's job, and what burdens or hardship does it carry. Find elements to show these things, cut them out and glue them down on the substrate. Ask yourself how you feel about this part. Find elements to symbolically show your feelings, cut them out and glue them to the collage. Thank the part and yourself for exploring this material. Find elements to symbolize appreciation for both you and the part.

4. **IMAGINE** you and your part as cooperative friends who came together to work to make sure you were safe and protected. Find element(s) to show your partnership. Knowing a part is usually developed at a time of fear, and when you feel you are both ready, ask the part if it is willing to shift its tasks. By this I mean to release some of their protective jobs and burdens now that you are older and are more mature. Ask if there is any concern on their part in doing so? Find an element(s) for this and glue it down.

5. **INQUIRE** of the part what it would like to do instead of carrying the burden. Does it want a new role or something else (maybe have some fun?). Give the part some time to respond and find elements to show what it would like to do instead. Cut them out and glue them down. To celebrate the shift your part has selected, Schwartz suggests that the part be offered the chance to transform the past energy into elements such as earth, light, fire, water, wind or anything else. If this appeals to the part then choose an element(s) to show this, cut it out and glue it down. You can repeat this with this part and others over time.

6. **WRITE** or use collage elements to create a supportive thought to encapsulate this experience. Put this anywhere on your collage. For example: "I can become familiar with all my parts, their roles and jobs. I can take the time to get to know them, thereby revising, as needed, their function in my life."

7. **PLACE** a triangle-shaped element anywhere on the substrate to symbolize your personal strength and to offer a comforting and familiar ritual.

8. **EXTEND** your transformation by completing the TAKEAWAY ACTION TOOLS (page 225).

9. **RETURN** here after completing the Takeaway Action Tools to read the ending quote below.

"There are no bad parts."

— Richard Schwartz, PhD.

CP Harrison, *A Cocteau I Didn't Know*, 2020, Analog Collage, Courtesy of the Artist

EXPLORING MOODS

A collage-making exercise-experience to learn about moods.

*"It was like a shadow, like a mist passing across her soul's summer day.
It was strange and unfamiliar; it was a mood."* — Kate Chopin

INFORMATION TO THINK ABOUT AND CONSIDER

It is important to know about moods, and to understand they are different from feelings. Moods are usually longer lasting events, or episodes, that can take place over many days. Moods may or may not be clearly associated with specific events or situations. They have a tone to them—qualities of light and darkness—much like what you hear in music, or see in a painting. Your mood might be cheerful and light, or it might be dark and heavy.

Emotions - Feelings are Different than Moods

Emotions, on the other hand, are often a short burst of energy. Feelings follow emotions and usually have some thinking, cognitive qualities to them. Both emotions and feelings are most often linked to a known situation or event, a "something". Emotions and feelings may have a tendency to be more intensely expressed than moods, but not always.

One way to differentiate between a mood and an emotion-feeling is to imagine a house with things happening on the inside and with weather happening on the outside. The change in the weather outside is like one's mood. Emotions and feelings are usually connected to events going on inside the house. In some cases, emotions-feelings may also be connected to the weather (mood) outside. One's mood, just like the weather, shifts and changes. Moods can be like a weather pattern; there for a short time, or remaining for a longer extended period. Emotions and feelings will take place and display different qualities or intensity depending on the situation, a "something", while a mood may not have as dramatic of a shift.

Here's an everyday example. One day you wake up experiencing a grey, cloudy, low energy mood, matching the weather outside. Unlike a gray cloudy day that indicates future rain, there may be no known source for the mood to occur. You may or may not be having any associated feelings in conjunction with the mood. The mood is just like the grayness of the day. Interestingly, you may be experiencing the mood (the weather) and have some feelings that can be related to the mood. Also, you may be having feelings that are connected to other events or situations, not related at all to your mood.

One Can Experience a Variety of Feelings During Moody Periods

You could have a wide range of feelings that lay on top of the mood that have no relation to the mood as well. For example, one could be in a heavy, grey, mood and still momentarily laugh at a joke, or cry over a sad story on the news, yet the persistent continuous mood might still remain.

Others May Note Moods

The outside world, the people with whom you interact, may notice and see you acting or behaving in a rather grey and cloudy-like manner. They may observe that you seem to have low energy, and that you are experiencing a mood of some sort. They may notice on your face a furrowed brow and a rounding of your back and shoulders. This could all be connected to the mood. Conversely, it could be connected to an emotion and feelings that are related to the mood. Or possibly something else altogether. Humans are complex! The people you know may be curious and inquire about what is going on for you and how you are feeling. They may ask you what events or situations are causing what they see as your unusual behavior. Or they may say you seem to be in a grey, dark mood. On the other hand, they may not notice anything at all due to what is happening in their own life. You may have to ask them to talk about what is going on.

If the distinction between moods and emotions-feelings seems vague, it may be distilled as follows:

Moods are one thing.

Emotions and feelings are another.

They can be connected and related to one another…. or not.

Moods Can Come On For No Reason

It can be surprising to have the experience of simply waking up in a mood which is not linked to a prolonged strenuous situation, or related to any flood of emotion connected to a specific event. This can be confusing, but true.

They Can Be Related to a "Something"

On the other hand, a mood can emerge from extended exposure to a series of events. Perhaps it might be ongoing sorrow due to loss. A mood might commence due to a change in hormones or a known (or yet to be diagnosed) mental health issue. The use and abuse of substances can affect moods. Ongoing trials connected to an extended event can understandably lead to a period of a certain mood.

Important Note: It is very important to consult with a medical or mental health professional if a mood episode persists for more than two weeks, or if a drastic, sudden change in mood comes on quickly and remains. If you have been diagnosed with one of the clinically known mood disorders, talk with your professional right away. Contact them as soon as possible if you have a sudden change in your mood.

Moods Can Be Transformed

The positive news is that moods can be transformed and changed. There are a number of things to do to lift a cloudy, heavy mood. Below you will find some proven techniques to add to your day that help improve and maintain mental well-being and related moods.

Many of these techniques are sensory-based and offer the brain additional information or stimulus. Your brain is like a generator, and when it gets new electrical input it can re-distribute the energy, changing the mood. This additional stimulus will unleash feel-good chemicals that may shift your mood. Each of the following, plus collage-making, can help.

MOOD CHANGERS

- Play music. Known as music therapy: see page 21 for what is good to listen to.
- Try what is called a Mona Lisa Half-Smile. Simply curl your lip upward.
- Smelling pleasing scents. Try orange, lavender, or cinnamon.
- Jump. Yes, you read that right! Try jumping jacks, jump rope or simply jump up and down.
- Go outside, expose yourself to sunlight, and put your feet in green grass.
- Snuggle with a soft blanket.
- Make a collage or simply cut out elements.
- Go for a walk.
- Drink soothing tea. Chamomile, Lavender, and Green are all known to lift moods and increase comfort.
- Accomplish one small goal. Empty the dishwasher, make the bed, or dust a table.

- Make a list of five people for whom you are grateful and send one or more of them a note, email or call them.

- Watch a funny movie.

- Tidy a drawer or two.

- Gather a bouquet of flowers or even just greens from a bush or tree.

- Light a candle.

- Take a bath or a shower.

- Give yourself a massage - pay special attention to your hands and feet.

- Go somewhere new or go somewhere that is uplifting, such as the library or a coffee shop.

CONTENT ROUND UP to REVIEW—RECALL—REMEMBER

- Moods may be connected to a specific event. Moods may also occur stand-alone, independent of a specific event.

- Moods are different from emotions-feelings, but you can have emotions-feelings while experiencing a mood.

- Small, but potent and positive activities can shift a mood.

- If a mood persists for an extended period of time, or you experience a sudden drastic change in mood, consult your doctor or mental health professional.

Beverly West Leach, *Hymns Of Praise: Make Art Not War*, 2022, Collage in a Tunnel Book, Doug + Laurie Kanyer Art Collection

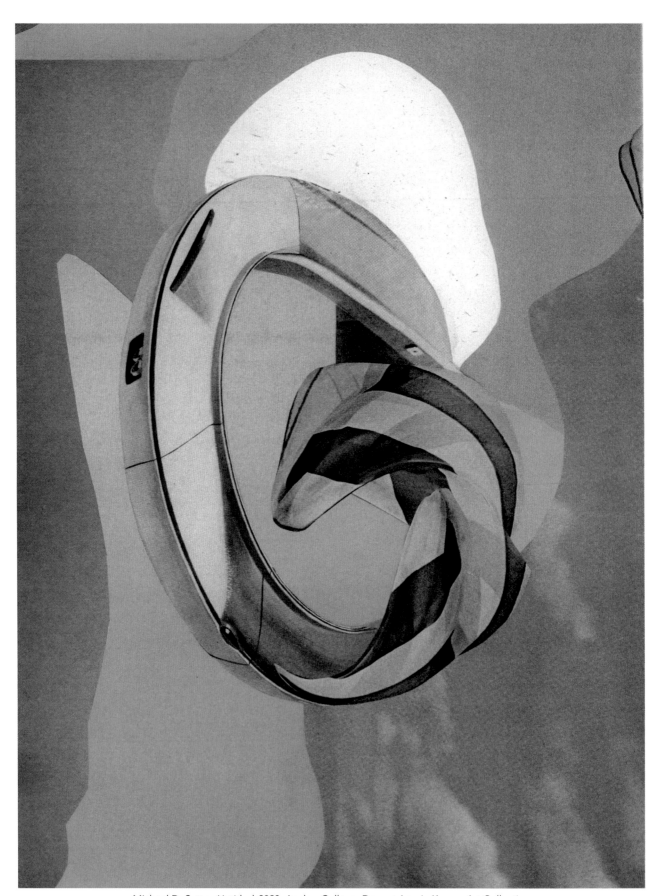

Michael DeSutter, *Untitled*, 2020, Analog Collage, Doug + Laurie Kanyer Art Collection

GUIDED COLLAGE EXPERIENCE–MAKE A COLLAGE

1. **GATHER** materials (glue, magazines, books and a substrate to make your collage on). Cut a small, triangle-shaped element from your source material. Place it anywhere on the substrate to provide a personal symbol of power and strength and to offer a comforting, familiar ritual to begin.

2. **FOR** this guided collage-making exercise-experience you will be creating a collage about your mood and associated emotions-feelings. Start by observing and grounding yourself into your surroundings. Consider these questions to center and ground yourself. What are you sitting or lying on? What makes it feel supportive to your body? What do you see and hear? What sensations are you noticing in your body? Choose an element(s) to symbolize what you are noticing, seeing and hearing. Cut it out and glue it somewhere on the substrate.

3. **THINK** of a name to symbolize your present mood or a moody period from the past. Choose an element(s) to symbolize the mood. Cut it out and glue it down to the top of the substrate.

4. **CHOOSE** an element to symbolize a building. The building represents your body that experiences both the mood and emotions-feelings. Cut it out and glue it down on the substrate.

5. **CHOOSE** elements to symbolize your emotions-feelings. Find elements to symbolize any physical sensations you notice. An example may be an elephant to symbolize the weighty tension in your gut or shoulders. Find elements to symbolize words to describe your feelings. Cut them out and glue them down below the element that represents your mood.

6. **CHOOSE** from the list of MOOD CHANGERS one or two you can use right now to shift a mood you may be experiencing. Choose an element(s) to symbolize your choices. Cut them out and glue them onto the substrate.

7. **CHOOSE** an element that will symbolize sharing and talking to others about what is going on for you. You could choose a mouth to symbolize sharing with a trusted individual by talking with them. You could locate a pigeon to symbolize writing a letter, sending an email or text.

8. **FIND** another element to symbolize who you will talk to about what is happening for you. Write the date next to it, a date that represents when you plan to reach out and share about the mood and emotions-feelings that are taking place. Do this to decrease any suffering you are experiencing.

9. **WRITE** or use collage elements to create a supportive thought to encapsulate this experience. Put this anywhere on your collage. An example: "I can learn to differentiate my mood from my feelings, and find ways to improve my mood and express my feelings."

10. **PLACE** a triangle-shaped element anywhere on the substrate to symbolize your personal strength and to offer a comforting and familiar ritual.

11. **EXTEND** your transformation by completing the TAKEAWAY ACTION TOOLS (page 225).

12. **RETURN** here after completing the Takeaway Action Tools to read the ending quote below.

> *"Where an emotion is a single note, clearly struck, hanging for a moment in the still air, a mood is the extended, nearly inaudible echo that follows."*
>
> — Thomas Lewis

Lee McKenna, *Loving Christmas Wishes*, 2019, Analog Collage, Doug + Laurie Kanyer Art Collection

EXPLORING MEMORIES

A collage-making exercise-experience to know more about memories and how collage-making helps.

"The faculty of memory cannot be separated from the imagination. They go hand in hand. To one degree or another, we all invent our personal pasts. And for most of us those pasts are built from emotionally colored memories." — Siri Hustsvedt

INFORMATION TO THINK ABOUT AND CONSIDER

Memories are a vital part of one's life. Think of a memory as information, filed and stored in the brain, which contains key knowledge and past experiences. Fun times with friends, where you put your keys, your birthday when you were 14; all are stored in memory.

Therapist Kendra Cherry offers the following definition: "Memory refers to the processes that are used to acquire, store, encode, retain, and later retrieve information. Human memory involves the ability to both preserve and recover information we have learned or experienced (Cherry, 2020)." There is an intricate and profound structure and organization to how a memory is kept and stored. There is both the process (implicit memory, which consists of emotional and procedural memory) and content (explicit memory, which consists of semantic and episodic memory) (NICABM, 2017).

Memory Encoding System

Memories are stored using a system that labels and encodes information for later retrieval. Much of this information is named and then stored outside of one's awareness. It is held in the subconscious. Once a memory is activated, the retrieval process takes place to locate information stored in either the short- or long-term vault. People often think that memories concern only sentimental or horrific things, but memories are so much more than that.

Memories are Sensory

Some memories are activated by sensory stimulation. The retrieval of a memory can therefore be activated by something that is heard, smelled, tasted, touched, or seen. You may experience this when you hear a song and it takes you back to your high school days, or when you catch a fragrance in the air and you're suddenly in your grandmother's kitchen (Menakem, 2017). The activated memory may involve a difficult time or joyful time. There can be a wide spectrum of memories. This is why a smell or a song can quickly ignite a potent memory.

Memories are Fluid

A key aspect of memories is they are fluid, meaning they seamlessly flow into one another, shifting and changing over time. You might find recent and long-past memories connecting, like a small stream connecting to a river. This can be a random process where unrelated memories flow together or re-consolidate (Miller, 2010).

Memories are Affected by Present Day Events

When a memory is recalled it is affected or shaped by the context of one's current life situation. Accordingly, the memory typically shifts to some degree. Those moments where the memory streams co-mingle and merge together may form a fresh memory in real time, a tributary of sorts. This association of two possibly unrelated experiences may form a new memory with contemporary elements (Miller, 2010). It is important to note that this does not necessarily make your memories "inaccurate". Rather, it is to say they are not cemented in stone, and that they are malleable and flexible.

Consider the following thought experiment. You recall a memory of your elementary classroom when you see a TV commercial for a favorite cookie that you often had in your lunchbox. You can see in your mind's eye your teacher, the other children, your desk, your cookie at lunch time, and then a favorite pencil. As you recall this memory from your youth, your thoughts quickly flow into the pencils you left on your worksite desk just hours ago. From there you see the orientation and placement of your desk. It is situated facing a westside window. You then begin thinking about how you are able to see the sun fading each day as your work session comes to an end. Then you imagine what you will make for dinner. One memory of your elementary school, ignited by a cookie commercial, flowed into making dinner.

Memories Contribute to Self-Identity

Memories are important, as they contribute to and shape your self-identity. Identity is how you see and understand yourself. It is your sense of self, providing you with sameness and continuity in personality over time. Identity is a script or operating system for your self-worth and abilities.

Memories Mingle with Emotions When a New "Something" Takes Place

When one is experiencing a new "something", such as a person, place, thing, event or situation, it causes one's emotions to be activated. When this happens, memories are accessed. To be able to attune, decipher and determine what to do in response to the "something", the brain activates the Emotional Response System (ERS). A component of the ERS is the accessing of memories to determine if it has had a similar experience to draw upon.

A "something" is happening in the here and now, and the brain digs into the memory bank for how one might proceed, based upon what it knows from before. That information can contribute to how one reacts to the "something" happening today. This is an amazing phenomenon, as what one has learned, experienced, and knows from the past can support tending to a "something" in the present.

Memories Are Compared, Contrasted and then Contribute to a Response

When a new "something" emerges, the brain will take an inventory. Such inventory is conducted in order to compare a new event and associated feelings with past events and accepted patterns of expressing feelings (Dahl, 2020). This is done in an attempt to reference the new event to past experiences, for the purpose of determining what and how to feel. If the brain finds that the new and old events are familiar, it will use the feeling it knows and has used from the past. The brain will "compare and contrast" the new event to old events to determine what to do with the new "something". If the brain finds no easy reference from the past to support how to express a feeling, it will develop a new feeling pattern.

This is why you can make significant new contributions to your feeling expression habits using collage-making. As writer Melissa Dahl says, "When you encounter something you haven't experienced before, your brain doesn't ask itself, 'What is this?' It asks, 'What in my experience (past memories) is this similar to?' If it is a similar experience, the brain will in effect say to itself, "I see, this is like before," and it may then link the new event to previous understandings and use those previous patterns of expressing feelings. If it is not similar, your brain will go on to build new concepts and patterns of feeling expression.

It should be noted that a number of things can affect what is retrieved and how it is applied to the current situation. The intensity of the current situation, coupled with the circumstance and what was stored from the past memory, can create an interesting mix. One's past experiences that are encoded in memory may have a large influence on how one responds. And remember that memories can span a lifetime. When one has a "something" today, a memory from an experience as a child could be retrieved.

Exploring One's Memories with Collage-Making is Helpful

Collage-making is an excellent tool to study and decipher memories. Collage is the equivalent of an excellent memory detective. It is a highly effective method of exploring, documenting, and clarifying events and related memories. As you make collage you use visual elements to assign meaning to both old and new bits of information. This helps to keep things precise and add deeper clarity. If you are sighted, your vision was your first language; seeing an event on a collage will tap into the keen language system of sight to pinpoint and decipher aspects of your memories.

Collage-Making Uses the Body

The miracle of collage-making is that it uses your mind (what you recall) and your body (your hands, eyes, etc.) to uncover and gain access to fragments of memories. These fragments, which are held in the various storage memory systems previously described are more deeply explored and connected via collage. Making a collage about a recent experience will help to implant the experience more efficiently in the memory for later recall. This process of collaging a new memory helps to attach and encode particular importance to an experience, giving it more value than other events. The collage process tells your memory bank, through the use of the entire body and related senses, that this is a key nugget of information worth remembering. In the end, you have a finished collage to visually jog your memory.

Collage-Making Being Sensory Adds Deeper Insight

Collage-making uses all of your senses, and is therefore uniquely equipped to assist in the mining of your memories. With collage-making you use all of your finely tuned sensory mechanisms to process the memory and associated feelings. The advanced sensory activity provides deeper insight into what took place. With collage-making, you are given visual and sensory cues that tap into this operating system. Rather than just talking about a memory, with collage-making you see, feel, hear, and touch the memories. The sensory aspect of collage-making offers a profound way to access what you remember about an event or situation and how you see yourself in the event.

Collage-Making Can Help Revise Memories

Collage-making can help you to deeply consider if you are operating from old, outmoded perceptions and memories. Collage is a platform to explore your memories with a newfound maturity, allowing one to reconsider the validity of the conclusions, beliefs, and decisions you've noted in your memory. It will help you to mine past experiences to gain deeper appreciation of what you've navigated, experienced or even survived.

Collage-Making Helps to Organize Memories and Heals Trauma

Collage-making can help to organize memories, which leads to healing and self-compassion. By exploring a memory from the past with collage, you will have deeper recall, assist in better understanding of yourself, and possibly assist in better understanding others. The act of using collage-making to explore hard events offers a place to put the experiences. Collage-making may take away the power of the potent memory and possibly unload a heavy burden. If the memory is trauma-based, you may be able to process it without the typical flooding of your Emotional Response System. Collage-making helps to dissipate deep trauma wounds by providing a landing place on the substrate, so that emotions and feelings don't morph. They are contained and are grounded.

Collage-Making Shows Memory Layers and Documents History

The build-up of collage elements, glued upon one another on the substrate, can symbolize historical layers in your life. The events you experienced, tucked deep in your memory, waiting to be documented and pondered, can go on to your collage. It helps one to reflect and consider memories of events and to discern if how one recalls events is the same as how one sees them today. You are expressing the truth of an event or circumstance as you see it. Only you know the real meaning of the collage element symbols, and you need not explain them nor discuss them with anyone else if you so choose.

Collage-Making is a Present Moment Activity Offering Perspective

Collage-making provides the gift of time in the present day to unveil new insights and ideas about issues, events, and life experiences. When collage-making is used to engage with a memory, you have the chance to contemplate and consider for an undetermined period of time as you arrange and rearrange the elements. When you are in the present, considering a memory without undue attachment to an outcome or assessment, you can contemplate, meditate and reflect. You may choose to postpone permanently gluing your elements down so as to be able to deeply consider the memory. This time of gentle and quiet contemplation will be both calming and add clarity to your memory.

Collage-Making Elements as Tools to Explore

One way to combine collage-making while considering memories is to place elements on the substrate and move them around for a time, prior to gluing them down. Dr. Steven Rudin, a collagist and retired psychiatrist, is a big fan of this approach. Dr. Rudin will take up to a year in his collage-making process when considering a memory. He moves elements around, considering what relationship they have with the other elements in the collage. He then ponders what thoughts or memories they bring forth for him.

In his collage-making process he is thoughtfully mining his memories while suspending judgement on what he recalls. He enlists the tools of curiosity and compassion to consider his reactions and feelings about the collage arrangement. He does so with reverence and self-respect. Eventually a story or memory may emerge, but he takes his time. He allows for the fluidity of memory to come forth and for new insights to flow.

You too can choose to cut out an abundance of collage elements, move them around, add more, pause for days, and then return to observe the relationship between the elements. Do so with curiosity, considering what they stir in you. Approach this process with self-compassion and acceptance. You can enjoy the creative process of observing, reflecting, and pondering memories while reveling in the new awareness you have developed about yourself and your world.

Collage Can Transform Memories to Fit for Today

Collage-making is transformational. The guided collage experiences in this book can help you to process recollections and memories in the context of who you are today. You will be able to consider past events and notice how fluid memories can be, how they attach to one another, and how they shape beliefs about events, people and earlier life conclusions. You will be able to dissect what you recall and what you believe about yourself and revise it to fit in the present.

CONTENT ROUND UP to REVIEW—RECALL—REMEMBER

- Memories are fluid and flow into each other over time. Older memories blend with memories of today. This means memories can be refined, revised and reframed if needed.

- Memories are stored in both the short- and long-term vault, and they are often accessed by a sensory experience.

- Collage-making is a great tool to mine, explore and consider memories.

GUIDED COLLAGE EXPERIENCE—MAKE A COLLAGE

1. **GATHER** materials (glue, magazines, books and a substrate to make your collage on). Cut a small, triangle-shaped element from your source material. Place it anywhere on the substrate to provide a personal symbol of power and strength and to offer a comforting, familiar ritual to begin.

2. **THINK**, on day one, of a pleasant memory you shared with others. Cut out elements to symbolize as many aspects and details of the memory you can recall. Do not glue them down, just place them on the substrate. Gradually recall more details and find additional elements to symbolize your impressions. They may be songs, scents, objects, clothing, people, or statements. At the end of day two, glue them all down on the top one-quarter of the substrate.

3. **CONTACT**, on the next day, one or more of those who experienced the same event. Ask them about the event and the specific things they recalled. Find elements to symbolize the things other people shared. Glue these elements down in the next one-quarter of the substrate.

4. **RECALL**, on the following day, the events you experienced while living the past number of days. Find and cut out elements for the things you recall. Glue these elements down in the next one-quarter of the substrate. Pause now for a few days.

5. **LOOK** at the collage a few days later. Find elements to symbolize the recollections you and others had that were the SAME and cut them out. Find elements to symbolize the recollections you and others had that were NOT THE SAME and cut them out. Glue these elements on the lower left-hand corner of the last one-quarter of the substrate.

6. **LOOK** at the elements for the events you recorded from a few days ago. Get up and walk around a bit. Return and sit for a time. Let your mind pause and wander. After a bit, when you have a new thought, anything that comes to mind, find an element to symbolize it. Cut it out and glue it on the right side of the bottom one-quarter of the substrate. Repeat this for the next number of thoughts. Pause a few days.

7. **RETURN** later and notice what has occurred. You have an example of how memories are fluid and flow together. You have considered a memory and recorded what you recalled. You asked others and found differences and similarities. You had new experiences of living in the recent days; all of this is blended together on the substrate. You have created a new memory tributary with collage-making.

8. **WRITE** or use collage elements to create a supportive thought to encapsulate this experience. Put this anywhere on your collage. For example, "I can consider and dissect my memories and work to understand their accuracy and relevance in my life today."

9. **PLACE** a triangle-shaped element anywhere on the substrate to symbolize your personal strength and to offer a comforting and familiar ritual.

10. **EXTEND** your transformation by completing the TAKEAWAY ACTION TOOLS (page 225).

11. **RETURN** here after completing the Takeaway Action Tools to read the ending quote below.

"The memories which lie within us are not carved in stone; not only do they tend to become erased as the years go by, but often they change, or even increase, by incorporating extraneous features."

— Primo Levi

CP Harrison, *There is no Death and Art can Prove It*, 2018, Analog Collage, Courtesy of the Artist

DENIED FEELINGS

A collage-making exercise-experience to gain knowledge about why people deny their feelings.

"We destroy ourselves when we stop feeling. If you bury your feelings within you, you become a graveyard." — Bernie S. Siegel

INFORMATION TO THINK ABOUT AND CONSIDER

To live well you need to know helpful information about feelings and helpful methods to express and accept them. Such information ultimately leads to better problem solving.

People Sometimes Deny Their Feelings

There are situations where people deny their feelings. They maintain the feeling does not even exist. Denial can come from the person who has the denied feelings, or it may be imposed upon them by the group with which they associate, when the group is unwilling to acknowledge and accept their feelings. For the purpose of this exercise-experience, we will focus on you, a person who may have feelings that you are denying.

Denied Feelings are Not Clogged Feelings

Before we move on however, it is key to differentiate between the 'denial' of feelings, and the 'clogging-ignoring-stuffing' of feelings. When a person is clogging their feelings they are aware of the feelings, not denying them. However, due to a variety of factors they have not been able to pause, pay attention to, and express them (see page 103 for more on clogged feelings).

People Deny Outside of Their Awareness

When a person is denying feelings, they simply do not have a conscious awareness of the feelings, and therefore cannot tend to them or address them. They basically have cut off access to the feeling in their present awareness. Sadly it is quite common for other people to invoke a casual and critical attitude toward one another with statements like, "He is just in denial." It is vital to be compassionate to others who use denial to manage and cope with life.

Denial Happens for Many Reasons

People deny feelings for a variety of reasons. The denial of feelings can be a coping mechanism instituted to maintain safety. People use denial to manage the heaviness of a situation that is overwhelming. Doing so creates an environment where the individual refuses the feeling or declines that the feeling and its source even exist.

Reasons Why Denial Takes Place:

- Attempting to avoid heavy, unimaginable doses of pain.
- Inability to trust others in their group to hear and accept the feeling.
- Overwhelmed by the magnitude of the issue causing the feelings.
- Unable to face the fear and potential outcome of telling the truth with your feelings.
- Lack of skills or maturity to confront the situation causing the feelings.

- Having learned to doubt or not trust one's feelings.

- Not wanting to bring shame on oneself, or those involved.

- Feeling as though one does not have a voice, or a choice.

- Lack of desire to confront or address the situation.

- Having a perception that their safety would be compromised if they felt their feelings and shared them.

- Past negative experiences when sharing certain types of feelings.

Denied Feelings Often Do Not Get Released

These and other situations can cause people to cut themselves completely off from expressing feelings, totally denying the feeling exists. When people deny feelings their feelings can fail to get released and stay buried deeply in their subconscious. As the weight of denial accumulates it can cause unintended consequences, such as mental and physical illness. Denied feelings can therefore pile up and can compromise your health.

Denial of feelings can keep you from being able to respond in a helpful way and can forge a pattern of repeating emotional injury. This repeat injury occurs when one is exposed to the same situation that caused the initial pain, but had not expressed one's feelings about the situation.

Collage-Making Can Help with Denial

Collage-making allows for denied feelings to be revealed and gently allows them to be considered. As collagist Frances Ryan said, "I make the collage, and then later I can see the story (feeling)." Hearing this might cause you to pause, maybe feel a bit agitated or uncomfortable. You may wonder, "What might be exposed in making a collage?" It is natural to feel this way when faced with the unknown. Still, those I know who explored collage-making discovered critical insights they needed to further their progress in problem-solving by uncovering denied feelings.

Collage-Making Can Bring Forth Awareness

Collage-making can help you understand what occurred by bringing the problem to light. Like a beacon blazing through the shadows of the subconscious mind, collage-making may spotlight the problem and illuminate the way to possible solutions. The pathway from subconscious to collage-making is quite profound.

With the knowledge of why you might deny your feelings, the importance of expressing feelings for your well-being, and the significance of having your feelings acknowledged by a trusted soul, let's move on to the collage-making exercise-experience. Some gentle advice: take your time with this particular material. Recognize that you and many others have used denial to cope with what they felt were astronomical obstacles. In those situations the denial made sense. The question moving forward is, "Do those earlier beliefs fit now?" Are you in a place where you can tenderly discover how you feel about feelings you may have denied? It is better for you to pause and take your time than to see this as a challenge.

CONTENT ROUND UP to REVIEW—RECALL—REMEMBER

- People deny their feelings for a multitude of reasons.

- When feelings don't get expressed they can accumulate and cause new hardships.

- Collage-making can help to reveal denied feelings and expand one's awareness.

GUIDED COLLAGE EXPERIENCE—MAKE A COLLAGE

1. **GATHER** materials (glue, magazines, books and a substrate to make your collage on). Cut a small, triangle-shaped element from your source material. Place it anywhere on the substrate to provide a personal symbol of power and strength and to offer a comforting, familiar ritual to begin.

2. **PONDER** why people use denial, recognizing many of the reasons are related to protection and safety. Find an element(s) to show a feeling you may have denied and the "something" it was connected to. Cut it out and glue it anywhere on the substrate. Please take a day or more to pause and rest. Return to this exercise later. Appreciate the courage you invested to explore it now.

3. **RETURN** and choose an element to symbolize the way you would have desired the "something" to have taken place. Ask yourself, how you would have hoped it had been handled. What was a better way for it to be managed so your feelings could have been heard, rather leaving you with one choice which was to deny? Find element(s) to show a helpful way for the event to be managed. Cut them out and glue them down anywhere on the substrate.

4. **FIND** elements to symbolize people who could have listened to your feelings had they known the situation. Or someone who might have been able to help you had they known about the situation. Cut the element(s) out and glue them anywhere on the substrate. NOTE: If you, like many, feel there was no one you knew who could have filled this role back then, know that you can choose someone in your life right now. Choose an element(s) to symbolize the person who can listen today. Cut and glue down the element(s) to symbolize these new people in your life anywhere on the substrate.

5. **FIND** an element(s) to symbolize yourself. Cut it out and glue it down anywhere on the substrate. Notice you have elements for what took place, the denied feelings, a better way to handle the event, and those who would have helped originally OR who can help now.

6. **CUT** out a heart shape element and glue it down in the middle of the substrate. Choose an element(s) to symbolize the denied feeling. Cut it out and glue it on top of the heart to show compassion and respect for the need to use denial. Make a plan to share with one of the people you identified to tell them about what took place and how you felt in the past and how you feel now. You might choose to write a date on the substrate when you might reach out to them.

7. **WRITE** or use collage elements to create a supportive thought to encapsulate this experience. Put this anywhere on your collage. For example: "I can discover and become acquainted with feelings I may have hidden and denied. I can now choose to share them with trusted others."

8. **PLACE** a triangle-shaped element anywhere on the substrate to symbolize your personal strength and to offer a comforting and familiar ritual.

9. **EXTEND** your transformation by completing the TAKEAWAY ACTION TOOLS (page 225).

10. **RETURN** here after completing the Takeaway Action Tools to read the ending quote below.

> *"Expression that comes from the deepest, darkest place that most of us would rather hide from the rest of the world is the substance that will most likely also deeply affect others."*
>
> — Ken Poir

Monique Vettraino, *Finding Calm While We Wait*, 2020, Analog Collage, Doug + Laurie Kanyer Art Collection

CLOGGED - STUFFED - IGNORED - OVERRIDDEN FEELINGS

A collage-making exercise-experience to become familiar with how and why one clogs feelings.

"Nothing destroys self-worth and self-love faster than denying (clogging) what you feel. Without feelings you would not know where you are right now in life, nor would you know what areas you need to work on. Honor your feelings, allow yourself to feel them." — Iyanla Vanzant

INFORMATION TO THINK ABOUT AND CONSIDER

When you experience a "something" a series of reactions may take place compelling one to make some choices. The brain, being so complex, registers the event and computes a path to address the event. If the event is in fact serious, requiring immediate attention, it will somewhat override any pause in thinking and propel you to react. This process is known as the Fight, Freeze, Flee, or Fawn Response, and it is designed to protect you.

In other situations, with much less concern, your emotional response may be a bit more paused or calculated, offering you time to plan and anticipate your response. A feeling is formulated and you then make a choice. For this exercise-experience the words stuffed, clogged, ignored and overridden are used interchangeably.

Options to Use Feelings

The choices regarding your feelings in this circumstance are varied and may be summarized as follows:

1. Respond to the situation immediately by taking action or making a response.

2. Observe for a time, staying aware if the need to respond is required.

3. Let it go, as you determined it either holds little importance or is not serious at this time.

4. Minimize the situation by discounting your feelings and perceptions, possibly due to the issue's severity or in an effort to diminish its importance.

5. Take note of the feeling, recognize it is important to you, but choose to not address it in the moment by clogging, ignoring, stuffing and overriding.

Choosing to Clog Feelings

When you take note but don't address the situation at the time of its occurrence you are choosing to override the choice to respond. In effect, you may be ignoring and stuffing the feelings, overriding them and storing them away. You retain a conscious awareness of their presence and they register in your body. You can feel the activation of the sensation caused by an initial emotional response to a situation. You actually experience the emotion(s) in your physical and mental self and form a feeling(s) response, but you essentially clog them.

Overriding the Feeling for a Time

The stuffing process consists of not expressing the feeling at the time you are having it. You store or shelve the feeling, hopefully for further consideration at a later time. In the best-case scenario, the situation and resulting feelings are reflected upon later and you take the Feelings Stepping Stones Pathway to process the experience. Regrettably, feelings that are stuffed and ignored can pile up, one upon another, going unattended which leads to deposits of clogged-up feelings.

As an example, let's say you are at a celebratory event for a friend. As you mingle and engage in conversation, one of the guests brings up a controversial and potent topic in the current news. The topic is political, religious or has overtones of tender circumstances. The discussion of this event colors the tone of the celebration. You can feel the air going out of the room and you begin to feel disgusted (or another feeling) at the conversation. You are aware of the emotional agitation registering in your body. You note your chest is tightening and your jaw becoming clenched. You find yourself making attempts to override and ignore your feelings. In the moment you choose to clog your feeling(s) in effort to not add more to the difficulty of the circumstance that is already awkward.

Feelings as Helpful Signals

You know that your feelings are signaling that this experience is not OK for you and likely for others. You begin to consider how to manage your feelings in order to address the situation. One solution would be to say, "The topic of this conversation is not appropriate for this gathering, I am feeling disgusted (or another feeling), let's talk about something else." Another solution could be to start another topic or tell a joke. Yet another might be to leave the group.

Sometimes People Clog Feelings to Survive the Situation at Hand

And then there is the option of stuffing, ignoring and overriding the feeling. You actually find yourself pausing when stuffing your feelings. You are pushing down the feeling and staying where you are. In the instant you choose to stay and stuff the feeling you could be adding to a pileup of other ignored feelings, leading to a clog.

Different From Denied Feelings

It is important to know stuffed-ignored-clogged feelings are different from denied feelings. A denied feeling is one where the feeling actually does not exist on a conscious level for the person. Denied feelings are buried in the subconscious and are not registered at all in one's awareness. A clogged feeling, in contrast, is one where you are aware of a feeling (similar to the examples cited above) but you stuff it (see exercise-experience Denied Feelings on page 99).

Unattended Clogged Feelings Can Pile Up

You may find you have not yet taken time to consider, ponder and mine a stuffed feeling or the situations that generated the same. You are certainly not alone in this discovery. You simply leave the feeling stuffed or ignored. Later another event occurs and you find yourself stuffing more feelings. Over time you may have developed a clogged, balled-up trench of unattended feelings.

This clogging process takes place for many reasons, so be gentle on yourself. Most people have stuffed, clogged, and unattended feelings from time to time. Be it lack of time, energy, the social situation you find yourself in, or another factor, an accumulation of clogged up feelings can take place. At some point an overflow or a flood of backed up, clogged feelings may happen.

Floods of Clogged Feelings Can Occur

It is not uncommon that a flood of feelings will occur over some unrelated concern or situation. It is likely that it was caused by the metaphorical clogged emotional drain. Imagine you bump your toe on the leg of a table. This unrelated event to your clogged feelings is the situation that opens up a portal for those ignored feelings to pour through from the past. This can cause an emotional mess, where buckets of clogged feelings pour out even though they have no relation to the stubbed toe. They are stored up, ignored feelings in the drain pipe of clogged emotions.

Take Time to Consider Ones Overridden Feelings Regularly

In a situation where you stuff a feeling to get through a situation or some other reason, make a plan with yourself to consider the event that caused the feeling. You may have wisely planned to make time to explore your thoughts and feelings at some later point. In revisiting the feelings, you can actually step back onto the Feelings Stepping Stones Pathway to analyze and consider the feeling, for the purpose of expressing, validating and accepting it. Essentially, you are taking the feeling that you stuffed-ignored and you are pulling it out for investigation and resolution. The overall goal is to release the weight of the clogged feeling, and then to consider if there is a problem to solve.

Use Collage-Making

Collage-making can be used to assist in this process of consideration and analysis of a clogged feeling. The exercise-experience to follow can be used for any situation in which you find the need to clog a feeling. Collage-making is an act of tending to a feeling and not stuffing it. It is like taking what would be trash sent to the local dump and instead recycling it, turning it into something productive. You are not sending it to the dump to be added to a clog of unattended feelings.

STERBs

In addition to stuffing and ignoring feelings you might find yourself turning to the use of Short-Term Energy-Relieving-Behaviors (STERBs) to manage the emotional tension and residue connected to the stuffed feeling. People turn to STERBs as alternative behaviors used to distract one from the feelings and events.

STERBs are things such as excessive shopping, binge watching TV, obsessive scrolling on social media, indulging in drugs or alcohol, over exercising, or even self-harm. STERBs most certainly will distract for a short period of time, but do not attend to the care of unresolved stuffed and clogged feelings. They are often habit forming and can become addictive, leading to more strain and hardship. STERBs in the end can compound the clogging of feelings, as you still have the original clogged feeling and have now added a pile of STERBs-related issues.

Another variable to consider is the effect of adrenaline and cortisol. When one avoids processing and understanding one's feelings these brain hormones/chemicals can remain and get stuck in your system. This can be associated not only with ongoing mental strain but can contribute to stress related illnesses (see the exercise-experience titled Avoiding STERBs on page 149 for more on the topic).

In conclusion, use collage-making and tools like the Feelings Stepping Stones Pathway featured on page 61 and those listed on Give Yourself a Hand on page 115 as ways to process and acknowledge feelings that tend to get stuffed or clogged. In making a collage you will find that your feelings are helpers and they can lead to solving problems, when considered, validated and expressed.

CONTENT ROUND UP to REVIEW—RECALL—REMEMBER

- When people ignore their feelings at the time they are taking place the feelings can become clogged, or stuffed.

- Sometimes people clog their feelings to survive the situation at hand.

- Unattended clogged feelings can cause an emotional flood that can occur over some unrelated concern or situation.

- Making a collage can be a way to tend to feelings that can clog up for a variety of reasons.

Monique Vettraino, *Amabie*, 2022, Analog Collage, Doug + Laurie Kanyer Art Collection

GUIDED COLLAGE EXPERIENCE–MAKE A COLLAGE

6. **GATHER** materials (glue, magazines, books and a substrate to make your collage on). Cut a small, triangle-shaped element from your source material. Place it anywhere on the substrate to provide a personal symbol of power and strength and to offer a comforting, familiar ritual to begin.

7. **PONDER** and consider the events of the last week. They could be a conversation, a project, a challenge, a celebration. Reflect, ponder and analyze some of the events and the feelings you expressed and acknowledged. Find elements to show you having honored your feelings, rather than stuffing and ignoring them. Cut them out and glue them anywhere on to the substrate.

8. **CONSIDER** once again the events of last week and note any feelings and situations you may have stuffed or ignored. They could be parts of conversations, projects, challenges, or celebrations. Reread the Feelings Stepping Stones Pathway on page 61 to assist you in processing your feelings rather than stuffing them, acknowledging that stuffing could lead to a clog. Take time now to find elements to symbolize these events, cut them out and glue them down anywhere on your substrate.

9. **THINK** about events from the distant past, the things you may have not yet explored and instead stuffed or ignored. Knowing that stuffing and ignoring could lead to a flood, process and honor those feelings. Find elements for those events to unclog the feelings, cut them out and glue them on your substrate. Find an element that looks like a drain, or a water faucet, or one that symbolizes a drain or water faucet. Cut it out and glue it on your substrate. On your substrate you now have elements to symbolize your feelings being acknowledged, validated, and accepted (unclogged) and you have a drain to represent feelings flowing. Notice the difference in how you feel once you have completed the steps above. Notice also how you have entered into a process of paying attention to feelings rather than ignoring, which may have led to a clog. Adopt the process of using collage-making often to note and appreciate your feelings so that they do not get clogged.

10. **WRITE** or use collage elements to create a supportive thought to encapsulate this experience. Put this anywhere on your collage. For example: "It is important to tend to my awareness of feelings and to offer myself space to consider them regularly."

11. **PLACE** a triangle-shaped element anywhere on the substrate to symbolize your personal strength and to offer a comforting and familiar ritual.

12. **EXTEND** your transformation by completing the TAKEAWAY ACTION TOOLS (page 225).

13. **RETURN** here after completing the Takeaway Action Tools to read the ending quote below.

"Express your feelings, no matter what. Make your every word beautiful, bright, and lovely. Make your every thought creative, caring, and lively."

— Debasish Mridh

CP Harrison, *Anthem in 2D*, 2021, Analog Collage, Courtesy of the Artist

RACKET FEELINGS

A collage-making exercise-experience to become aware of how groups influence the expression of certain feelings.

"What you resist, persists." — Carl Jung

INFORMATION TO THINK ABOUT AND CONSIDER

In most groups with whom you may associate there are feelings that are permitted to be expressed and others that are not. There can be different rules for a feeling expression in each group. There are many explanations for this phenomenon, but essentially the expression of some feelings is just fine in certain groups, while not accepted in others.

Feelings Still Exist Even Though Not Permitted

What we do know is a feeling that is not accepted to the group is still a feeling; it EXISTS. Not being able to identify, express and accept feelings can result in not feeling heard or being mis-understood by others. It can lead to confusion. You could begin to doubt yourself or feel unsettled or resentful toward others. This can cause discord in the group and within yourself.

Racket Feelings - Cover Ups

Authentic feelings are your true, real feelings, expressed in the here and now, that fit a particular situation. When a feeling is not accepted within the group, you may instead express another feeling that is permitted. The feeling expressed in this situation is called a Racket Feeling (Berne, 1961). Racket Feelings are those used by people to cover up true feelings, which for some reason are not permitted in a group. Such group might include your family, a social group, a work group or otherwise.

The use of the word racket is valuable. In this context, the term racket is synonymous with a business that seems to be legitimate upon first inspection, but is covering up another illegitimate business or enterprise. The Racket Feeling that is being expressed is a cover for the real feeling you are feeling deep down, that is not affirmed in a group.

Developed in the Family and Other Key Groups

Racket Feelings are initially developed in childhood, when you learned from your family that some feelings are not to be expressed. In the words of therapist Ian Tomlingson, "In most families there are guidelines as to which feelings are OK and which are not. (Tomlingson, 2010)". One way these messages are sent to the child happens when the child receives a negative response from a parent or another caregiver for expressing a particular feeling. For example, says Tomlingson, "If Abby is ignored when she is feeling sad, but given a lot of praise and attention when she is happy, she is likely to learn to be (and express) 'happy' and avoid expressing sadness." She may even express happiness when she is in fact sad. Think about a person at a funeral who has cheery facial expressions, when forlorn or downcast would better fit the situation.

Another way families can give children signals as to which feelings are OK is by the way they model their own expression of feelings. Families will use a certain feeling they deem OK, when in truth they may feel another way. The child observes their family members and absorbs the unspoken rules as to which feelings are OK to express. The child develops a vocabulary of OK (in the group) Racket Feelings, and gets the message to not express the more authentic feelings for specific situations.

You may have seen people acting as if they are mad when in reality they are scared. This is what happens when Racket Feelings are expressed rather than the true, real emotions. This can be wearing on one's well-being over time; one can become numb and out of touch with their True Self and their feelings. The opportunity to address the situation appropriately may be missed. If you are expressing 'anger' rather than expressing 'scared' you will not be addressing the circumstances that caused the fear.

Humans are made to be in community and groups. Regrettably, they will often select a Racket Feeling (or use a Racket Feeling out of habit) to continue to be part of the group, rather than express their true feelings and risk disapproval. The great news is you can help yourself by evaluating any Racket Feelings you have become accustomed to using and choose more authentic feelings that better fit the situation.

CONTENT ROUND UP to REVIEW—RECALL—REMEMBER

- In some groups certain feelings are permitted to be expressed and some are not.

- A feeling that is used to cover up a truer feeling not allowed to be expressed in a certain group is called a Racket Feeling.

- People can choose to use the feelings they are actually feeling in the here and now and challenge the use of Racket Feelings.

- Using the exact words to describe a feeling to others helps one to feel heard and understood. You can challenge any Racket Feeling and discover the best feeling word to fit the situation.

Laurie Kanyer, *Just Passing Through*, 2016, Analog Collage, Private Collection

GUIDED COLLAGE EXPERIENCE–MAKE A COLLAGE

1. **GATHER** materials (glue, magazines, books and a substrate to make your collage on). Cut a small, triangle-shaped element from your source material. Place it anywhere on the substrate to provide a personal symbol of power and strength and to offer a comforting, familiar ritual to begin.

2. **DRAW** a large circle on your substrate. Find a collage element to symbolize you, and glue it in the middle of the circle. Find collage elements for as many groups you interact with and glue them inside the circle.

3. **TAKE** time to imagine in your mind's eye interacting with the members of each group. Ask yourself what the reaction of the group members might be or has been in the past when you were feeling a heavy emotion, let's say the feeling of despair. Could you express despair and be accepted? Place the letter Y for the word "Yes" for the groups that would accept your expression of despair. Place N for "No" for the groups that would not accept your expression of despair.

4. **IMAGINE** in your mind's eye the group who would not accept your expression of the feeling of despair. Ask yourself what other feelings might be accepted by the group (Racket Feeling). Find an element to symbolize the Racquet Feeling, and glue it down by each group. See if you can identify why this group caused you to have to choose to use a Racket Feeling and choose an element for the reason. The aim here is to alert you to how and where in your life you use Racket Feelings and why. Consider if you might be able to talk to them about this now that you are older and have more skills. Alternatively, talk to another person you trust about this feeling. Use this knowledge to continue to find just the right feeling words to express your feelings and become aware of how Racket Feelings keep you from your true emotions.

5. **WRITE** or use collage elements to create a supportive thought to encapsulate this experience. Put this anywhere on your collage. For example: "I can take the time and create the space to reflect and preserve my true feelings."

6. **PLACE** a triangle-shaped element anywhere on the substrate to symbolize your personal strength and to offer a comforting and familiar ritual.

7. **EXTEND** your transformation by completing the TAKEAWAY ACTION TOOLS (page 225).

8. **RETURN** here after completing the Takeaway Action Tools to read the ending quote below.

"If you never bother to say the words, why should anyone believe you ever felt them?"

— Richelle E. Goodrich

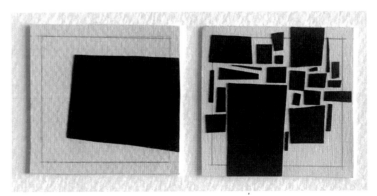

Elise Margolis, *Cheer Up! Together We're Not Alone*, 2020, Mini Collage, Doug + Laurie Kanyer Art Collection

Laurie Kanyer, *A Tour*, 2020, Analog Collage, Doug + Laurie Kanyer Art Collection

PART 3
Exercise-Experiences on Caring for Emotions

"Feelings can't be ignored, no matter how
unjust or ungrateful they seem."

— Anne Frank

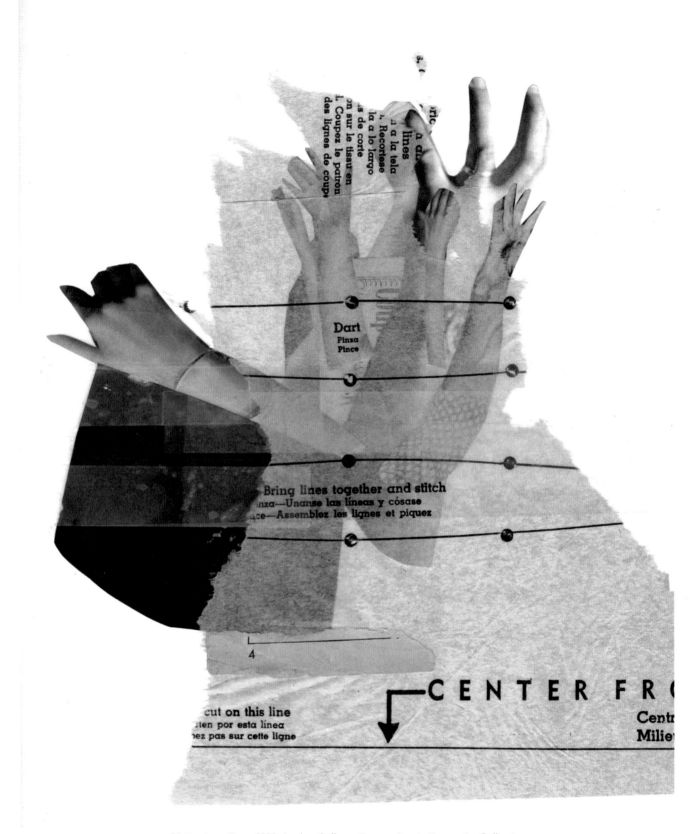

CP Harrison, *Rose*, 2020, Analog Collage, Doug + Laurie Kanyer Art Collection

GIVE YOURSELF A HAND

**A collage-making exercise-experience to practice the skill of monitoring
one's emotions, feelings and overall brain health.**

"Be patient with yourself. Self-growth is tender, it's holy ground. There's no greater investment."
— Stephen Covey

INFORMATION TO THINK ABOUT AND CONSIDER

Give Yourself a Hand is a comprehensive checklist of items you can use to experience optimal mental health. It contains proven items to choose and use all in one place. Like the care of your physical body, the care of the mind consists of several things you can immediately use to improve your mental health. This model will help you to determine a plan to help you feel emotionally well.

A Helpful Hand

The Give Yourself a Hand model uses your hand as a metaphor to help you remember all of the things to consider when tending to your emotional health. By adding even one of the self-care items (listed below) it is as if you are actually reaching out to your own self, to give yourself a hand, so you feel better.

Using Give Yourself a Hand Will Enable You to:

Identify and celebrate your strength by noting all the things you are already doing.

Remind you of self-care methods you previously used but are not currently active and using. This will prompt you to use them once again.

Inspire and challenge you to start using proven techniques known to support and improve your emotional well-being.

Motivate you to look for and secure help from professionals and peers.

Learn detailed information to make sure you get the best care from medical and mental health professionals if you should need them.

Build resilience while decreasing vulnerability by offering you a list of foundational self-care tasks to add layers of protection and assistance. The depth of the impact of a "something" may be diminished by regular use of the techniques listed here. What you do on this list has the cumulative effect of helping you to be more resilient.

Detect what you may or may not be doing, that contributes to how you feel or affects personal mental health concerns. Outside of one's awareness one could be doing things that actually contribute to not feeling well. This list will offer you knowledge about such things.

Discover that self-care is a way to tend to oneself in the present, and in doing so it helps to heal wounds from earlier. Self-care is a profound example of self-love.

Evaluate if you need to get help urgently so you can begin to feel better sooner. **NOTE:** If this is you, i.e., you don't feel well, jump ahead to MIDDLE FINGER and RING FINGER to assess your need for immediate professional help. The care of the brain and emotions is no different than the care of the heart. I have frequently stated that the brain can have a "brain attack" and there is help to correct the function of the brain just like the heart having a "heart attack." From time-to-time professional help is needed and is readily available.

HOW TO USE THE MODEL

A. **START** by holding up your hand.

B. **READ** the material to follow connected to each finger on the hand. Each finger represents something known to support and improve emotional health.

- The Thumb represents physical care needs.

- The Pointer Finger represents your social care needs.

- The Middle Finger represents medical care needs.

- The Ring Finger represents talk therapy/counseling care needs.

- The Pinky Finger represents the gathering of quality, up-to-date information on your condition. The Pinky Finger also represents finding peer support from others who have had similar experiences.

C. **MARK** the items in each list as follows:

- Place a STAR (*) by the things you are already doing.

- Place a QUESTION MARK (?) next to the things you might shift, change, improve, consider or need more information about.

- Place a PLUS MARK (+) by the one to two things you want to consider to start doing.

IMPORTANT - REMEMBER - KNOW: The intention here is to simply provide you with a comprehensive list that is informational only. It is not prescriptive. It is a one-stop, quick-access spot to consult for the purpose of supporting your emotional wellness. It is not intended for you to feel you have to accomplish all the items listed.

This tool is like a tour guide giving you options and suggestions only. Avoid feeling any pressure. The importance of having a round-up of things collected on emotional wellness is NOT a to-do list. It is to help you. It offers you some gentle reminders and information, all in one spot. The list provides an invitation to think, choose and use what is best for you, in your own time frame, for your specific needs.

The list to follow is comprehensive in nature, yet we readily acknowledge that the suggested items may not be available for all people everywhere in the world. For example, access to a qualified talk therapist may not be available to you where you. Honoring this truth, we also know people are creative and will find ways to tend to their emotional well-being in ways that work best for them. Use this book and other resources to support your well-being.

THUMB - Physical Self-Care Needs

This section, Thumb, offers insightful information on things to do to improve your physical well-being in order to benefit you emotionally.

READ and MARK

WATER - Drink enough water. It is vital to your production of hormones in the brain, called neuro-transmitters. If you are not drinking enough water you can experience slower reasoning and thought-processing.

FOOD - Eat quality food, in the correct amounts. The connection between food, gut and mind health has been widely documented.

SUBSTANCES - Monitor your use of alcohol, drugs, tobacco or caffeine. Make sure to read page 149 on STERBs. Avoid using them to calm yourself or distract from life's concerns. Seek support to reduce or halt the use of these substances.

SLEEP - Get seven to nine hours of sleep each day. Research techniques to improve your sleep health, which will in turn improve your mental health.

BATHE, SHAVE, GET READY - Tend to yourself with daily grooming. When you groom yourself you are showing self-respect and self-honor. This has a big impact on your emotions, overall outlook, and self-image.

GARMENTS and CLOTHES - Wear comfortable, soft and clean clothes. Discard anything that does not fit or anything you have not worn in the last year. In particular, discard any piece of clothing you wore during times of hardship. What you clothe yourself in enhances how you feel.

OUTDOORS - Go outside in fresh air, sunlight, and night sky gazing. You need at least 20 minutes outside each day.

EXERCISE - Get some exercise, or mild movement, for 20 minutes each day. You can do this in 10-minute intervals throughout the day. Even simple movements such as tidying your house or washing the car are effective! Note: If you are having a dramatic emotional flood, research indicates that using a sustained burst of 20 minute aerobic exercise will shift the emotional energy (Linehan, 2015).

BREATHE DEEPLY - Breathe deeply in through your nose and exhale out of your nose. Nose breathing filters dust and allergens and increases the amount of oxygen to the lungs. Look up a yoga breathing exercise called "nadishodhana" which uses alternative nasal breathing.

MEDITATION - Learn about meditation or just dedicate time to quiet reflection, coupled with patterned breathing. It will still and quiet your mind. The affordable *Calm* App is especially recommended. *Calm* has meditation segments and up-to-date information on mental health and sleep patterns.

QUIET TIME - Spend quiet time by yourself. This is different from meditation where you are consciously breathing while focusing on a unique word. This is a quiet time where you just sit quietly and settle the events of the day. Even 10 minutes of silence a day will help. Set a timer and be still and quiet, whether at home or at work. Take your breaks at work during the day.

COLLAGE-CARE METHODS - Choose to use the collage-making process routinely to pace and modulate your emotions, feelings, and life experiences. Practice the skills and tools herein to experience the multiple and proven benefits.

ENVIRONMENT - HOME - Make sure your home is safe, tidy and organized. De-clutter and discard anything that does not inspire or bring joy. Throw away anything negative, anything that reminds you of hard times, or negative people and experiences. Look up the writings of Marie Kondo. Her method takes some time, but it is refreshing and renewing to the mind.

MAKE YOUR BED - Make your bed daily. It is a small but mighty victory. It has been shown to have benefits for those experiencing depression. Getting back into a made bed at night is a sign that you are taking care of and showing respect for oneself.

INSPIRATIONAL BELONGINGS - Have in your environment things you can SEE that uplift and inspire you emotionally. What the eye can see, the heart and mind can remember.

MEDIA - Monitor what you are viewing and avoid heavy, unhealthy topics. Stop watching things that are frightening, negative or harmful. Take breaks altogether from TV (including the news).

HALF-SMILE - Smile like the woman in the famous Mona Lisa painting. The Half-Smile is a simple technique where you relax the muscles in your face, beginning at your forehead and proceeding downward. It was designed by American psychologist Marsha M. Linehan, who discovered that your body position can change how you feel. Let the corners of your mouth turn up just slightly, breathe in, and adopt this calm and peaceful expression on your face. Use this technique for 10 minutes daily to improve your mood. Note: This is not a smirk, it is a soft, willing facial expression that changes your mental state.

POINTER FINGER - Social Self-Care Needs

This section, Pointer Finger, offers you insightful information on interactions with others in order to benefit emotionally.

READ AND MARK

INTIMATE RELATIONSHIPS - Choose an intimate partner who is respectful, responsible and pleasant to be with over time.

FRIENDSHIPS - Choose friends who are respectful, responsible and pleasant to be with over time. Many people believe they need an army of friends, but no more than five close friends is recommended in your intimate friendship circle.

EXTENDED FAMILY and FAMILY OF ORIGIN - Monitor any pressure, influence or undue expectations from your extended family. You may occasionally need a pause or some distance.

UNNEEDED RESPONSIBILITIES - Evaluate if you are in social relationships where you are carrying more than your share of the load in the relationship. Ask yourself if there is quality in sharing the responsibility of the relationship. Note if you are being taken advantage of by someone.

SAYING NO - SET BOUNDARIES - Set clear boundaries with people on things you do not want to do, or are not comfortable doing.

EMPLOYMENT - See and choose an employment environment that advocates quality social behaviors.

EXPECTATIONS - Evaluate the expectations you place upon yourself. Particularly notice those coming from external social pressure. Do not let people impose upon you. Ask yourself if it is reasonable to expect as much from yourself or others.

SPIRITUAL GROUP - Associate with religious or spiritual organizations that uphold beliefs and practices that support positive self-care and emotional well-being. Ask yourself if they are uplifting and encouraging. You may find that joining a religious spiritual group is supportive.

DECREASE ISOLATION - Call a friend to talk to or meet at a park. Visit people who you enjoy and feel comfortable with on a regular basis. Isolation is known to increase emotional distress. People need to see and be with others to feel well emotionally.

FUN - Do things you like to do. Play board games, read books, go fishing, make art. Go out for a simple, inexpensive meal.

THINGS TO LOOK FORWARD TO - Plan something fun to do in the near future. The positive brain hormone of dopamine is increased when one experiences anticipation. It does not have to be an expensive vacation. Going for a walk with a friend increases your dopamine level.

HUG - PHYSICAL TOUCH - Give or get a hug from another person. Get a massage or even pet a dog or cat. The positive brain hormone oxytocin is poured through the body through physical touch. You can even give yourself a hug by putting your right hand on your left shoulder and your left hand on your right shoulder.

SOCIAL MEDIA - Curate your contacts on social media. Find others on social media who are uplifting and inspiring to you. You might choose to take a break or halt being on social media altogether.

MUSIC - Choose inspiring music to listen to that is good for your emotional self. Monitor the messages in the lyrics to protect your emotional health. Music is also associated with an increase in the happy hormone of oxytocin—listen to happy, joyful and delightful music.

MEDIA - Evaluate what you allow into your mind. Revise your choice of TV or other media such as movies, video games or magazines to make sure the things you see do not harm your mind.

PRACTICE GRATITUDE - Start a gratitude record (even a collage) where you write what you are grateful for. Research proves that expressing gratitude on a daily basis improves your mental status. You may prefer to do a gratitude collage. Expressing gratitude confronts the negativity of the world and any negative self-talk.

DO SOMETHING NICE FOR SOMEONE (within limits) - Doing something nice for others helps one to feel emotionally well. You could send a note, card or email to someone from time to time. One should be careful to monitor this however, to avoid neglecting yourself in order to serve others.

MIDDLE FINGER - Medical Self-Care Needs

This section, Middle Finger, offers you insightful information on medical care to improve your physical well-being in order to benefit emotionally.

READ and MARK

MAKE AN APPOINTMENT WITH YOUR DOCTOR – Connect with your medical care professional when you do not feel well emotionally. Go sooner, rather than later to avoid delaying care and extending the suffering. Bring evidence of insurance, your identification and list of medications.

COMMUNICATE OPENLY - Be upfront by sharing with your medical team exactly how you are really feeling. Only you and your medical care professional know what is best for you.

OTHERS - Take someone with you to support you and gather information. Have them write down and record what you need to do so that they can help you track the process over time.

BLOOD TEST - Ask your doctor for a blood test. Get a complete lab panel. Many disorders or deficiencies in the body can affect emotional health. Two common issues that can affect emotional well-being are problems with the thyroid gland and Vitamin D deficiency. A simple blood test can detect these problems. A prescription medicine may be needed to improve your condition.

MEDICATIONS - Talk with your medical team about the use of psychotropic medication used to treat many emotional conditions. Many people have experienced benefits from taking these medications.

TRACK EFFECTS OF MEDICATIONS - Work closely with your medical team to track the effects of the medication. It is key to acknowledge that it may take some time for you to see the results. Invest in developing the skill of patience.

REPORT CHANGES - Communicate with your doctor, as needed, to change to a different medication if you don't see anticipated results or have bothersome side effects. It is not uncommon for a person to have to make medication shifts until you find just the right fit. It may take some trials to find the best fit for you. Remember that it took time for your condition to develop, and may take time for the deficiency to be amended.

GET REASSURANCE - Be reassured that you likely will not need to be on medication for the rest of your life, as your brain heals. But if you do, remember it is no different from a person with a heart condition taking medication to help them.

> **NOTE:** Never stop these types of medications without consulting your doctor. With the support of your doctor you may be able to make plans to slowly decrease the medication over time.

REPORT CHRONIC ILLNESS OR INJURIES - Living with chronic illnesses or injury can affect your emotional state and emotional health. Be sure you ask a medical care professional how and to what degree these conditions affect you emotionally when coping with chronic illness or extended pain.

REPORT SLEEP CONCERNS - Talk to your medical practitioner about the quality of your sleep. If your sleep patterns have shifted, ask your medical professional for help. There are abundant ways to solve this problem and improve your sleep.

RING FINGER - Talk Therapy and Counseling Self-Care Needs

This section offers you insightful information on talk therapy and seeking care from a mental health counselor to improve your emotional well-being.

READ and MARK

TRAINED PRACTITIONER - Locate a professional counselor who is trained to determine and treat emotional issues.

EVIDENCE-BASED TREATMENT - Inquire of your counselor as to their use of evidence-based, well-researched, and well-tested counseling treatment models. We know they work when people are actively engaged. I have a deep appreciation for the following evidence-based therapeutic models, which have been studied and tested for quality results:

- Cognitive Behavioral Therapy (CBT) developed by Aaron T. Beck, MD

- Somatic Experiencing developed by Peter A. Levine, Ph.D

- Dialectical Behavior Therapy (DTB) developed by Marsha Linehan, Ph.D

- Internal Family Systems (IFS) developed by Richard Schwartz, Ph.D

CALL PROMPTLY - Talk with a counselor to expedite your healing and decrease emotional pain over time. Once decided, call as soon as possible to make an appointment, as it may take some time to secure one—good therapists are in high demand.

OFFERS PROFESSIONAL COMPASSION and EMPATHY - In talking to a counselor, you are conversing with a professional and not looking to others who are not trained in mental health. Ask yourself, would you ask a friend to stitch a deep cut? Clearly you would seek a medical doctor to treat your wound. In the same way, a trained mental health counselor may be best equipped to care for your emotional concerns.

GET RECOMMENDATIONS - Ask your doctor, friends, family members or others for recommendations of a quality therapist. Select a therapist who is trained and experienced in your specific concerns. For example: if you are grieving, seek a therapist with training and experience in grief. If you are depressed, find a therapist who treats depression. Often therapists treat a number of concerns.

INTERVIEW and ASK QUESTIONS - To the degree that is meaningful to you, ask the therapist where they were trained. How long have they been in practice? What experience do they have in treating people with your specific concerns? What credentials and specialty certificates does he/she hold? Has he/she had significant success with helping patients feel better? What therapeutic counseling models (modalities) do they use?

Know you are paying for a service and deserve to work with someone with whom you feel comfortable.

INTUITION - Use your intuition to determine if you feel this is a person who will be able to help you.

WHEN YOU FIRST MEET - The first meeting is called an Intake. The goal is for the therapist to gain an understanding of your needs. Anticipate that there will be some paperwork to fill out. The therapist will ask you questions about your concerns. Bring evidence of insurance, your identification and list of medications.

OVER TIME YOUR THERAPIST MAY:

Challenge your thinking, negative self-talk and inaccurate thinking patterns.

Affirm your dignity and worth.

Listen to your feelings.

Hear your experiences.

Help you to explore the 'parts' of yourself.

Suggest some Somatic exercises to release cumulative stress in your body.

Offer honest feedback.

Teach and encourage you to try new skills, often giving you mini homework assignments to practice.

Point out your strengths and celebrate your growth.

Confront any negative decisions.

Help you to think critically to make decisions.

Offer ideas and suggestions to solve problems.

Support you in asking for help.

Make referrals to other providers.

Help you to evaluate relationships.

Offer information on your particular emotional concern.

Highlight things to track progress.

Encourage you in a compassionate, empathetic yet firm manner.

Offer other resources to read or study.

COMMUNICATION - CALL AS YOU NEED - DON'T WAIT — Call your therapist if something arises between sessions such as:

A new stressful event emerges.

You feel poorly.

Your thinking and problem solving become impaired.

You feel worse after a session.

A new emotional feature emerges.

Your self-talk is becoming harsh, negative or off track.

You need further clarification on something that came up in the session.

(SEE the APPENDIX for a List of 24-Hour Hotlines to help)

CHALLENGES FROM TIME-to-TIME - From time-to-time talk therapy may feel uncomfortable and hard. Tell your counselor if you are uncomfortable as soon as possible so they can help. Your counselor can answer questions, clarify dialog and provide information. Occasionally you may feel stretched and maybe even awkward. This is your brain doing the work to heal, and healing can sometimes be uncomfortable. Stick with it, ask clarifying questions and tell the therapist when it is hard.

CONFRONT RESISTANCE TO CHANGE - Some mental health concerns carry the feature of resistance to change. And some of the parts in your mental makeup may not yet trust enough to make shifts. Your therapist is equipped to help you with change and any resistance you have. Your counselor may do this by compassionately challenging and encouraging you in an effort to shift your mental patterns.

Understand that the resistance to change, and the feelings that accompany it, may have been a behavior you developed earlier in your life to protect yourself. Extend compassion to yourself. Know that, although resistance may have worked in the past, avoiding change will delay healing.

TIMELINE - Depending on a number of factors the timeline for treatment and frequency of visits will vary. It is common for one to see a counselor for an extended period. It is not uncommon for people to see more than one counselor over their lifetime. It is also not unusual to see the same counselor for years. Just like a medical professional you see over time, understand that mental health care is no different.

WHAT TO DO IF YOU DON'T IMPROVE - If you find you are not improving or have profound negative feelings about the counselor, seek care from someone else. Keep in mind however that discomfort in counseling is not unusual, similar to one might experience from physical therapy for an injury. What is key is to not abandon counseling but find a therapist who will partner in your care.

PINKY FINGER - Up-to-Date, Accurate, Research-Proven Information and Peer Support

This section, Pinky Finger, offers you insightful information about gathering up-to-date information in order to benefit you emotionally.

READ and MARK

PEER SUPPORT - Find others who have experienced similar life trials and have had success in improving their well-being. Join a support group to gather suggestions, up-to-date information and inspiration. Hearing about their success stories and experiences will show that you are not alone in your trials. Ask your counselor for a recommendation of a group, or if they are leading a peer group.

WRITTEN MATERIAL and BOOKS - Ask your Medical Provider, Therapist or Peer Support Group for recommendations on clearly written, up-to-date and research-proven materials about your emotional condition. Often your professional caregivers and peer support team can recommend books with quality information to assist in your well-being. This will help you to track your symptoms and optimize care.

EVALUATE - Remember to evaluate information. Look for material that is researched and studied.

USE FOR A LIFETIME

Give Yourself a Hand can be used over your lifetime as a way to monitor, place, track and refresh how you care for yourself emotionally. You can look at this list regularly for a comprehensive guide to care for your emotional well-being.

CONTENT ROUND UP to REVIEW—RECALL—REMEMBER

- Give Yourself a Hand is a comprehensive list of ways to tend to one's emotional well-being.

- It uses your hand as a quick reminder of the ways to tend to one's emotional wellness.

- It supports examining one's physical, social, medical, psychological and informational needs to improve emotional well-being.

- People can make significant improvement to their emotional well-being by selecting one or two things to add to or subtract from their life, that are proven and known to help.

GUIDED COLLAGE EXPERIENCE—MAKE A COLLAGE

4. **GATHER** materials (glue, magazines, books and a substrate to make your collage on). Cut a small, triangle-shaped element from your source material. Place it anywhere on the substrate to provide a personal symbol of power and strength and to offer a comforting, familiar ritual to begin.

5. **LOCATE** from your source material a page with a significant amount of pattern. Place your hand on the page and trace your hand. Cut out the tracing and glue it onto the middle of the substrate, with all your fingers facing the top.

6. **LOOK** at the list above and locate the items beside which you placed a PLUS MARK (+). Choose one or two of the things you intend to start doing right away. Find elements to symbolize those things, cut them out, and glue them near the finger to which they relate.

7. **LOOK** intently at the collage. Choose a date you plan to begin the one or two things you intend to do. Write the date at the top of your collage.

8. **WRITE** or use collage elements to create a supportive thought to encapsulate this experience. Put this anywhere on your collage. Example: "I deserve to take really good care of myself and can offer care to myself as an act of self-love."

9. **PLACE** a triangle-shaped element anywhere on the substrate to symbolize your personal strength and to offer a comforting and familiar ritual.

10. **EXTEND** your transformation by completing the TAKEAWAY ACTION TOOLS (page 225).

11. **RETURN** here after completing the Takeaway Action Tools to read the ending quote below.

"If you never bother to say the words, why should anyone believe you ever felt them?"

— Richelle E. Goodrich

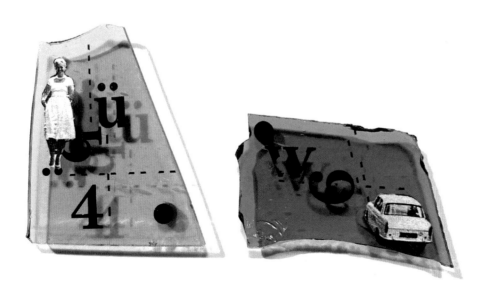

Lisbeth Søgård-Høyer, *Moving towards you*, 2020, Mini Collage on Glass, Doug + Laurie Kanyer Art Collection

Mauricio Mo, *In Memory of*, 2020, Collage Book, Doug + Laurie Kanyer Art Collection

ABOUT SELF-TALK

**A collage-making experience to learn about patterns
of self-talk and ways to replace harmful self-talk.**

"Don't be a victim of negative self-talk; remember, you are listening." — Bill Proctor

INFORMATION TO THINK ABOUT AND CONSIDER

You have an internal dialogue called self-talk. It is a constant back and forth conversation with small voices in your head. The voices consist of the constantly running thoughts that advise, motivate and instruct. They counsel, coach, and help to decipher what is going on around you. They tell you about yourself and the world in which you live. Self-talk is designed to help you navigate the world, while at the same time shaping your decisions so you can move forward.

Your self-talk formulates conclusions, impressions, and opinions about yourself, about others, and about the "somethings" you face. These inner directives talk to you throughout the day. They are there to help guide you during both simple and complex life decisions.

This inner voice is a combination of conscious thoughts and Early Life Impressions, life conclusions, biases, and personal values-beliefs. One way to look at these inner voices is like a coach helping to offer directions on how to negotiate through life. One's inner-voice self-talk helps you to create a framework for facing the nuanced aspects of life.

Helpful Self-Talk

In the best of situations your self-talk is supportive and encouraging. Its aim is to offer assistance and encouragement with words of strength. Your self-talk can help by reminding you of the times you have negotiated difficult situations in the past, and helps to bring forth strategies to use today.

In this case they are your superpowers. Helpful self-talk can be like a cheerleader, offering foundational courage and insight. When functioning in this positive capacity they can assess the inner wisdom from your True Self, supporting you to move in a way that fits and feels just right for you.

More Than One Voice

Most people believe there is one singular inner voice, but more and more researchers have proven there are many inner voices with a variety of self-talk platforms (Schwartz, 2021). This is why you can feel confused by all the voices in your head with their competing opinions, directions and options for any given situation.

Stop for a moment and think about your last trip returning home from somewhere. As you headed home you might have said to yourself, "Let's go this direction". Then another part of you might say, "You should turn left and go through the neighborhood since the other way takes longer." If you go your original route, and then run into traffic, the second voice may say "I told you so." And so forth. Your self-talk is actually a conversation among a number of parts of yourself.

Harsh Self-Talk

One's self-talk can occasionally become harsh, dictatorial, and even abusive. This is a very interesting phenomenon and it can be confusing. Why would anyone say hard, hurtful or harsh things to oneself?

Let's start by saying that you have a pure and very True Self within. This True Self is your original soul. As you grew and experienced things you developed personalities to protect and care for your True Self. This happened in your early childhood years, when one's personalities and parts were developing and had limitations in their sophistication and knowledge of the world.

Designed originally to help, guide and protect your True Self, these personalities created a series of behaviors, rules and structures about how you need to function. Over time they developed words that comprise your self-talk. As an example, imagine for a moment that you are a four-year-old child at a gathering. The adults are talking. You naturally want to be part of the conversation. You are young and learning. Not knowing exactly how to act to join in, you get a bit loud and interject with a noisy "Hey!".

The person who is talking at the time glances at you. They do not speak, rather they merely look directly at you and glare. You catch their look, and are left to derive a conclusion about their glance. Others may have said to you, "be quiet," "be good," or ignored you altogether.

From that look, and the words spoken or unspoken, you make an assessment about how to proceed. You develop an impression of you, your group, how to act, and so forth. Depending on how this went for you, the event produced a powerful impression. You then create some self-talk to be used in a similar situation. Your original intent of being with others possibly netted a hurtful experience. You may or may not have felt wounded.

If you felt wounded, to accommodate for the wound and shield yourself, you then developed a "part" to help protect you. The personality part develops a potent impression, which contains words to use in your self-talk commentary moving forward. Until it is reconsidered, this self-talk may be used for a lifetime when faced with similar situations, and it can be either harsh or supportive.

Your self-talk could develop a number of statements. Such statements may include something like "They are rude, be aware of people like this," or "I should watch and wait before I speak," or "I am so (put in your own hurtful negative words)." You could use one or all of these statements in your self-talk. Note that some of these statements are more neutral and direct, while others are harsh and hurtful.

Self-talk is about finding a way to put you in a position to avoid pain. One's self-talk may have adopted some harsh, heavy and even hurtful tones to keep you "in line". The goal is for you to avoid pain, while ironically the words used in one's self-talk can in fact be painful. This is in effort to manage your behavior and to cause you to halt. This circular logic is hard to believe, but it makes sense to the younger you who developed the self-talk.

Self-Talk Offers Structure

In the best, most desirable circumstances, the personality parts that one develops are helpful and calmly firm. They offer clear structure and rules on how to behave, in a kind yet direct tone, to help you avoid awkward or hurtful situations. The structure and rules developed contribute to the content in your self-talk. It is there to help prevent you from inserting yourself into potentially hurtful or embarrassing situations. An example of this helpful self-talk could be something like "When others are talking, I need to wait until they are done speaking, and do so in a calm tone." This is helpful, structuring self-talk.

Negative Self-Talk

The difficulty comes when the self-talk, in effort to protect and manage, is so negative that it increases the undesirable trend. It can actually tear at your self-worth and self-esteem. It can be hard to imagine that the voice in your head is actually the voice of a scared or angry four-year-old. This however, is human development as we presently understand it. Have you ever confronted a scared, annoyed, confused four-year-old in the throes of a heavy reaction to a "something"? This is what one's self-talk can be like. It can consist of statements that have no basis in reality, that are irrational or distorted. They came about during a painful situation that took place in the past, and their deeper intent is to help. Unfortunately, this does not always happen and one can have a critical pattern of shaming and blaming self-talk.

In summary, the topic of Self-Talk is a complex one.

What to Do?

When faced with negative, hurtful, self-talk, it can be helpful to approach yourself with compassion. It was a small child in a sophisticated situation who created these internal self-talk statements. If you can accept that your younger self was doing what if it felt it needed to be done in the circumstance, you can move forward with empathy and curiosity. Rather than shutting down the negative self-talk, you can seek to understand where it came from and work to make adjustments to fit it into the present. As an adult you can now take leadership and release the younger you from the negative self-talk pattern. The collage-making exercise-experience to follow will offer ways to document, observe and invite new self-talk declarations.

TYPES OF NEGATIVE SELF TALK

It can be helpful to get perspective on some of the more severe and heavy self-talk types. Researchers have studied and discovered some typical patterns of self-talk, and you will find a list of these to follow. Knowing about these common patterns can help you to know that you and others have similar self-talk tracks. Knowing the types will help you to not feel isolated and to detect some of the patterns in yourself. Please note that this list is a generalized view. You may have other self-talk patterns that are unique to you.

Here are the categories of negative self-talk, as defined by *The Feeling Good Handbook* by David D. Burns, M.D. (Burns,1989):

- **All-or-Nothing Thinking** – Seeing things in black-or-white categories. If a situation falls short of perfect, you may see it as a total failure.

- **Overgeneralization** – Seeing a single negative event as a never-ending pattern of defeat by using words such as "always" or "never."

- **Mental Filtering** – Picking out a single negative detail and dwelling on it exclusively, so that your vision of reality becomes darkened, like the drop of ink that discolors a beaker of water.

- **Discounting the Positive** – Rejecting positive experiences by insisting that they "don't count." If you do a good job, you may tell yourself that it wasn't good enough, or that anyone could have done as well. Discounting the positives takes the joy out of life and makes you feel inadequate and unrewarded.

- **Jumping to Conclusions** – Interpreting things negatively when there are no facts to support your conclusion.

- **Mind Reading** – Without checking it out, arbitrarily concluding that someone is reacting negatively to you.

- **Fortune-Telling** – Predicting that things will turn out badly.

- **Magnification** – Exaggerating the importance of your problems and shortcomings, or minimizing the importance of your desirable qualities.

- **Emotional Reasoning** – Assuming that your negative emotions necessarily reflect the way things really are: "I feel terrified about going on airplanes. It must be very dangerous to fly". "I feel so inferior. This means I'm a second-rate person."

- **"Should" Statements** – Telling yourself that things should be the way you hoped or expected them to be. After playing a difficult piece on the piano, a gifted pianist told herself, "I shouldn't have made so many mistakes." "Must's", "Aught's", and "Have to's" are similar offenders. "Should" statements that are directed against yourself lead to guilt and frustration. "Should" statements that are directed against other people or the world in general lead to anger and frustration. An example: "He shouldn't be so stubborn and argumentative!"

- **Labeling** – Labeling is an extreme form of all-or-nothing thinking. Instead of saying, "I made a mistake," you attach a negative label to yourself: "I'm a loser." You might also label yourself, "a failure" or "a jerk." Labeling is quite irrational because you are not the same as what you do.

Human beings exist, but "losers" and "jerks" do not. These labels are just useless abstractions that lead to anger, anxiety, frustration, and lower self-esteem.

You may also label others. When someone does something that rubs you the wrong way, you may tell yourself: "He's an S.O.B." You then feel that the problem is with that person's character or essence, instead of with their thinking or behavior. You see them as totally bad. This makes you feel hostile and hopeless about improving things and leaves very little room for constructive communication.

Personalization and Blame – This is a description of holding yourself personally responsible for an event that isn't entirely under your control. When a woman received a note that her child was having difficulty in school, she told herself, "This shows what a bad mother I am," instead of trying to pinpoint the cause of the problem so that she could be helpful to her child. Personalization leads to guilt, shame and feelings of inadequacy.

People also blame others or their circumstances for their problems, and they overlook ways they might be contributing to the problem. An example might be "The reason my marriage is so lousy is because my spouse is totally unreasonable." Blame usually doesn't work very well because other people will resent being scapegoated and they will just toss the blame right back in your lap.

Collage-Making Can Help

Making a collage about what you say to yourself—about yourself and others—can help you to know more about the accuracy of your internal dialogue. You will be able to consider and challenge habitual patterns in your responses to circumstances. This knowledge may allow you to make necessary shifts in your thinking or to consider your thoughts more in-depth. Collage-making can reveal your conclusions and help you to see if they are true or need some revision, just like a quality counselor or loyal friend might do.

As you learn to better identify negative self-talk patterns, you can then learn how to start answering them with rational arguments and challenging the statements. In this manner, you can work to turn your internal conversation back to being positive in your life, instead of a running negative commentary.

CONTENT ROUND UP to REVIEW—RECALL—REMEMBER

- Each person has a voice or voices constantly speaking to them, and the conversation can be positive, negative or neutral. It is often called self-talk.

- This running dialog of self-talk is often formed in early childhood and adolescence and can contain words said by others and conclusions you develop yourself. These are called "Early Life Impressions".

- There are many types of negative self-talk statements and all of them can be challenged. You can change those patterns.

- You can get help to challenge your negative self-talk with the help of your support team or professional counselors.

GUIDED COLLAGE EXPERIENCE—MAKE A COLLAGE

1. **GATHER** materials (glue, magazines, books and a substrate to make your collage on). Cut a small, triangle-shaped element from your source material. Place it anywhere on the substrate to provide a personal symbol of power and strength and to offer a comforting, familiar ritual to begin.

2. **REVIEW** the list to identify any negative self-talk patterns you find yourself using. Choose elements to symbolize the patterns you tend to use. Cut them out and glue them down in a vertical line, from top-to-bottom on the substrate, on the LEFT-hand side.

3. **CONSIDER** the exact statements you say to yourself, whether these statements are about yourself or others. Find elements to symbolize the statements. Cut them out and glue them down in a vertical line, from top-to-bottom on the page, in the MIDDLE of the substrate, next to the type of self-talk. You might try to tally the frequency of the negative self-talk patterns.

4. **CHOOSE** an accurate, positive, helpful statement to replace the negative self-talk statement. Find elements to symbolize the accurate, positive, helpful statement. Cut them out and glue them down in a vertical line, from top-to-bottom on the page on the RIGHT-hand side of the substrate, next to the type of negative self-talk. Feel free to also write down the accurate, positive, helpful statement, to help you continue to identify more accurate words to say to yourself. Consider finding someone to talk with about these patterns. It might be helpful to take a screenshot of your collage on your phone of the POSITIVE statements to use when you are out in the world.

5. **WRITE** or use collage elements to create a supportive thought to encapsulate this experience. Put this anywhere on your collage. Example: "I can challenge and coach myself to speak more constructively to myself and call into question negative self-talk."

6. **PLACE** a triangle-shaped element anywhere on the substrate to symbolize your personal strength and to offer a comforting and familiar ritual.

7. **EXTEND** your transformation by completing the TAKEAWAY ACTION TOOLS (page 225).

8. **RETURN** here after completing the Takeaway Action Tools to read the ending quote below.

"Would you ever talk to others the way you talk to yourself?"

— Laurie Kanyer

Sarah Perkins, *Finding Joy in the Smallest of Things*, 2021, Mini Collage, Doug + Laurie Kanyer Art Collection

CP Harrison, *Chill*, 2020, Analog Collage, Courtesy of the Artist

FINDING CALM

A collage-making exercise-experience to practice establish
calm by using the small muscles of the hands.

"Human freedom involves our capacity to pause between the stimulus and response, and in that pause, to choose the one response toward which we wish to throw our weight. The capacity to create ourselves, based upon this freedom, is inseparable from consciousness or self-awareness." — Rollo May, *The Courage to Create*

INFORMATION TO THINK ABOUT AND CONSIDER

Collage-making requires cutting items out of a magazine or a book. This action of physically cutting out elements supports the healing of emotional strain, stress, and anxiety. The use of the small muscles in the hands while cutting elements facilitates the pacing, regulating, and modulating of stress chemicals which are related to emotional strain and anxiety (Kanyer, 2004). This action helps to disburse and cleanse the body of these potent chemicals and offers calmness to one's system.

Pacing Potent Hormones

When the brain feels a potent emotion, it transmits strong chemicals throughout the body to signal the person to pay attention and to possibly act. The strength of these chemicals can be dramatic and can at times hamper clear thinking and decision making. One such stress hormone is called Cortisol. We know that about 15 minutes after the onset of stress, Cortisol levels rise and often remain elevated for several hours.

It is interesting to note that, in times of danger, this mechanism of chemical flooding can be a life-saving function of the brain, causing it to signal the body to seek safety. If you are in danger or frightened, chemical flooding moves through the body to help you seek safety. This is called the Flight, Freeze, Flee or Fawn Response. On the other hand, some chemical flooding impedes helpful actions, processing, and thinking. The intense weight of these hormones on the rest of the body can be wearing and harmful.

Repetitive Motions Help Bring Forth Calmness

We know that repetitive motions, like that of cutting out elements for a collage, helps to pace the chemicals in order to regulate, to settle, and to modulate the potency of emotional strain (Kanyer 2004). This is important, as not all chemical floods require swift action. Therefore, by doing a repetitive motion like cutting or even tearing paper, you can help pace the chemicals of the brain. It can calm one's nerves and improve emotional well-being.

Many people enjoy the satisfaction of slow, intentional, and precise cutting. It is relaxing, calming and satisfying. Noted Belgian collagist Native puts it this way: "Personally, I experience collaging as a wonderful resource to help me to manage states of anxiety due to chronic illness. The creation process brings me serenity. Putting various elements together is like reuniting fragments of myself and my past to create something new and meaningful. Collage is not only a creative practice, but a companion on a healing journey." She says in a film she made on collage, "My mind can escape through creation."

Anxiety Can Be Contagious

The other thing to know about anxiety is that it is communicable. An anxious tone is just as contagious as a calm tone. There is great benefit to the group with whom you are associated to invest in having an intentional calm practice. Being calm is a choice, and people can gain usable calm skills, like collage-making.

Anxiety as a Family Structure

Some families develop an anxiety pattern that puts an emphasis on over-functioning. Possibly due to birth order, someone in the group takes on more of the responsibility than is humanly possible. They often take charge and can become very direct. Conversely, other people under-function. They do not use their established skills and talents to support problem solving. Both of these responses are developed early in life out of a need to manage problems, but both limit quality problem solving and undermine teamwork. Knowing this will help you to consider if these earlier family patterns fit for you in the present.

A Calming Process:

You can learn calming techniques to avoid or reduce anxiety. The value of cutting out elements for a collage to calm oneself is immense. You can activate the process with the following steps:

   A. **Pause** and consider if you have enough information to form an appropriate response, for the purpose of avoiding the emotional energy of anger and frustration.

   B. **Focus** your awareness on the present moment. Nourish and reassure your brain that you are not in danger by taking six (6) slow, deep breaths.

   C. **Practice** daily calming behaviors to build the mental muscle memory necessary when faced with strain. You can choose to use the exercise-experience that follows, and other exercises in this book, on a regular basis to establish a calm-pattern-pathway for when anxiety attempts to hijack your emotions.

Note: The guided collage-making exercise-experience to follow can become a daily exercise to decrease anxiety. The action of cutting by itself may be helpful. While the elements you cut out can become part of a final collage at some point, simply cutting items supports your brain in processing daily emotions. If life events are deeply concerning right now, the repetitive small muscle motions of cutting out elements will focus the eyes and pace the hormones. Like taking a yoga class or going for a walk, it can help you to decompress from the day or when deeply burdened, dispel the weight of emotional strain.

CONTENT ROUND UP to REVIEW—RECALL—REMEMBER

- The gentle act of sitting and cutting collage elements can help to calm and pace potent brain chemicals connected to anxiety. By cutting elements out you can reduce the effect of strong chemicals in the brain on your entire system.

- Anxious feelings can be contagious and stifle the expression of calmness.

- Slow, deep breathing at the onset of a disruption helps to signal to the brain you are safe and can reduce anxiety.

GUIDED COLLAGE EXPERIENCE–MAKE A COLLAGE

1. **GATHER** scissors, source material and some envelopes only. In this activity you will not be doing some of the steps featured in other exercise-experiences in this book.

2. **SET** a timer for a half hour. Breathe in through your nose and out through your nose. Simply sit and cut out elements for a half hour. Take your time cutting in slow, paced precision. Cut simply for the purpose of pacing hormones related to emotions. Just sit and cut. You could choose to search for and cut only from a particular subject matter; for example, find and cut out only hats or cars or flowers or trees or something else you choose. Searching for single-themed elements will also engage the small muscles of your hand to turn the pages. Similarly, focusing on a single subject will set a meditative tone for a time. Caution: Do not use scissors if you are feeling like hurting yourself or others. Tear paper instead.

3. **CONSIDER** that symbolically, as you cut and trim from the source material and small pieces fall away, imagine them to be the events of the day, the heavy emotions and feelings connected with those events detaching and drifting away.

4. **AFTER** a half hour (or more if you wish) sort the elements by subject and place them into an envelope. Label the envelope, its contents to use in the future. Later you will delight in your own cleverness and planning when it comes time to use those sorted elements in collage-making. Consider by comparison the feeling of contentment you feel when you go to find a tool you need and can locate it with ease….the confidence and lack of strain can be a powerful emotional boost. When you go to your envelope file and easily find the collage element you need, it is a little wink to enhance your self-esteem.

5. **EXTEND** your transformation by completing the TAKEAWAY ACTION TOOLS (page 225).

6. **RETURN** here after completing the Takeaway Action Tools to read the ending quote below.

"Sometimes getting to the other side seems impossible. You know there's a way.
You can actually see the steps in your mind - but it all seems out of reach.
Pause. Relax. Remember to do what you can in the moment you're in.
Before long, you'll arrive at your destination,
ready for the next challenge."

— Lashawnda Jones

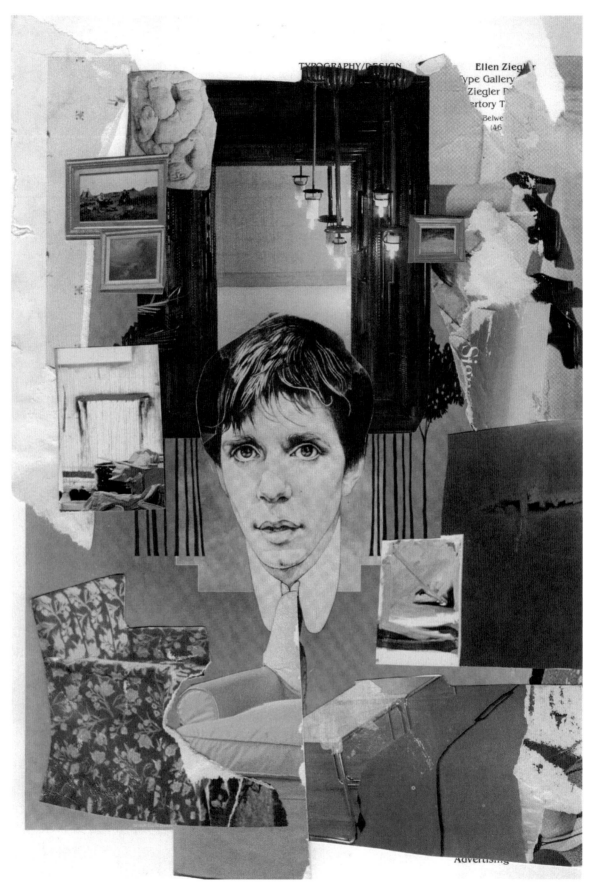

CP Harrison, *Outsider Ease*, 2020, Analog Collage, Courtesy of the Artist

GROUNDING ONESELF

**A collage-making exercise-experience to ground and balance oneself
in the face of anxiety or potent hardships.**

"As you start to walk in the way, the way appears." — Rumi

INFORMATION TO THINK ABOUT AND CONSIDER

Have you ever had an experience where you feel outside of your body due to the potency of what you are going through? When one is facing hardship and drastic life changes, the mind can develop a number of mechanisms causing one to not feel alive, or even feel emotionless. It can feel as though you are suspended in another world or someone else's story. The power and potency of life events have temporarily re-circuited your ability to be in touch with yourself. This is often called disassociation.

Big Changes Can Unsettle One's Balance

When coping with life-altering change like loss of a job, an unexpected health issue, the death of a loved one, or another form of heavy loss—you can almost feel non-existent. Numbness is a word people often use to describe this phenomenon. You may say to yourself "I can't believe (fill in the blank)" or "This can't be my life." The situation may be so life-altering that it exceeds the brain's ability to comprehend it all.

Using collage-making during times of huge shifts and changes can help to ground you, to bring you back into yourself. It helps you to move toward healing and integrate the event. Some say time heals all sorrows and unexpected twists in life. I say, action, like collage-making, heals and helps!

Here is why.

Witnessing Oneself

When collage-making, you actually observe or witness your hands cutting and pasting. This witnessing offers the mind the proof you exist, even when it does not feel like it. Collage-making supports you becoming balanced or grounded at times when you feel unbalanced, or when you feel that the floor is melting away. It shows you that you are here, in the present moment.

Evidence You Exist

The collage-making process and the resultant completed collage is the evidence that you are in the "here and now". It is proof that you are living this story and that you can have both feet on the ground as you move forward to make adjustments. Collage-making will ground you and be a support to help you move through the stages of grief associated with heavy changes.

Helps to Insert New Realities

When you have had a large change in your life your brain must open its metaphorical file drawer. It has to insert a new file into how it sees and knows the world. Collage-making, and the final finished-product collage, helps. The collage-making and the finished collage is like locating a new piece of paper to fit into the file drawer of how you understand your life.

Being Overwhelmed is Not Necessarily Connected to a Known "Something"

There are other times when a feeling of overwhelmedness comes on unexpectedly. It may be associated with a "something" or not. The source of the feelings of overwhelmedness can be analyzed at a later date, but in the moment one must have access to a tool to balance oneself. Floods of overwhelmedness can provoke a feeling of profound numbness. Overwhelmedness can be accompanied by a flood of rapid-fire emotional sensation. In this case a grounding activity is called for, and the exercise to follow will help.

Taking Account of Your Surroundings

When feeling profoundly overwhelmed, enough to bring you to a halt or pause, taking account of your surroundings is known to help. The collage-making activity to follow can be used any time you experience a heavy "something". The activity can also be used when you find yourself in a situation with anxiety, panic or distress that is not connected to a known "something."

CONTENT ROUND UP to REVIEW—RECALL—REMEMBER

- When making a collage you see yourself creating it and this can be grounding.

- The collage-making process and the resulting collage are evidence that you exist in time, when you do not feel like you exist.

- Collage-making helps you to accept a new reality connected with change.

- Collage-making can help to modulate and regulate feelings of overwhelmedness and anxiety not connected to a known "something".

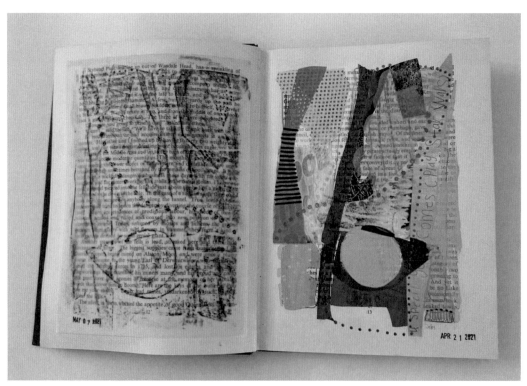

Molly McCracken, *English Lakeland Personal Stratigraphy Maps in Color*, 2021, Collage in Book, Doug + Laurie Kanyer Art Collection

GUIDED COLLAGE EXPERIENCE–MAKE A COLLAGE

1. **GATHER** materials (glue, magazines, books and a substrate to make your collage on). Cut a small, triangle-shaped element from your source material. Place it anywhere on the substrate to provide a personal symbol of power and strength and to offer a comforting, familiar ritual to begin.

2. **LOOK** around the room in which you are sitting, whether it's in your home or other environment. Notice the chairs, lamps, tables, the walls, the ceiling. Take your time as you make this inventory.

3. **SEARCH** in your source material to find elements that symbolize the objects in your environment. For example: find element(s) for a chair, a sofa, a rug, a desk or other items in your environment. Naturally, you may not find exact replicas of what you have in your environment. Simply locate elements to symbolize what is in your environment. Cut them out and set them aside.

4. **ARRANGE** the elements in a similar pattern to how the items are placed in your home or environment. Don't overthink this. Once you have found a similar layout to the room you are in, glue each element down on the substrate.

5. **RETURN** to your source materials and find element(s) to represent you. Cut them out and place them somewhere on the substrate. Feel free to add more elements to show objects in your environment until you feel more balanced and grounded.

6. **WRITE** or use collage elements to create a supportive thought to encapsulate this experience. Put this anywhere on your collage. For example, "I can ground and witness myself using collage-making."

7. **PLACE** a triangle-shaped element anywhere on the substrate to symbolize your personal strength and to offer a comforting and familiar ritual.

8. **EXTEND** your transformation by completing the TAKEAWAY ACTION TOOLS (page 225).

9. **RETURN** here after completing the Takeaway Action Tools to read the ending quote below.

"Although no one can go back and make a brand new start, anyone can start from now and make a brand new ending."

— Carl Sandburg

Native, *Passers By*, 2020, Mini Analog Collage, Doug + Laurie Kanyer Art Collection

Carol White, *What if the Moon Falls*, 2014, Analog Collage, Doug + Laurie Kanyer Art Collection

EMOTIONAL PAIN CAN BE INVISIBLE

A collage-making experience to learn how interdependence can help combat invisible emotional pain.

"Pain is like water. It finds a way to push through any seal." — Katie Kacvinsky

"People assume you aren't sick unless they see the sickness on your skin, like scars forming a map of all the ways you're hurting. Sometimes monsters are invisible, and sometimes demons attack you from the inside. Just because you cannot see the claws and the teeth does not mean they aren't ripping through me. Pain does not need to be seen to be felt." — Emm Roy

INFORMATION TO THINK ABOUT AND CONSIDER

Emotional pain can be invisible to others. It frequently differs from physical injury, which is easier to observe with bandages, crutches, or casts. It is no wonder that others have a difficult time extending compassion toward a person who is hurting emotionally. Others simply may not be able to see the depth of one's suffering or imagine the hurt one feels. Unless those in their life are experiencing the same exact situation, or have had a similar event in their life as a reference point, it can be hard for one to find true empathy.

Emotional Pain Can Be Difficult to Observe

When emotional pain is intense and others cannot easily observe it, it may manifest in more pain. It is as if it has to be acknowledged by others to make it real. This pain, and the absence of compassion, understanding, or help, can be crushing.

Additionally, there are cultural mores or beliefs that may compound the issue of emotional pain. Specifically, the belief that being totally independent and not sharing one's pain or asking for help is a noble characteristic. It is certain that one of the human developmental stages of childhood is to be able to independently care for oneself; to do things on one's own. You may have heard accounts of people who have had hardship and then are lauded for never complaining or becoming a burden. They may in fact be taking independence a little too far, or there may have been no one in their sphere who they could ask or trust to help.

The truth is yes, humans need to be able to do things independently. Being able to bathe comes to mind as an example. But consider this other truth: most adult activities require some teamwork and help from one another. Famed author (and one of my mentors) Jean Illsley Clarke talked about the developmental stage of adulthood being that of Interdependence (Clarke, 1995).

Sharing Ones Pain Helps

Interdependence, as it relates to emotional pain, translates into sharing your pain with another by becoming vulnerable with them. The goal of this vulnerability is to work as a team to get help and understand what is going on. It is where another person can come alongside you interdependently, to assist you, knowing that you too may be called on to help them in the future. This is not dependency, where you need others' help with everything. It is where you work to build a trusting relationship where you help each other to build a life of well-being.

The exercise-experiences in this book are geared to help you to strengthen your knowledge of emotions, and then use this knowledge to build and live in interdependent relationships for the health of all. It is likely that, in your life, you will experience some emotional, invisible wounding. When living an interdependent life with others you are able to share the emotional pain and then see the pain as a signal to get on a road with others to sort out the wound. The group, knowing of the wound, can use the Empowerment Triangle (page 213) to work as a team to transform the pain in your life. In doing so, others gain skills and use their strengths while helping you to become stronger.

Others Care and Can Help

Even though your emotional pain cannot be seen, you can still work to share it with someone. It may be a friend, family member or a professional such as your doctor or a mental health therapist. The concept is to have someone come alongside you and seek to transform your pain. The exercise-experience to follow is designed for you to make a collage about some pain you are experiencing that is likely invisible to others. In making the collage you will be able to see it first, and it will give you the affirmation that it is in fact real.

You can use this visible knowledge on the collage as a motivator to seek support. Making the collage might be all you need to move forward in your transformation of sorting it out while talking to others. Or you might find the words to explain might be too overwhelming, and merely showing the collage to others keeps you from having to speak. Whatever you choose, this will likely offer you the support to get relief and use the pain to solve a problem.

CONTENT ROUND UP to REVIEW—RECALL—REMEMBER

- Emotional pain can be invisible to others and collage-making about your pain can help others to understand.

- Sharing one's emotional pain with others will offer support to decrease one's suffering.

- Interdependence is when people work together to help each other in life.

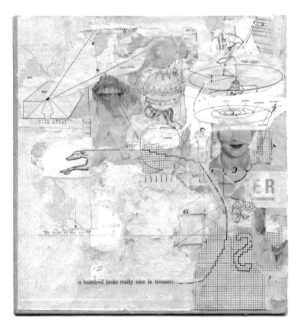

Oliver Lunn, *A Hundred Looks Really Nice in Trouser*, 2019, Collage, Doug + Laurie Art Collection

GUIDED COLLAGE EXPERIENCE—MAKE A COLLAGE

1. **GATHER** materials (glue, magazines, books and a substrate to make your collage on). Cut a small, triangle-shaped element from your source material. Place it anywhere on the substrate to provide a personal symbol of power and strength and to offer a comforting, familiar ritual to begin.

2. **CHOOSE** element(s) to symbolize how emotional pain can be invisible. Cut them out and glue them to the bottom 1/4 of your substrate.

3. **CHOOSE** as many elements as you want to show the invisible emotional pain you may be experiencing right now or have experienced in the past. Cut them out, and glue them onto the next 1/4 of your substrate. Add elements to symbolize what caused your pain, how long it has been going on, your self-talk and Early Life Impressions about it, and any other aspects.

4. **FIND** an element to symbolize a door, a mouth, and clouds. They don't have to actually be these items. Choose elements that are symbolic with meaning to you. The door shows a new path to walk through to share your feelings about the pain. The mouth will symbolize using words (or this collage) to let others know how you feel. The cloud, for looking up in the sky, and having the hope you will transform your feelings about the pain. Cut them out and glue them in the middle of the next 1/4 of your substrate. Find elements to symbolize others to work interdependently with you to help sort it out, and transform your feelings. Place and glue these elements on either side of the door, mouth and cloud.

5. **MOVING** across the substrate from left to right, in the last 1/4 of the collage:

   • Add an element to show you connecting with others to discuss what you are experiencing.

   • Add an element to show others helping and believing you.

   • Add an element to show your transformed emotions, a plan to resolve the challenge.

6. **WRITE** or use collage elements to create a supportive thought to encapsulate this experience. Put this anywhere on your collage. An example: "I can begin to recognize when I am in pain. I can begin to shed light on the pain I have that is hard for others to see. I can work to find people who will listen and help."

7. **PLACE** a triangle-shaped element anywhere on the substrate to symbolize your personal strength and to offer a comforting and familiar ritual.

8. **EXTEND** your transformation by completing the TAKEAWAY ACTION TOOLS (page 225).

9. **RETURN** here after completing the Takeaway Action Tools to read the ending quote below.

"Whenever I get frustrated or annoyed with someone's actions, I remind myself that I don't really know what's going on in their life. I try to take a breath, not take it personally, and trust that they are doing the best they can."

— Mary-Frances Makichen

Liberty Blake, *LOVE Rat*, 2021, Collage on Panel, Doug + Laurie Kanyer Art Collection

SHIELDING FROM SHAME

A collage-making exercise-experience to learn about shame and ways to combat it.

"We can endure all kinds of pain. It's shame that eats men whole." — Leigh Bardugo

INFORMATION TO THINK ABOUT AND CONSIDER

Shame shapes what we believe about ourselves, as prescribed by others. It is a form of social control aimed to keep you in a lower place. It threatens to distance you from the affection of the group if you act in a certain way that does not benefit them. As renowned author, counselor and educator Connie Dawson says, "Shame dims our original light. It is a colorless shroud that covers our eyes and holds us back from seeing what we see and knowing what we know. It is a murky layer that has a way of binding us up and keeping us from becoming the person we are meant to be (Dawson, 2016)."

Shame is Used to Control and Manipulate

Shame uses schemes to make people feel worthless. Statements such as saying, "You're a failure as a person" or "You are bad to the core" or "You are completely inadequate" are often used. Please do not let these harsh words you just read descend upon you and soak in.

Shame can be summed up as "stinking thinking", disparagingly projected to manipulate you and take away your ability to think and feel clearly. It differs from guilt, which occurs when one does something wrong or makes an error, but can make appropriate reparations, amends and apologies.

Historical Perspective of the Use of Shame

From a historical perspective, shame may have been used hundreds of years ago to keep members of a group safe. In the distant past it was believed that if you thought for yourself you may do something impulsive, and the impulsive behavior might result in putting the group or yourself in danger. Accordingly, families and other groups used shame to keep members from thinking for themselves by making them feel badly about themselves.

Shame Rules

Connie Dawson has developed a list of "shame rules". She says these rules are kept "secret" by the group and are rarely challenged. Says Dawson, "They rarely go named, are never discussed or negotiated (Dawson, 2016)." Interestingly, shame rules can change in the blink of an eye by the person who is working to keep an upper hand on those whom they lead. The rules of shame are toxic, sticky, and disabling.

Summary of Connie Dawson's Shame Rules

Dawson concludes with this grave warning about Shame Rules: "All of these rules are inhumane because they can't possibly be carried out without causing damage to human beings". The Rules are as follows:

Rule One: Be Perfect

This is an interesting rule as no one can achieve perfection. No human has ever been without error. Mistakes happen. By asking people to achieve perfection, we find ourselves focusing on the goal of perfection, rather than learning to think for oneself or asking for forgiveness when a mistake does happen. The rule of perfection is designed to focus on the standards of others and invites absolute compliance and reliance on the definitions of others.

Rule Two: Blame Others

If you have to be perfect that means you cannot fail, ever. Therefore, you must at all cost avoid any spotlight being focused upon your failures. To maintain a seemingly perfect profile, people who shame others will seek to find fault in others, even if it is fabricated.

Rule Three: Ignore Feelings

If shame was originally designed to keep us safe, then that meant listening to your feelings had to be eliminated. Feelings and emotions are signals to alert you to "do something" or "pay attention" to something that needs tending to solve a problem. In an earlier time it was believed that if you listened to your feelings, you might become impulsive and act unpredictably, which could put you and others in danger. It was felt that if you paid attention to feelings you might go against the group mentality. Shame tells you to NOT pay attention to your feelings and to not ask for care or get your feelings attended to. Shame keeps you denying what you need, and obscures what you know from your feelings and emotions.

Rule Four: Keep Secrets, Tell Lies and Do Not Tell

Shame uses lies. It ignites and spreads suspicion and uncertainty. It is the opposite of healthy loving relationships in which you have trust, certainty, security and honesty. The secrets and lies cause people to fear and doubt themselves, and then to become suspicious of others based on lies and secrets told to them. In a shame-based group, lies are told to keep people uncertain and to cause doubt. Secrets are used to keep people from working together and to spread suspicion.

Rule Five: Be Unclear and Un-Accountable

In shame-based groups people tend to not follow through on promises. They will not make reasonable agreements. They will withhold information readily available to them or not share information they have. People who shame seem to be inviting others to challenge them on their behavior, but they are betting you won't.

Rule Six: Be in Control

During moments of strain, one may want to maintain balance by being in control. This makes sense to some degree. Shame-based control, however, is different. This type of control is frightening and abusive. Coupled with the use of all the other steps, people use fear to maintain control. They become bullies. Sadly, for those using shame-based control tactics, it may turn on them as there are so many things to try to manage to gain and maintain control.

Rule Seven: Deny Reality

Often called gaslighting, this is where the person who is trying to maintain control using shame denies events, perceptions, or stirs up confusion. Essentially, the aim of this rule is to make others feel irrational, and it aims to keep others guessing. People who use shame will deny the truth so others feel that what they know to be true has been skewed or denied.

Rule Eight: Use Guilt When it is Really Shame

People trying to control others will attempt to use shame disguised as guilt to get you to go against your beliefs and against what is in your best interest. They aim to manipulate you to go against your best interest or values by saying they are "guilting" you, when they are in reality using shame. They aim to get you to question your needs and to shame you when you have your own thoughts, feelings and life desires.

Rule Nine: Threat of Being Cut Off from the Group

Dawson's final Shame Rule describes a circumstance where the person who uses shame says you are undeserving of the company of the group because you are a source of dishonor.

Connie Dawson's Healthy Rules to Combat Shame

Healthy, non-shaming groups support the safety of people using their feelings. They do so inspirationally, providing a way to gain insight, expand knowledge, teach negotiation skills, solve problems, inspire teamwork and expand pride in skills developed.

Healthy Rule One: Room for Mistakes

Offering people room to make mistakes and still have the support of others is paramount according to Healthy Rule One. Such behavior offers one the chance to learn skills and make reparations if needed.

Healthy Rule Two: No Blame or Shame

If there is an error, Rule Two describes how the group uses a tradition of encouraging people to take responsibility without blame or shame and offers help to solve problems.

Healthy Rule Three: Feel Your Feelings

In healthy groups there is room for people to share their feelings and be heard. And if someone feels unsafe, in danger or afraid, this is addressed immediately.

Healthy Rule Four: No Secrets

In Rule Four people share information to help both the individual and the group, as opposed to keeping secrets and imposing shame on someone. In stressful times the use of conference calls, group texts, shared emails, and as often as possible face-to-face gatherings are used to share information so all have access to information. Additionally, know that secrets are designed to never be found out. It is as if one is being asked to take this information to the grave. A healthy process is to say "We do not keep secrets". Tell those who want to keep secrets that you understand their feelings, but point out it undermines the group's health and well-being.

Healthy Rule Five: Follow Through

When people move to a passive role and do not keep their promises—acting unaccountable—healthy groups encourage members to tap into courage to step up and take responsibility. Healthy groups use boundaries with consequences and extend compassion as people work to be accountable. Healthy groups insist members make amends when they fail to follow through. As a result, people are seen as valuable regardless of their behavior, even while they are being held responsible for their actions.

Healthy Rule Six: Shared Problem Solving

It is natural to try to be in control of things, especially to attempt to avoid pain. However, this is a form of over-functioning, developed to control others in order to maintain power. It is unhealthy. It will lead to people finding it challenging to trust, as shame is often used to control others. Healthy groups work to call out or point out those who are beginning to over-function, trying to take total control. They are lovingly firm in offering to divide tasks during problem solving, and listen to how the over-functioning person feels. It is likely that they are experiencing fear, and that could lead them to using shame.

Healthy Rule Seven: Seek to Discover the Truth

Healthy groups seek to discover what is true and combat denial of reality. This denial of reality is often called gaslighting. When people attempt to change the truth, the group can work to remain calm and to adopt the view of respecting someone even when their view on a topic is different than theirs. When you feel your reality is being denied, speak up. Say, "I know what I know. I was there and I know what I saw. I respect your point of view, but I trust my perspective on things and I have formed an opinion that is sound."

Healthy Rule Eight: Accountability and Repair

If you experience someone shaming you rather than holding you accountable when an error is made, or when you are guilty of an offense, ask them to clearly outline the offense and ask for them to outline how you can repair the situation. If they label you with ugly names and criticism say "I will listen to this when it is offered with clear information about what I did wrong. I fully reject any discussion that is an attack on my person."

Healthy Rule Nine: Value the Individual and the Group

Healthy groups gather to discuss concerns and do not use shame or the threat of being cut off from the group. They call group meetings to discuss the situation. If someone as an individual needs some space, the group honors this need, with a goal of eventually working to gather to discuss the situation further.

What to Do If You Have Been Shamed

Author Brene Brown says shame thrives in secrecy, silence and judgement (Brown, n.d.). What, then, is oppositional to shame? Brown encourages us to establish self-care steps to combat shame using the following:

Step One: Know Your Shame Triggers

A hint that you are being shamed is when you come away feeling as though you are "not enough". That is, "Not smart enough", "Not good enough", "Not fast enough", "Not rich enough", and so forth.

Step Two: Tell Your Story

Brown says shame cannot thrive in secrecy and silence.

Step Three: Reach Out to Someone You Trust

Have a REALITY CHECK to determine what is really true and to determine your part in a concern. Choose a person who can be empathetic and has great listening skills. They must know you well, and be deeply kind-hearted. Shame cannot thrive when exposed, emphasizes Brown. Combat shame with empathy!

Step Four: Talk to Yourself as Someone You Deeply Love.

Would you ever talk to someone you love in the same tone as you talk to yourself when feeling the throws of shame? Most likely not be vulnerable with them. The goal of this vulnerability is to work as a team to get help and understand what is going on. It is where another person can come alongside you interdependently, to assist you, knowing that you too may be called on to help them in the future. This is not dependency, where you need others' help with everything. Rather, it is the establishment of a healthy, trusting relationship where you help each other to build a life of well-being.

CONTENT ROUND UP to REVIEW—RECALL—REMEMBER

- Shame is used by people to control and manipulate others.

- Unhelpful Shame Rules are often kept secret, are rarely challenged and often change to fit the needs of those who are attempting to control others.

- To recover from being shamed people can adopt healthy, non-shaming rules which enable people to safely express feelings.

- Healthy, non-shaming group rules provide a way to gain insight, expand knowledge, teach negotiation skills, solve problems, inspire teamwork and expand pride in one's self.

- Telling one's story decreases the power and potency of shame. Shame cannot survive in silence.

GUIDED COLLAGE EXPERIENCE—MAKE A COLLAGE

1. **GATHER** materials, glue, magazines, books and a substrate (the paper you make your collage upon). Cut a small, triangle-shaped element from your source material. Place it anywhere on the substrate to provide a personal symbol of power and strength. Doing this will offer a comforting and familiar ritual to begin this experience.

2. **ORIENT** your substrate vertically. Draw a LARGE triangle with the two points facing the top of the substrate and the single point facing the bottom. This symbolizes a protective SHIELD against the venom of shame. It will symbolically guard you against the secrets, lies and gaslighting that accompanies shame.

3. **FIND** elements to symbolize the true, lovable aspects of who you really are. Find elements to symbolize your positive character traits. Find elements to show your skills, your accomplishments, and things you love. Cut them out and glue them inside the large triangle.

4. **REVIEW** Connie Dawson's Healthy Rules to Combat Shame and find element(s) to symbolize the ones you like and want to remember. Cut them out and glue them inside the triangle.

5. **THINK** about who you can call to do a reality check when someone has shamed you, or your shame triggers get pushed. Who will tell you the truth about how lovable and capable you are? Plan to tell your story to this person so that shame cannot be propagated in secrecy. Find an element(s) to symbolize all the people you know and trust who you can talk with and who remind you who you are. Cut out and glue the element(s) for these people somewhere below the large triangle.

6. **FIND** a page in your source material that has a great deal of pattern on it and that greatly appeals to you. Tear out the page and draw a heart shape on it about the same size as the triangle on your collage. Cut the heart shape out, and then cut it down the middle. Glue each side of the heart shape onto the sides of the triangle.

7. **BRAVO!** You have made a collage to symbolically represent a shield to protect you from shame. You have inside the triangle some elements to symbolize a) the truth of who you are, b) a group of people to confront the lies of shame—your defenders of the truth, and c) Healthy Rules to Combat Shame. You have on the outside of the triangle a heart to show love and protection to combat shame.

8. **WRITE** or use collage elements to create a supportive thought to encapsulate this experience. Put this anywhere on your collage. For example: "I can be keenly aware of the schemes of shame and establish healthy rules to enhance my belief in myself."

9. **PLACE** a triangle-shaped element anywhere on the substrate to symbolize your personal strength and to offer a comforting and familiar ritual.

10. **EXTEND** your transformation by completing the TAKEAWAY ACTION TOOLS (page 225).

11. **RETURN** here after completing the Takeaway Action Tools to read the ending quote below.

"Shame is a soul eating emotion." — Carl Gustav Jung

Miranda Millward, *Always Ask*, 2022, Analog Collage, Doug + Laurie Kanyer Art Collection

ABOUT STERBs

A collage-making exercise-experience to learn about behaviors people use to decrease pain.

"When you have a persistent sense of heartbreak and gut wrench, the physical sensations become intolerable and we will do anything to make those feelings disappear. And that is really the origin of what happens in human pathology. People take drugs to make it disappear, and they cut themselves to make it disappear, and they starve themselves to make it disappear, and they have sex with anyone who comes along to make it disappear. Once you have these horrible sensations in your body, you'll do anything to make it go away."
— Bessel A. van der Kolk

INFORMATION TO THINK ABOUT AND CONSIDER

It is natural to seek a solution to decrease the pain and hurt in life. Doing so is in effort to protect oneself from the depth of pain one might be experiencing or to avoid additional hurt. To halt the pain or decrease the severity, one might be tempted to turn to mind-numbing behaviors to distract and dissipate the emotional energy. These actions can be defined as Short-Term Energy-Relieving Behaviors, or STERBs.

STERBs Are A Distraction from Pain

A STERB is any behavior designed to defer the depth of pain you are feeling by offering a temporary distraction. A STERB can appear positive on the surface. In fact they start quite innocently. You have heard people say, "Lets go out for a glass of wine, I just need to not feel this feeling." They can appear to be quite benign, like studying or exercising, or having a known negative effect like excessive drinking, gambling, or smoking. Sadly, STERBs rarely lead to recovery from pain or solve the origin of the hurt (Eissinger, 2019).

People are Often Not Aware They are Using a STERB

An individual may use a STERB totally outside of one's awareness. When the pressure of emotional energy builds up you may find yourself turning to STERBs, as society often reinforces them. Without a productive alternative to modulate and regulate the associated feelings, you may end up using a STERB. Without a way to show the pain, to accept the feeling and get relief, you may feel that turning to STERBs is the only answer.

STERBs Don't End Pain Indefinitely

A STERB may offer a short-term diversion, but they do not bring you closer to resolution of the initial pain and can actually make it worse. STERBs are non-verbal expressions of needs for support, comfort, and relief from hardship. Collage-making is a healthier and productive alternative to facing and illustrating pain.

STERBs such as binge drinking, eating, gambling, excessive spending, over-exercising, compulsive sexual behaviors, and self-harm can actually create additional adversity and hardship. STERBs are often addictive. New challenges like chemical dependency, unexpected re-traumatization, shame, or relationship strain can develop when a STERB is used.

Some typical STERBs:

- Drinking or Using Drugs

- Sleeping

- Eating

- Excessive Exercise or Extreme Sports

- Sex

- Self-harm by cutting

- Gambling

- Smoking

- Shopping

- Video Games

- Social Media/Playing on the Internet

- Workaholism

- Isolation

- Anorexia or Bulimia

- Keeping Busy

- Binge Watching TV/Movies

- Helping Others too Much

STERBs are illusions, a temporary technique to cope, yet they are often not effective or restorative. They can become self-destructive or harmful. Ironically, they are often promoted on TV and the media in marketing campaigns, tempting one to purchase things to divert the pain. Making a collage offers you a safe way to express and show your intense feelings, instead of hurting yourself by using a STERB.

Collage-Making Is An Alternative

Collage-making offers you a cathartic outlet; in the process, you create a vessel in which to place and contain your pain. Making a collage about the event(s) causing the emotional strain will allow for a safe, healthy release of heavy emotions. You can also choose to show the collage to others to help them see how you feel. In the process, others can begin to understand, support, and care for you (see the exercise-experience titled Give Yourself a Hand on page 115 for healthy alternatives to STERBs).

CONTENT ROUND UP to REVIEW—RECALL—REMEMBER

- It is natural to seek ways to reduce one's pain and hardship.

- People may be tempted to use a STERB to distract from their pain.

- STERBs are often addictive and add another layer of pain over time.

- Give Yourself a Hand exercise-experience on page 115 offers healthy alternatives to STERBs.

- Using collage-making to consider painful topics and hardship is an alternative to the use of a STERB.

GUIDED COLLAGE EXPERIENCE—MAKE A COLLAGE

1. **GATHER** materials (glue, magazines, books and a substrate to make your collage on). Cut a small, triangle-shaped element from your source material. Place it anywhere on the substrate to provide a personal symbol of power and strength and to offer a comforting, familiar ritual to begin.

2. **GATHER** elements that symbolize any emotional pain you have felt in the past, or are feeling now. Feel free to document as many episodes of emotional pain you desire and add additional details as you wish. You don't even have to remember the exact situation to heal from it. Once you have gathered all the elements, glue them down in the top 1/4 of the substrate.

3. **REVIEW** the list of STERBs and find any you have used in the past, or are tempted to use now. Choose elements to symbolize the STERBs and glue them down on the next 1/4 of the substrate. If you find the STERBs are becoming a habit, rate them from one to ten—one being of little concern and ten ones that are developing into a larger concern. Put the number 1 to 10 near the STERB.

4. **LOOK** at the STERBs you have glued down in step 3. Come up with alternatives to those STERBs. Find elements to symbolize your alternative ideas. Glue them down in the next 1/4 of the substrate. SEE the exercise-experience titled Give Yourself a Hand on page 115 for healthy alternatives to STERBs. An example; rather than going to the gym with the intent of doing extreme cardio or lifting excessively to numb yourself, call a friend and ask them to go for a gentle walk with you. Tell your friend you have been in emotional pain and need someone to talk to. Or, if you are tempted to overspend, rather than heading to the mall, watch your favorite movie or comedian on TV, or watch a movie about someone who is experiencing similar emotional pain.

5. **ON** the last 1/4 of the substrate reflect on the emotional pain and the information about STERBs. Work to recognize any trends you might have to avoid seeking help with these hardships. Remember even though you are feeling strongly, others can't see your pain. They are very likely willing to talk and help you. Choose elements to symbolize who you could talk to, and new thoughts on avoiding STERBs. Cut them out and glue them to the substrate.

6. **WRITE** or use collage elements to create a supportive thought to encapsulate this experience. Put this anywhere on your collage. An example: "I can recognize when I am in pain and know others will only be able to help if I share with them. I can work to find people who will listen and help rather than using a STERB."

7. **PLACE** a triangle-shaped element anywhere on the substrate to symbolize your personal strength and to offer a comforting and familiar ritual.

8. **EXTEND** your transformation by completing the TAKEAWAY ACTION TOOLS (page 225).

9. **RETURN** here after completing the Takeaway Action Tools to read the ending quote below.

"You know what truly aches? Having so much inside you and not having the slightest clue of how to pour it out."

— Karen Quan

CP Harrison, *16 ft*, 2020, Analog Collage, Doug + Laurie Kanyer Art Collection

PERMISSION TO PLAY TO REDUCE THE STRAINS OF LIFE

**A collage-making exercise-experience to emphasize the value of play
in enhancing emotional well-being.**

*"As adults we have quite a bit of work to do, and play seems to function as a protective
mechanism against the costs of this work. Play is a buffer against stress, a support
during life transitions, a means of forming bonds and alliances, a jump-start
for creativity and problem-solving."* — Christine Caldwell

INFORMATION TO THINK ABOUT AND CONSIDER

Would it not be amazing if, as we grow, we are able to retain the notion from childhood that everything is fun and play? It would be marvelous to approach life with the enthusiasm and curiosity of childhood play.

One might think that when you have your four-year-old up to the kitchen counter making cookies you are showing them the skill of baking, the work of making a cake. The child sees the sweet substances to be felt, smelled, and tasted from the perspective of sheer fun. They are learning, but mostly learning while playing. When you sit with a toddler at the computer keyboard, they don't see typing as work, or a project to be tackled, they see the keys as items to be poked and tapped, creating sheer joy.

The Work of Childhood

The work of childhood is essentially play. Sadly, the work of adulthood is typically toil. The concept of work is a mindset found in the age and stage of life. Imagine if one could see the tasks of the day as a child would. Suddenly, putting away the dishes is just like stacking blocks. Vacuuming is just pushing a noisy machine around. Typing a memo is just playing with the keys on a keyboard. Doing a presentation is just pretending you are in a performance.

Life in Perspective

Life can, in essence, really just be play. It is fundamentally about how you see it. Says Dr. Carla Hannaford, author of the book *Smart MOVES*, "When we play, dopamine is released, which induces elation and excitement and orchestrates nerve development and alignment all over the brain. When we are able to take in our fill of sensory stimuli, process and integrate it with richly developed base patterns, express new insights in a creative way, both physically and verbally, we are then truly at play (Hannaford, 2007)."

Let's reverse a typical adult task to get a different perspective or viewpoint on the drudgery of life. Many people love outdoor sports such as boating, camping, skiing, or swimming. In fact, many people live for their moments on the slopes, right? Stop for a moment, close your eyes, and visualize all of the tasks one must accomplish to be able to get on the ski slopes. Is there not an abundance of work to be done to be able to go skiing, or for that matter even to go swimming? Consider and reflect upon your attitude when packing up to prepare the gear for a fishing trip. Do you see it as work, or are you not really full of anticipation and full of childhood joy?

What if you deeply considered it and recognized that it might be more about how you frame or view a task? When you are folding clothes for the week you have a certain attitude. When you are folding clothes for a ski trip you have a different attitude. When you are preparing for a ski trip you are like a child gathering toys to play with; when you are putting away clothes for the week you might be seeing it as drudgery and work.

Life as a Playground

Renowned researcher and author Shawn Achor has conducted a significant amount of work in the field of positive psychology. He maintains one can choose how one sees things in life. He believes people can make a choice to see life as a child sees things; all the world is a playground (Anchor, 2018). As Alan W. Watts shares, "This is the real secret of life—to be completely engaged with what you are doing in the here-and-now. And instead of calling it work, realize it is play (Oppong, 2022)."

It is often our vocation or job that causes us to lose this idea. It may come from the pressure to perform in school, quotas to hit on the job, or the competitiveness of sports. People begin to say to themselves, "I have to work to get ahead!" Despite the fact that life may not be "fun" on some level, it is time to find ways to be a kid and play. Maybe it means a new job, or finding a new hobby. Linda Naiman, founder of Creativity at Work, offers this perspective: "When we engage in what we are naturally suited to do, our work takes on the quality of play. And it is play that stimulates creativity (Naiman, n.d.)."

CONTENT ROUND UP to REVIEW—RECALL—REMEMBER

- The work of a child is play, and they learn about the world by having fun and being curious.

- One can shift one's mindset from seeing the tasks of adulthood as the drudgery of work to one of curiosity and play.

Liberty Blake, *LOVE YOU PB*, 2022, Analog Collage, Courtesy of the Artist

GUIDED COLLAGE EXPERIENCE—MAKE A COLLAGE

1. **GATHER** materials, glue, magazines, books and a substrate (the paper you make your collage upon). Note, for this exercise-experience you will also need CRAYONS or COLORED MARKERS (or both). Cut a small, triangle-shaped element from your source material. Place it anywhere on the substrate to provide a personal symbol of power and strength. Doing this will offer a comforting and familiar ritual to begin this experience.

2. **SCRIBBLE** with the crayons or colored markers on the substrate for five full minutes, more if you can. Simply make marks and notice the colors overlap and mix. Choose to use the colors you love the best.

3. **LOCATE** the silliest or funniest elements you can find in your source materials. Or find elements that feel exciting and joyful to you. Cut them out and glue the silly, funny, exciting, elements anywhere on top of the colorful marks. Don't concern yourself with the composition of how it looks, just enjoy the process.

4. **LOCATE** the crayons or colored markers once again and scribble all over the substrate for a full five minutes, more if you are able. Feel free to scribble on top of the elements you glued down. Again, just make marks; notice the colors, and see how they overlap and mix. Choose the colors you love best.

5. **ASK** yourself what else you want to do. Do you want to color the back, add more elements? Ball the whole thing up and wrinkle it? Do you want to tear it up and throw the pieces all over? Do you want to get scissors and cut it and then glue the pieces on a new substrate? You can do whatever sounds fun! Remember you are just playing, with no set outcome, just for the fun of it.

6. **ONGOING PRACTICE:** Make a series of collages representing yourself playing at different time periods of your life.

7. **WRITE** or use collage elements to create a supportive thought to encapsulate this experience. If you haven't playfully balled or cut it up, put this anywhere on your collage! For example: "I will consider the quality of my life, my attitude toward daily activities and work, toward a life that is full of fun and play."

8. **PLACE** a triangle-shaped element anywhere on the substrate to symbolize your personal strength and to offer a comforting and familiar ritual.

9. **EXTEND** your transformation by completing the TAKEAWAY ACTION TOOLS (page 225).

10. **RETURN** here after completing the Takeaway Action Tools to read the ending quote below.

"Play is the highest form of research."

— Albert Einstein

THE MOMENT

Kathy Starr, *The Moment*, 2019, Analog Collage, Courtesy of the Artist

PART 4
Exercise-Experiences
to Resolve a Challenge

"Turn your obstacles into opportunities and
your problems into possibilities."

— Roy T. Bennett

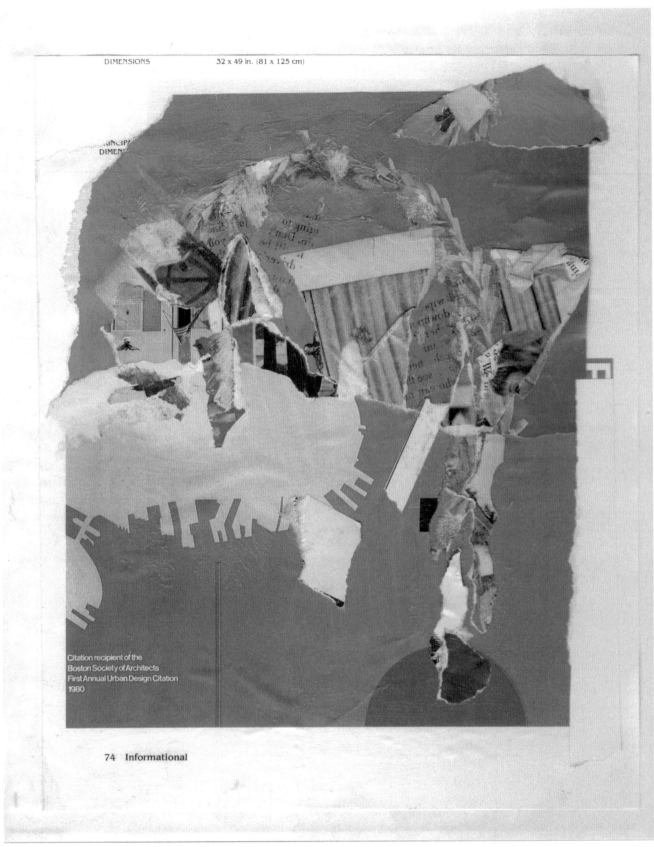

CP Harrison, *Alas, I must stand in grace*, 2020, Analog Collage, Doug + Laurie Kanyer Art Collection

INTRODUCTION TO PART 4:
SEGMENTS TO RESOLVE CHALLENGING "SOMETHINGS"

A collage-making exercise-experience to identify whose challenge it is to resolve and to move from denial to empowerment.

CONSIDERING THE EMOTIONAL AND PRACTICAL STEPS OF RESOLVING A CHALLENGE

Most books on resolving challenging "somethings" focus on moving quickly to resolution, creating and implementing a plan, and then evaluating the plan when it is completed. They often overlook the emotional and mental aspects of the process. Most do not offer coping mechanisms to modulate and pace the emotional tone and the feelings that emerge.

This book emphasizes emotions, feelings and transforming life experiences. Accordingly, we give great consideration to the emotional and mental processes one goes through. The consideration of emotions and feelings is interwoven with other known traditional steps. Therefore, this part of *Collage Care: The Method* contains exercise-experiences to resolve challenges with the typical processes, as well as ways to attend to the emotional and mental aspects.

Articulated in Separate Segments

The process of resolving a challenge has herein been broken down into five unique Segments. It is done this way to deeply articulate the steps and effort it takes, emotionally, mentally and practically, to resolve a challenge. You will thus have a guide to follow to consider decision-making, emotions and action steps. This will decrease confusion, as you will now know more about the emotional and mental mechanisms of solving challenges in addition to the practical planning steps.

Use the Segments in Order at First

The first time you use a Segment do the first four exercise-experiences in the exact order they are presented. They are presented in a thoughtful sequence. After using the Segments in written order for the first time, feel free to return to them later, as individual tools to use separately.

The Segments of Resolving a Challenge

Segment One - Identify Who Owns the Challenge. Moving from Disbelief-Denial to Empowerment while Resolving a Something.

Segment Two - Observation and Investigation of a Challenging "Something". Accurately Naming and Defining the Challenge.

Segment Three - Acceptance of a Challenge. Using PMAs as a Way to Care for Feelings, Thoughts and Behaviors During a Challenge.

Segment Four - Identifying Ideas - Getting Help - Making a Plan to Resolve a Challenge - Celebration and Evaluation.

All of the Segments are vital to the process of resolving a challenge. Even though they are presented sequentially in this book, it is important to know that in real life the Segments overlap and intertwine.

You will also find two (2) additional exercise-experiences, one titled "Asking for Help and Finding Quality Solutions" and another titled "The Suggestion Circle". These two exercise-experiences will favorably supplement the segments.

Time Expectations

Remember that most challenging "somethings" take time to develop. These exercise-experiences will take time to complete. You are invited to pace yourself with this material. Read a bit and then pause as you need. The length, depth, and breadth of each segment in real life will differ from one challenge to another. Be kind and gentle to yourself and set reasonable time expectations.

DEFINITIONS AND WORD PREFERENCES

"Challenge" Rather than "Problem"

We prefer to use the word "challenge" versus "problem". A challenge provides an opportunity to overcome something, as well as a chance to use and gain skills. Look at a challenge as if it were a duel or a battle, a sporting game, or an imposed or chosen special project. A challenge is something that needs to be resolved, conquered or completed. Challenges come with the understanding of the need for endurance, patience, courage and fortitude. In a challenge one often needs support, information or assistance from others. Resolving a challenge is the process one goes through to address a "something". In the Appendix on page 236 you will find a detailed discussion on the value of using the word "challenge" and how it engages a strength-based focus and a mindset of forward thinking.

"Something"

The definition of a "something" is a challenge (chosen or imposed) which consists of a person, place, thing, event, project, or a situation causing one's Emotional Response System to be activated (see page 47 for an in-depth discussion). A "something" is largely synonymous with the word problem, insofar as it causes thoughts and decisions to be formulated and behaviors to come forth. Another word for a "something" is a "challenge" or "problem".

"Resolution" Rather Than "Solution"

We prefer to use the word resolution versus solution. The word solution denotes only one right, correct answer, as in a mathematics equation. Resolution means to come to an end point or a conclusion relating to a particular "something."

APPROACHING CHALLENGES AS REMINDERS AND OPPORTUNITIES

One way to approach a current challenge or a "something" is to recall and remember that you have solved challenges in the past. Doing so will ignite confidence. The new challenging "something" can be seen as an opportunity to practice and extend your skills, as well as refine techniques you already have. This is not to discount the heaviness of the "something". It is mentioned here to assist in shaping how you can approach and view the concern.

THE SEGMENTS OF RESOLVING A CHALLENGE OFFER A NUMBER OF HELPFUL THINGS

- Provides a structure to use to help resolve the challenge. Outlined in these Segments are suggested steps to support your thinking and feelings while working to resolve the "something."

- Helps the development of additional skills to maneuver and resolve a challenge. It is assumed that most people do not receive formal training and information to resolve "somethings," so this is the equivalent of a basic primer on the topic.

- Offers some emotional ease when faced with a "something". Collage-making is a way to release tension. It will comfort you as you are in fact "doing something" toward an end while in the middle of a "something".

- Provides for emotional self-care while experiencing hardships and challenges (see the Appendix for "Collage Care Gems: How Collage-Making Helps, Heals, and Transforms" on page 231).

COLLAGE-MAKING MIRRORS RESOLVING A CHALLENGE

Collage-making is a great tool to experience and practice the skill of resolving a challenge. It is comparable to working on a complex puzzle. When you find the "right" piece to fit on your collage it affirms your ability to locate viable options to resolve challenges.

Another wonderful outcome of collage-making is, as you look through source material to find elements for your collage, you will likely come across some novel ideas, new information, and possible solutions to help you with the challenges you are facing. The source material may be filled with articles or stories of others who have resolved challenges. This will assure you that you are not alone and will be an encouragement. Have you ever seen a "before and after" in a home magazine? They show you how things were (the challenges) and how they ended up (the resolution)!

As you make a collage you are actually witnessing and tracking yourself using the skills needed to resolve challenges. You will observe yourself searching, finding, selecting and placing elements. This is further testimony to the fact that you can resolve challenges. It shows you that you can do it. You have observed and witnessed the evidence. Finding the elements and seeing the collage emerging will be a great motivator. It will encourage you to continue to search for just the right, most fitting elements to make your life better.

When one resolves a challenge one might not totally restore things to the way they were. However, in collage-making one observes the transformation and a new "wholeness". And in collage-making, where you take an element from a book, another element from a magazine, and maybe a third element from a different source, it demonstrates that it may take a variety of sources to come together to resolve challenges. This shows you it takes creativity to resolve challenges and inspires you to keep searching, discovering and inventing new solutions to tend to challenges.

The collage-making process will offer you a space of mindful meditation to help pace any anxiety. When you see your finished collage, it will be a visual reminder and proof you can resolve your challenges and that "somethings" do come to a conclusion. One aspect of resolving a challenge is the ability to tolerate and endure the situation, and this material will assist you.

Let's Get Started — Turn to the next page to begin.

Jake Kennedy, *A Good Walk*, 2021, Analog Collage, Doug + Laurie Kanyer Art Collection

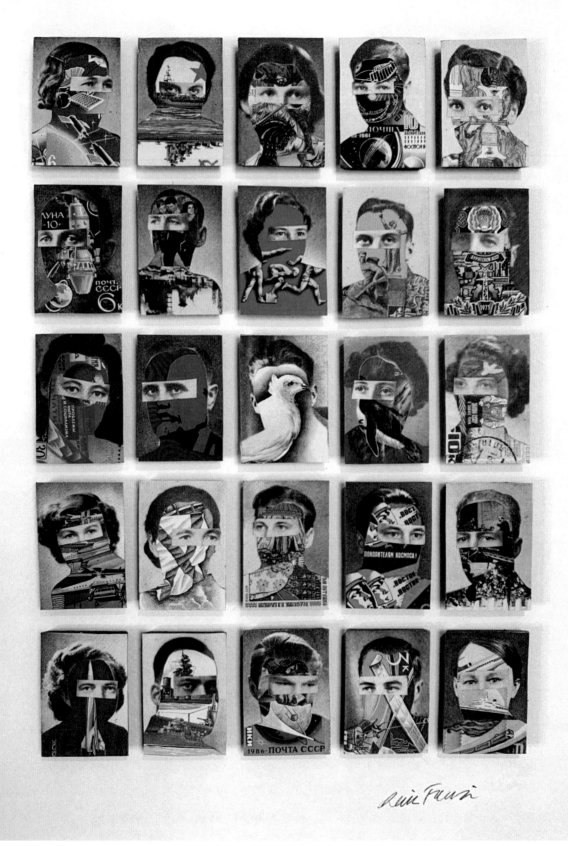

Riikka Fransila, *Too Afraid to Speak*, 2022, Analog Collage with Stamps, Doug + Laurie Kanyer Art Collection

162

RESOLVING A CHALLENGE - SEGMENT ONE

**A collage-making exercise-experience to identify whose challenge it is
to resolve and moving from disbelief-denial to empowerment.**

"Life is what happens to you when you are busy making other plans." — John Lennon

INFORMATION TO THINK ABOUT AND CONSIDER

The First Segment to resolving a challenging "something" consists of two distinct and related parts.

The first part of Segment One is about deciphering if this "something" is actually a challenge for you to take part in resolving. It is referred to as "Whose Challenge is it to Resolve - Confirming One's Role".

The second part of Segment One is about the emotional and mental effort one needs to invest to move from "Denial-Disbelief to Empowerment."

SEGMENT ONE - PART ONE: WHOSE CHALLENGE IS IT TO RESOLVE - CONFIRMING ONE'S ROLE

It is important to determine if the challenging "something" is really yours to be involved in resolving. Since it will take time, energy and resources to resolve a "something" it is wise to make sure this is actually your challenge, and not someone else's.

Think First - Be Absolutely Sure

A "something" can seem to materialize out of thin air, visiting itself upon you. Because of this it can activate your Emotional Response System, or ERS (see more about this on page 47). The activation of your ERS can then propel one to action. One might forget to fully think or clearly evaluate your involvement. While it is certainly vital to respond swiftly if the "something" is extreme, such as an emergency health or safety issue, it may not be so good in a non-emergency situation. In such cases one must take the time to determine if this is really your challenge to resolve.

If you are a helpful sort of person, known for having skills and abilities, and are willing to resolve challenges, it may be your natural mode of operation to get involved right away. There are drawbacks to this tendency. One needs to be absolutely certain of their role and to be able to evaluate one's tendency to be involved for a multitude of reasons. Pause now and consider times you or others got involved in resolving a challenge that truly was not theirs to solve. What was the outcome?

Whose Challenge is it?

Famous psychologist Dr. Thomas Gordon was the founder of Gordon Training International. He was especially recognized for developing one of the first skills-based training programs for parents called PET: Parent Effectiveness Training. Gordon was keen on helping parents to determine what he referred to as "who owns the problem" (author's note: we prefer the word "challenge" as opposed to "problem").

The goal was for caregivers to avoid resolving challenges that were really "owned" by their children (Gordon 1994). His insight led many caretakers to take a thoughtful pause prior to engaging in any act of resolving challenges for their children. Gordon's use of the title "who owns the problem" indicates possession, rather than shame, blame and causality. What he is attempting to clarify is who ultimately has the primary role to resolve challenges.

Ask Yourself These Questions to Determine if it is Your Challenge to Resolve:

- Does it have a concrete, clearly observable, negative effect on you personally?

- Does it affect your ability to function?

- Does it keep you from getting your personal needs met?

- Does it impact your well-being (mentally, physically, spiritually, emotionally, socially, vocationally)?

- Does it impact your safety (mentally, physically, spiritually, emotionally, socially, vocationally)?

If so, this is your challenging "something" and you need to be involved in resolving it. If not it is someone else's "something" to resolve.

It May Be Someone Else's Challenge

If you determine this is not your "something" to resolve, then the challenge is someone else's. Give yourself time to reflect and ponder on this truth. Others need to resolve their own challenges. They need to have the opportunity to do so for their own personal growth and development. Your involvement may disrupt the natural opportunity others need to gain experience in resolving a challenge.

This does not mean you cannot be a resource for support, encouragement, or information. It means that if you claim primary responsibility and become involved in the task of resolving a challenge that is not directly connected to you, there may be strain for you and others. Claiming primary responsibility may disable the other individual from the development they need, as a person, to gain skills and experience in the process of resolving a challenge (see page 213 on the Empowerment versus Drama Triangle).

SEGMENT ONE - PART TWO: MOVING FROM DENIAL-DISBELIEF TO EMPOWERMENT

Extending Emotional and Mental Energy to Resolve Challenges

When you have determined the challenge is yours, you then have to go through the emotional and mental exercise of moving from denial-disbelief to empowerment. This is because one's mind and thought processes will need to insert the new "something" into its reality. It is you who has to work to resolve it. It is now your challenge to engage with and possibly also to engage with into the future. You will have to come to believe it to be true, then begin to mentally comprehend that it is really happening to you.

To cope with the complexity involved one goes through a number of emotional and mental phases. Going through these phases enables one to commit to the entire process of resolving the "something". The phases may be summarized as follows (Clarke, 1995):

- **Phase One** - Experiencing disbelief or total denial - "There is no challenge, it does not exist."

- **Phase Two** - Acknowledging the challenge, yet discounting the severity - "The challenge is neither that serious nor very important."

- **Phase Three** - Acknowledging the challenge, yet feeling helpless to resolve - "There is no solution."

- **Phase Four** - Acknowledging the challenge, yet not seeing one's role - "There is nothing I can do."

- **Phase Five** - EMPOWERMENT: Acknowledging there is a challenge one needs to be part of resolving and making a commitment to do the work. Empowerment is about finding your voice, the ability to speak up in the middle of a challenge. "It is clear I have a role. I will commit to doing the work to gather the facts. If needed, I will find a way to resolve it and make a plan. I will do the work to participate in amending and resolving this challenge."

Why Do People Use Denial and Disbelief?

Challenges often take an undetermined time period to fully reveal themselves. Sometimes a new "something" will not immediately manifest or fully reveal its effects. It may seem like for a time that it is a slight possibility, or there may be a subtle hint of a challenging "something" developing. It may not be immediately clear that this is a challenge that could truly bring change and be unsettling. It might be a "maybe something". When this happens, one could question its reality for a time in order to fully confirm the reality. When it is a "maybe" one might be able to mentally shelve it or discount its severity for a time.

Challenges Unsettle Predictability

Humans thrive in predictability and the ability to anticipate what each day will bring. When a new "something" comes forth, one is compelled to grieve the loss of "what was," and the loss of what was known. One has to move from what was predictability known, into what is unknown. The change brought on by a "something" can be difficult for people, as it upsets the balance of known predictability.

Challenges Can Be Overwhelming

The enormity of the "something" might be so overwhelming that one attempts to deny, disbelieve or discount that it even exists. This behavior is a coping mechanism. Even though one knows it is clearly their own challenge to resolve, the enormity of the "something" could be too much emotionally and mentally to comprehend. It may be beyond one's capacity. In this circumstance one may find themselves wanting to shelve what they are seeing for a time. One may have no idea what to do and may freeze in the face of what feels like a tidal wave of change.

Challenges are Occasionally Shared

Even though one takes ownership of a challenge, it may still involve others. Similarly, one might hope or wish that others will help or shield the effects of the challenge. To cope with the formidable task of working with others one might minimize one's role, discounting or denying it. If there is not a clear leader, or one who bears the most potential impact and responsibility, one might reserve their involvement for a time. All of these responses are understandable when faced with the unknown of needing to potentially resolve a challenge with others. To resolve a challenge involving others one adds an additional layer of complexity and uncertainty to the "something".

If it is determined that the "something" is shared amongst a group of people, the questions from Gordon listed previously must be answered affirmatively by all. Similarly, all of the Segments offered in this book will need to be cooperatively processed with the group.

Moving to Empowerment Takes Effort and Courage

The process of moving from disbelief to empowerment is tender, humbling and significant. Tackling a challenging "something" takes character and courage. Extend compassion to yourself as you mount the mental and emotional vigor to move forward. When you are in the middle of experiencing the effects of the "something", it weighs upon you, and may be impacting others you care about.

Challenges Bring New Beginnings with Work and Unknowns

To become empowered you have to mentally leave what you know of life in its present form. One must weigh the current discomfort of the concern against the potential for even more. One may not yet be fully sure of one's role. One must to a degree imagine the future uncertainty brought on by the "something" and one's effort to resolve. It takes great courage to step into empowerment, with all of its heavy tasks: initial observation, finding solutions, implementing a plan, moving from what is known into the unknown, and with no assurances.

This is why disbelief, denial, and the discounting of a challenge is useful for a time. It is not laziness or lack of concern. Denial offers much needed time to cope with the enormity of the situation. It is a contextual protective factor. Working to resolve a "something" can be big work, depending on the nature of the challenge.

What is Empowerment?

One definition of the word empowerment is to have or claim the authority or power to act connected to a "something". When you are empowered to resolve a challenge it is clear that you are the one (or one of the ones) who are to resolve this challenge. You know it is yours to take on.

Empowerment is Commitment

Empowerment involves a personal commitment to investigate a challenge to determine if there are steps that are needed, and if there are, to take those steps. You are engaged in actively observing and working on a resolution over time. When you are empowered, you access and accept the "call" to be involved in resolving the named challenge.

Moving Through the Phases of Denial to Empowerment Takes Time

Author Jean Illsley Clarke once said that, "If a challenge is not in the realm of critical health and safety (a non-emergency), it can take people who are motivated to solve the "something" two weeks to move through each one of the phases from denial-disbelief towards empowerment (Clarke, 1995)." What constitutes one's motivation varies from person to person. The phases mentioned above were developed by Clarke. These phases are on a spectrum that are uniquely experienced by each person. Naturally, and importantly, the time lines vary by person.

Clarke uses the word 'denial' to describe the process one goes through mentally to be able to accept a "something" to be true. People do not deny in order to shirk responsibility or out of a lack of courage. They deny due to the potential that "something" could be emotionally and intellectually overwhelming. People also deny if they have limited skills, support, resources, or experience with the "something" they are facing. They could be feeling scared or fearful. Or they just need time to begin to insert reality into their awareness.

Kindness and Respect is Needed

Extending grace and compassion to oneself and others during this time is a kind and thoughtful thing to do. Naturally, when a challenge is in the realm of health and safety, it requires people to move through these steps quickly and take immediate empowered leadership to help.

CONTENT ROUND UP to REVIEW—RECALL—REMEMBER

- It is very important to determine if you are the one to be involved in solving a challenge. Ask yourself, "Can I, with all assurances, confirm that this is a challenge I am to be involved in resolving."

- Some challenges are owned by more than one person. This can impact the process of resolving a challenge as all people will need to be empowered to do so.

- There are emotional and mental phases one goes through prior to engaging in solving challenging "somethings". This process is called moving from denial-disbelief to empowerment.

- It takes time and courage to move from denial-disbelief to empowerment.

GUIDED COLLAGE EXPERIENCE–MAKE A COLLAGE

1. **GATHER** materials (glue, magazines, books and a substrate to make your collage on). Cut a small, triangle-shaped element from your source material. Place it anywhere on the substrate to provide a personal symbol of power and strength and to offer a comforting, familiar ritual to begin.

2. **THINK** back on a challenge you resolved in the past. Read the questions designed by Thomas Gordon and choose an element(s) to symbolize how you knew, with full certainty, that it was your challenge to be involved in resolving. Glue the element(s) at the top of the substrate on the left-hand side.

3. **ASK** yourself the questions designed by Thomas Gordon as it relates to a current challenge you are experiencing. Choose an element(s) to symbolize your answers to Gordon's questions, to determine if you need to be involved in resolving this current challenge. Glue the element(s) at the top of the substrate on the right-hand side, across from the first one.

4. **THINK** back on a challenge you resolved in the past. Reread the Phases of Moving from Denial/Disbelief Toward Empowerment, by author Jean Illsley Clarke. Choose an element(s) to symbolize your journey through the phases of denial/disbelief as it was connected to a past challenge you resolved. Glue the element(s) below the previous ones on the left-hand side of the substrate.

5. **CONSIDER** a current challenge you are experiencing. Choose elements to symbolize where you are currently in Jean Illsley Clarke's Moving from Denial/Disbelief Toward Empowerment. Glue the element(s) below the previous ones on the right-hand side of the substrate.

6. **RESPECTING** where you find yourself in moving from denial to empowerment, find an element(s) to symbolize what you think might be needed for you to get closer to empowerment for the current challenge. Glue the element(s) below the previous ones in the middle of the substrate.

7. **WRITE** or use collage elements to create a supportive thought to encapsulate this experience. Put this anywhere on your collage. An example: "I will determine who owns the challenge before I engage in it and will be aware of where I am from denial to empowerment."

8. **PLACE** a triangle-shaped element anywhere on the substrate to symbolize your personal strength and to offer a comforting and familiar ritual.

9. **EXTEND** your transformation by completing the TAKEAWAY ACTION TOOLS (page 225).

10. **RETURN** here after completing the Takeaway Action Tools to read the ending quote below.

"This life is not about the problems and/or the struggles we pass through, but the way we behave towards the situation is what makes us heroes"

— Anath Lee Wales

Susan Ringer, *Observatory*, 2022, Analog Collage, Doug + Laurie Kanyer Art Collection

RESOLVING A CHALLENGE - SEGMENT TWO

A collage-making exercise-experience to observe, investigate, and define a "Something".

"The best way out is always through." — Robert Frost

INFORMATION TO THINK ABOUT AND CONSIDER

The Second Segment in resolving a challenging "something" contains three distinct and related parts.

Having completed Segment One, you have now determined that you are empowered to be involved in resolving a challenge, and that it is a "something" in which it is your responsibility to be involved. This next Segment helps you figure out what exactly is happening, acknowledging your feelings, and labeling and defining the "something". This Segment takes you deeper into the process of resolving a "something."

On an almost daily basis clients in my groups or individual sessions would say, "I have to tell you about "something". The "something" was a person, place, thing, event, circumstance or a situation that activated an emotional response and caused related feelings. The "something" was either from the just recent past, or lingering from days, weeks, years or even decades.

I would typically say to those I served, "Ok, let's map and sort this "something" out." At other times I would say, "Let's investigate and document it." Using this structured process of observation, investigation, and mapping achieves a myriad of benefits.

Segement Two - Part One: Observe, Investigate, Gather

The first part of Segment Two is about observing, investigating and gathering information on what you are noticing or experiencing, related to a challenging "something". You will be visually mapping your answers to questions about what took place by placing collage elements on a substrate. This will allow you to know exactly what happened or is presently happening. You need to determine what the various aspects of a challenge truly are, who is involved, and what happened. This helps you to further prove to yourself, and possibly others, that this is in fact a challenge, it is real, and it is happening to you. It will fortify and affirm your empowerment. The exercise-experience to follow contains a series of informative questions to help you to compile the facts connected to a "something".

Segement Two - Part Two: Tending to Emotions and Feelings

The second part of Segment Two tends to your emotions and feelings. You will be visually mapping on the substrate your answers to questions about what you felt related to the "something." You will be documenting your emotional sensations, memories, and impressions connected to the "something". As you see the collage elements emerge on the substrate connected to your emotions and feelings, you are acknowledging, expressing and witnessing them. Additionally, you can see them as fitting and justified based on the circumstances connected to the "something". There is an extended benefit of being able to show and tell others how you felt using an image.

Segement Two - Part Three: Labeling and Defining a "Something"

The third part of Segment Two helps one to clearly label, name and define the challenging "something". You need to accurately name and define the challenge to resolve it. This will allow you to be focused on a precisely defined mission toward a resolution. Having a clearly understood label and definition of the "something" will also help you to describe it to others. This will give you the opportunity to generate ideas, get support and develop a plan that fits this specific, investigated challenge.

The collage-making exercise-experience below will take you through all the parts. You will observe, investigate and gather information on the who, what, where, when and why. It will confirm, acknowledge and offer acceptance of your emotions and feelings. In doing so you will be able to tend to and offer care to yourself on an emotional and mental level. It will also help you to clearly label, define and name the challenging "something".

SEGMENT TWO - PART ONE: OBSERVE, INVESTIGATE, GATHER THE FACTS CONNECTED TO A CHALLENGING "SOMETHING"

When a challenge emerges there is a period of time one needs to deeply investigate and observe it. The exercise-experience is a thoughtful way to deepen one's awareness and clearly observe what is taking place. When you experience a "something" it is valuable and helpful to gather information to discern the cause of it, for the purpose of figuring it all out. Very often, the cause is not of your own doing. Clearly documenting the events of the challenge will help you and others refrain from blaming, judging or shaming oneself by observing and examining the actual facts.

Through thoughtful investigation, such as you will conduct in the exercise-experience, you are afforded an opportunity to see things as facts. One needs to track the severity, intensity, and frequency of a challenge to determine the need to move to address it or not. Since resolving a challenge takes time, energy and engagement in the unknown, it is wise to observe and expand one's awareness for a time. Once you have the information gathered you can determine if you need a short interval to pause and watch, or to move to the other segments of resolving a challenge.

Investigating Like a Detective

A good comparison of this investigative process is the whiteboard used on detective TV shows. Detectives put all of the known aspects about a "something" (the case with which they are confronted) on a whiteboard to be mapped, documented and sorted out. They want the details visible, to be able to be observed and deciphered.

There is a great benefit, when a "something" arises, to put everything about it in one place. In doing so all can witness the key aspects of the "something". One's mind can come to accept that the "something" really did take place when seeing all the details. The "something" is revealed and might need to be investigated, noticed, and responded to in a way that fits best. The exercise-experience will be asking you to put all the things about a challenge on a collage substrate.

Short-Term and Long-Term Observation

The exercise-experience offers both short-term and long-term observation. Having documented the "something" on the substrate, with all of the various facts and details, one can observe the effect over time. You will have the ability to return later to the collage you made. This offers an opportunity to ponder and reflect. One can complete the exercise quickly, perhaps in an hour, to get it all out. Conversely, one may take a number of days, depending on one's needs and the situation.

Later, if the effect of the "something" still has an aura of heaviness which remains or lingers, one can come back to repeat the process. You can add more detailed elements to the substrate as you continue to consider the material. In the end, the entire "something" can be put "out of sight and mind" if one chooses to discard the final collage. In this act, you become the victor. Additionally, if you keep the collage, one can see it as a reminder of your courage, fortitude and strength.

SEGMENT TWO - PART TWO: TENDING TO EMOTIONS AND FEELINGS

When faced with a "something" in life, a series of potent emotional responses can come forth, and feelings can emerge. The weight of the "something," coupled with everything else one is facing, can be overwhelming. One's ability to pace or regulate emotions could be stretched due to the potency of the circumstance. The magnitude of the "something" might feel as though it is more than one can bear.

Thoughts can become extreme and unyielding. By mapping the challenge one's emotions and feelings are validated, acknowledged and affirmed, not staying stuck in whirling emotional energy.

This mapping allows for some space to open up, keeping one's feelings from becoming clogged, ignored or denied. It also prevents one from acting impulsively or out of character due to the pressure of the "something". This exercise-experience offers you a way to do productive activities in the middle of a challenge. It decreases feelings of helplessness by offering you something to do. It is active and affirming.

Offers Space and Increases Objectivity to Release Emotional Tension

Holocaust survivor and psychiatrist Victor Frankl is attributed with saying, "Between stimulus (a "something") and response (emotions, feelings, thoughts and behaviors) there is a space." The exercise-experience examines and provides some space between what is taking place with the "something" and what one decides to do. It offers you a window to explore your feelings about the problem, outlines what the facts and details are, and then provides a chance to define it. Whether you determine you need to move on to the other segments of resolving a challenge or not, this exercise helps you to know why your feelings were activated. This can be reassuring.

Releasing Emotional and Mental Tension

When all of the items related to a "something" are put on the whiteboard, or in this case a collage substrate, one will experience the release and documentation of all the details swirling around in one's head. You will also be pacing and regulating the emotional hormones that flooded your body due to the challenge. When a "something" is distressing, the exercise-experience helps to serve as a bridge away from the initial hardship. It releases the burden of carrying all the details and subsequent emotional energy in your mind and body. The collage you make becomes a safe container for the "something" to be held, so that it does not pour over into other aspects of one's life.

Decreasing the Potency and Power of a "Something"

Being able to gain an unbiased perspective of the "something" serves to expel its potency. Seeing is believing, and using this exercise you will be able to actually see what you are experiencing. It will help you and others to in fact "know what you know". You are not imagining it.

Most importantly, it helps one feel emotionally better. Being able to reduce the discomfort of the "something" by using collage-making while figuring it out, is deeply beneficial. By seeing it all in one place one can illuminate what is believed to have happened, clarify with others, and decipher what caused it by showing all of the known aspects on the collage substrate. Others can inquire and ask questions and more details can unfold. Additional aspects may be revealed over time, when all of the details are exposed visually.

Increased Confidentiality

A fascinating and somewhat ironic benefit to collage-making is that it enhances confidentiality. Since collage-making elements are symbolic, they cannot easily be read or interpreted. When dealing with a challenge it is beneficial to be able to confidentially investigate it and express oneself. This adds a layer of privacy and discretion to "somethings" that are potent. If one decides a plan of action is needed, such a plan is more rapidly identified by seeing the "something" right in front of your eyes.

SEGMENT TWO - PART THREE: LABELING AND DEFINING A "SOMETHING"

To be able to make a plan to resolve a "something" you need to know what you are facing by giving it a name and defining it. It is vital to clearly define and name what the "something" is as accurately as possible to be able to resolve it. When you have gathered all of the information you can then describe it to others in a clear way, thus getting help and suggestions. By using the exercise-experience you will be gathering and seeing the who, what, where and more. Once all of the details are documented, one can then determine a name, label or definition.

It is important to name and define the "something" in a few sentences. This allows for specific targeted solutions to be identified along with steps to be discovered to match the precise challenge. Clearly, in an emergency, one names and defines swiftly and just yells out "Fire" for example, calling for help. However, in non-emergency situations one has the time to precisely consider what to call the "something" and how to define it. In naming and defining sentences you can include some of what has been observed.

CONTENT ROUND UP to REVIEW—RECALL—REMEMBER

- The investigation of a "something" offers one distinct benefits. Such benefits include, but are not limited to, the following:

- Affords one an opportunity to gather information about what is going on in an organized fashion.

- Grounds you and decreases stress and strain by capturing all of the details and facts about a "something", in one place on the substrate.

- Clarifies what happened by showing all of the aspects of a "something" on the collage substrate, thereby reducing the internal heaviness and burden.

- Serves as a record of the events, to prompt and clarify memories and impressions over time.

- Provides a safe container, on the substrate, for the challenge so it will not pour over into other parts of life.

- Allows one to see and observe, at a distance, what happened.

- Affirms emotions and feelings.

- Provides a way to accurately label, define and name the challenge. This helps one gather ideas specific to resolving the "something".

- Fortifies and clarifies your beliefs. Beliefs shape one's decision-making and need to be considered as you adopt a plan of action moving forward.

- Offers a chance to get some space from the "something," to be able to think and make decisions.

- Helps you to be able to describe what is happening to others in a clear way.

- Indicates the need to possibly make plans for what to do moving onward, once causes are fully discovered.

GUIDED COLLAGE EXPERIENCE—MAKE A COLLAGE

NOTE: It is expected that this exercise-experience could take an extended period of time of investigation and discovery. Like a detective, more and more information will emerge, and other causes of the "something" may be revealed. Once you have completed this exercise-experience you may decide to pause and observe for a period of time. In any case, unless the challenge is an emergency, take your time in using this exercise-experience so you can gather all the information that is helpful to you.

1. **GATHER** materials, to include glue, scissors, magazines, books and a substrate (the paper you make your collage upon). **NOTE:** For this exercise-experience it is advised to get a large substrate to hold all the details and to make the collage elements smaller so everything fits.

   Start by first cutting a small, triangle-shaped element from your source material. Place it anywhere on the substrate to provide a personal symbol of power and strength. Doing this will offer a comforting and familiar ritual to begin the experience.

2. **LOCATE** and cut out element(s) to symbolize all the aspects related to a "something," with guidance from the list below. Read the list and then hunt for elements to symbolize each one. Glue each of the elements vertically on the left-hand side of the substrate. The reason to use the left side only here is to offer space to continue to add other elements over time, as the cause and effect of the "something" is revealed or discovered. The blank space to the right side also will symbolize open opportunities ahead, to think and choose any future options as you learn more.

   NOTE: For the list below there may be questions that are not applicable to this specific "something". In that case skip the question and go on to the next one.

   ### Investigation of a "Something" - Part One: Observation and Investigation of the Facts Connected to a Challenging "Something"

   What: What took place?

   When: When did this "something" take place?

   Who: Were other people there? If so, who?

   What: What did you do? What did the others do?

   Where: Where did this "something" take place?

   Why: Do you know why this "something" happened or is currently happening?

   Causes or Contributors: Are there any known, clear causes or contributors related to the "something" that you are aware of in the present? If so, what are they?

   Frequency: How often, or how long has this "something" been going on?

   Preceding events or earlier aspects of the "something" that took place: Are you able to identify anything that preceded this "something" that one might look out for in the future? Is there a pattern to be documented?

   Consequences: Are there any known consequences of the "something"? If so, what are they?

   ### Investigation of a "Something" - Part Two: Tending to Emotions and Feelings Related to a "Something"

   Emotional Sensations: What were (or are) the emotional responses or sensations that you experienced or noticed in your body related to this "something"?

Feelings: What was your first Primary Feeling? Were you: happy, mad, sad, or scared? What were your Secondary Feelings? (See page 230 for a suggested list of feeling words.) How do you feel about the "something"? How do you feel about yourself related to the "something"? How do you feel about others related to the "something"?

Thoughts: What are you currently thinking or saying to yourself about yourself related to the "something"? What are you currently thinking or saying to yourself about others involved in the "something"? What information are the various parts of yourself telling you about you, people and the "something"? If you find yourself issuing judgement, blame or shame to yourself or others, choose an element to symbolize a redirection of your thoughts towards observation, wisdom, curiosity and consideration.

Beliefs and Values: What do you believe about the "something"? How are your personal set of values affected by the "something"? Knowing one's values helps to shape decisions and resolve a challenge.

Memories and Early Life Impressions: What memories or Early Life Impressions (conclusions about yourself, others or how one should behave) are you recalling after experiencing the "something"? How are your memories and Early Life Impressions contributing and shaping your responses? Are there things from your memories or Early Life Impressions that are helpful and true, or need to be revised in light of this new "something"?

Other: Choose elements to symbolize other aspects not listed here.

3. **LOCATE** and cut out element(s) to symbolize your effort in documenting all of the details of the "something". Step 2 of this exercise took strength, courage, time and a great deal of energy. Glue all the element(s) down in the middle of the substrate. Say to yourself, "Thank you for showing and telling me about this "something".

    Reserve the right-hand side of the collage to add more elements later. As with any investigation, more details will be discovered and you can then return to document the new information.

4. **LOCATE**, cut out, and glue the next element(s) in the middle, next to the ones you placed for step 3, to symbolize what you now discern about the "something". Viveka is the Sanskrit word for discernment, which means "seeing things as they are". What insights have you gained that are now clear after this analysis? Insight is seeing into "something" from our True Self without rigid standards, opinions, or social pressures.

    Investigation of a "Something" - Part Three: Naming and Defining the "Something" to Decrease Confusion and Establish a Clear Mission

5. **LOCATE**, cut out, and glue the next element(s) to symbolize a NAME for this something and an element to symbolize how you DEFINE the "something". Place this anywhere you choose on the substrate. Add more elements to clearly remind you of how you define this problem.

    A recommendation here on how you might express this to yourself or others. Consider describing the "something" you are experiencing as a challenge, not a "problem". Say, "I am experiencing this challenge (name the challenge)", rather than "I have this problem". The word problem has so many negative connotations. To say you "have a problem" indicates ownership. The definition of the word "have" is to possess, own, or hold. When one says, "I have a problem" it can indicate to others that you possess the problem. It literally means that, "you own" or "hold" on to it. The truth is you are a person who is going through an experience brought on by a "something". You don't want to own, hold or possess a problem. Additionally, ownership can also denote a person's character traits, as if this "something" describes you (see the benefits of using the word challenge on page 236).

6. **CONSIDER** and decide, having completed this exercise, if you need to move on to the other Segments to resolve this "something". Or CONSIDER, after having completed the exercise, if you need to pause and see what takes place in the near future.

7. **WRITE** or use collage elements to create a supportive thought or an affirmation to encapsulate this experience. Put this anywhere on your collage. Example: "I can document the aspects of an emotional "something" to reduce the effect of it on my life."

8. **PLACE** a triangle-shaped element anywhere on the substrate to symbolize your personal strength and to offer a comforting and familiar ritual.

9. **EXTEND** your transformation by completing the TAKEAWAY ACTION TOOLS (page 225).

10. **RETURN** here after completing the Takeaway Action Tools to read the ending quote below.

"The greater the obstacle, the more glory in overcoming it."

— Molière

mr.babies, *untitled*, 2017, Analog Collage, Doug + Laurie Kanyer Art Collection

Luciana Frigerio, *Untitled*, 2020, Collage in Vintage Clock - Front and Back View, Doug + Laurie Kanyer Art Collection

RESOLVING A CHALLENGE - SEGMENT THREE

**A collage-making exercise-experience to learn about Acceptance
and Present Moment Activities.**

***"Radical acceptance rests on letting go of the illusion of control and a willingness to notice
and accept things as they are right now, without judging."*** — Marsha Linehan

INFORMATION TO THINK ABOUT AND CONSIDER

Before we conduct a deep dive into the topics of Acceptance and Present Moment Activities (PMAs), let us first commence with some important definitions and clarifications. For our purposes in this exercise-experience, the words "somethings" and "challenges" are used interchangeably. Also, please note that we are using "acceptance" and "acknowledgement" interchangeably as well.

When a "something" arises, one begins a journey. Whether it is a "something" that comes outside of one's intentions, or an unanticipated concern arriving within planned parameters, you find yourself headed in a new direction. The scope and range of what will be required, in the context of this new direction, may be vast or it may be modest. To accommodate, resolve and integrate the new "something", one goes through a series of stages. The stages take place from the initial moment of noticing the "something" to the ultimate celebration of the situation resolving.

The discussion of "Acceptance" here relates to addressing and resolving a "challenge". Acceptance can also apply to non-challenging things in life. A common example would be when a project or perhaps a relationship in your life does not meet certain expectations or ideals. Or if an anticipated thing turns out differently than what was hoped or planned. Things that are disappointments or "other than" what was expected may carry with them potent feelings. In this example, using Acceptance can help. As you read this material, which focuses on Acceptance as part of resolving a challenge, feel free to apply this material to other aspects of life beyond resolving a challenge.

There are five Segments in the process of resolving a "something" or a challenge. This exercise-experience addresses Segment Three - Acceptance and PMAs as a Way to Care for Feelings, Thoughts and Behaviors During Resolving a Challenge.

Acceptance as a Tool to Modulate Distress While Resolving a Challenge

The goal of the work in this book is to transform, evolve, and to seek actions to facilitate change. Accordingly, it may seem ironic or even odd that "Acceptance" is brought into the conversation. Isn't Acceptance giving up? Isn't Acceptance actually the denial of a "something"?

The answer to these questions is "no". Indeed, Acceptance can actually become your superpower when finding oneself in the middle of a "something". This is especially true when working to modulate strong feelings and thoughts connected to a challenge. As you will see, Acceptance, as used here, is an active choice of release. In this application it is used to regulate thoughts, feelings and behaviors that ultimately will disarm some of the suffering when experiencing a "something." It is not "hyper-positivity" nor is it the ignoring of reality. It offers you objectivity, and detaches you from being too connected and defined by a challenge.

A "Something" Arises and Starts an Emotional Response

When a challenge arises, there will be associated emotions and feelings connected to it. Depending upon the details and nature of the "something" there can be a bounty of potent, powerful, even overwhelming emotions and feelings that present.

Not only does one have the task of managing all the aspects of a new "something", one has to also manage oneself and one's emotions-feelings. Additionally, it is not uncommon for other unexpected things to come up while dealing with the new "something". These new variables might simply be annoying, or they may be more considerable. For example, you are on your way to an unexpected medical appointment and there is a traffic jam, causing you to think you will be late. Or you forgot to deposit a check in the bank and you accidentally overdraw your funds.

The Components of the Emotional Response System (ERS)

The components of the Emotional Response System (ERS) include an initial burst of sensory-body emotions followed by emerging feelings. Your memories related to a similar "something" from the past, are then added. Your Early Life Impressions, which shape your beliefs, values and more are also connected, and thoughts emerge. All are co-mingled and attached with the "something". It is vital to the overall resolution of the "something" that you are able to pace your ERS and then be able to engage your cognition to produce an optimal response. The aim is to be able to make a conscious response to a "something" using the tremendous energy of the ERS to fuel your efforts rather than derail them.

Acceptance is Key Coping Skills

Acceptance is key to resolving a challenge. These traits have the effect of regulating the potent charges of the ERS and any tangled thoughts that might be occurring in the cognitive centers. They are remedies, blocking anxiety from creeping in and hijacking the process. Acceptance and acknowledgement help you to know that this challenge does not define you or your overall life. Acceptance is a quintessential ingredient to decrease distress, to live well during a "something", and to rise above the hardship, both during and after (Linehen 2020).

Broad Scope Acceptance and Acknowledgement

Marsha Linehan, the famed inventor of Dialectical Behavior Therapy (DBT), found in her research the deep value of adopting two behavioral patterns that may seem to be in opposition to one another. It is applicable here, while using Acceptance and at the same time maneuvering the challenge. When working to resolve a challenge one needs both. To "Accept" means to acknowledge the challenge as outside of one's control, while at the same time continuing one's efforts to resolve it. You Accept into where you are in the process and you Accept all of who you and others are in the present moment.

To be able to tolerate the emotional discomfort of a challenge one can "Accept" it in the present moment. You can say to yourself, "Yes, there is a challenge and yes, I am having an abundance of feelings, memories, and more. I accept it all and myself in the middle of it. It is just so." You don't give up the process of resolving a challenge. You do not deny the thoughts or feelings attached to the challenge. You accept it all as true. The challenge, feelings and other aspects of the ERS are fully noted and embraced.

Acceptance is Similar to Non-Attachment

My daughter Kirsten Dahlhauser is a yoga trainer and instructor. She says, "In yoga philosophy there is an emphasis on 'non-attachment', rather than 'attachment'." In many ways non-attachment is like Acceptance. In yoga there is the concept of "santosha" where one consciously and actively chooses contentment in the middle of a "something". Contentment or choosing Acceptance for where you are increases calm and decreases suffering. Says Kirsten, "You can actively choose 'acceptance' for what is and 'non-attachment' to the outcome." This does not mean you stop the process of working to resolve the challenge. What you do is humbly accept the process and engage one's will to not be attached to the outcome.

Using Present Moment Activities to Stay in the Here and Now

It is vital to stay present and grounded while resolving a "something". One can accomplish this through Acceptance, coupled with the use of Present Moment Activities (PMAs). Both methods work to modulate and pace emotional energy. Examples of PMAs are meditation, deep breathing, gentle yoga, and slow-paced walking. Collage-making is a profound and effective form of a PMA. PMAs are active calming activities.

By invoking Acceptance and using PMAs, one has the ability to let things be as they are right now without the type of deep rumination that leads to worry and anxiety. Acceptance and PMAs offer you a method to remain present. As stated earlier, this does not represent "giving up". Instead, through the active use of PMAs and Acceptance, one avoids spiraling emotionally. PMAs calm the Flight, Flight, Fleeze, Fawn Response tendencies of the ERS. They allow you to observe what you are feeling and thinking with calm space. The combination of Acceptance along with PMAs helps one avoid the energetic power of dramatic emotions and thoughts. One is able to allow them to dissipate and melt away.

Present Moment Activities Can Aid Acceptance

Using PMAs (often referred to as "Mindful" activities) you can face the illusion of controlling the challenge and move to Acceptance. I prefer to use the term Present Moment Activities rather than "mindful", as many of my clients commented that they already have a "mind full" of a "something". Hence the more accurate term.

Using PMAs can help to unhook yourself from a number of things that can unsettle your emotional stability. As Linehan says, "You have to accept things to change things (Linehan, 2020)." Linehan and I are in agreement that it is best to employ Acceptance and to actively utilize a PMA like collage-making (Kanyer 2021) to pace the emotions and thoughts connected to a "something."

Noting and Accepting Helps to Stay Grounded

When utilizing the tools of Acceptance and PMAs one is actually able to notice and acknowledge, rather than deny the "something". This is often a spiritual step where one sees and accepts the present situation as true, while staying grounded in the present moment with a PMA. You clearly realize that the situation may be unfair, yet you accept it as so, and then use PMAs to modulate the tension.

PMAs enable one to gain perspective and invoke Acceptance. Applying PMAs to a "something" will help one to accept two things that may seem in conflict. You may lack the control to make a challenge go away right now, so you accept, while at the same time knowing it will ultimately change. You stay in the moment with PMAs, rather than future-tripping, which is engaging in anticipatory anxiety about future "what ifs".

Curbs Outbursts

Acceptance and PMAs help one to avoid behaving in a way that will make things worse. They are effective in avoiding clogging, denying or ignoring your feelings. Acceptance and PMAs can also help avoid making extreme behavioral actions that don't fit with your character or that complicate matters. Rather than an outburst with extreme actions, saying things you don't really mean or doing things you will later regret, you accept and use a PMA to regulate the force of the emotions, feelings and thoughts. PMAs are essentially active calming activities that can prevent any strong behavioral outburst which could make the challenge worse.

Halting the Emotional Snowball Effect

The tools of Acceptance and using PMAs help one interrupt or decrease the potential for things to get bigger, to metaphorically becoming a monstrous snowball. Feelings and thoughts are seen, witnessed and acknowledged as they are. Using the tool of Acceptance and PMAs, the situation does not grow and become bigger or worse, as one might think or believe. With Acceptance the power of the "something" to balloon up and grow is dissipated.

One does not need to "scream" at oneself internally to take notice. By stepping into Acceptance and using PMAs you can halt the intensity of the emotion and the thoughts. This can help you to more closely align your behaviors to avoid acting in a way that could make the situation worse.

Tending to Your Feelings and Thoughts with Perspective Offered by PMAs

When a feeling or thought is observed and accepted using a PMA, it can be witnessed as a mental event. Such a mental event can then be viewed with a proper perspective. This keeps one from seeing feelings and thoughts connected to "something" as a defining, overbearing tyrant in your life. You gain a "mountain-top" viewpoint, a grander perspective, rather than denying. This will give you a chance to decrease the register of the feelings, and the corresponding tyrannical aspect of inaccurate thoughts. You are essentially saying to yourself, "I see the depth and weight of something in my life. It is extensive (or labeled it in a way that makes sense for you). I accept and acknowledge it to be so. I fully note and accept its imprint on my life. I will take care of myself right now and keep moving toward a resolution over time."

This is active. It is not discounting, denying, stuffing, or clogging. It is seen as the truth. Seeing oneself and feelings that come about using Acceptance is an action that decreases pain and heads off suffering. Suffering often happens in life when one holds on to the pain and fails to accept.

Acceptance and PMAs Require Practice

"This takes practice!" says Linehan. "Acceptance is acknowledging or recognizing facts that are true, and letting go of fighting your reality." She goes on to say, "Acceptance is accepting all the way, with your mind, your heart, and your body; accepting something from the depths of your soul, opening yourself to fully experiencing reality as it is in the moment (Linehan, 2020)". This has to be done over and over again in life, especially when working to resolve a challenge. Using PMAs often, even daily, or minute by minute, will help when challenges arise to accept and get needed perspective.

The process may look like this: you say "I am experiencing a challenge, but I am OK. I am whole. I accept this challenge just as it is. I recognize and accept what I have influence on right now, and what I do not. I accept myself and all that comes with me. While I am in this period of a challenge, I will stay present (using PMAs) where I am at now, seeing what is true, and invest in the things that will support my well-being."

PMAs in the Book - Collage-making is a PMA

Collage-making is a profound example of a PMA. It has many layers of effectiveness to in "deflating" otherwise inflated emotions (see the Appendix on page 231 for a complete list on how collage-making helps). It helps one to stay in the present moment when faced with a "something". Think about how "in the present" one needs to be when using scissors to precisely cut out elements. Every exercise-experience in this book uses collage-making as a PMA to help to modulate and pace the emotional energy that comes with the exploration of various topics. When you use collage-making you have to stay present as you search, cut, tear and glue elements.

While collaging on a particular subject and aspect of a "something", you ultimately witness on the final collage the evidence of the situation. You can see what you are thinking and feeling and all the aspects of the "something". Additionally, the collage becomes the container for the thoughts and feelings. You don't have to hold it all in your head. PMAs support the regulation and management of strong feelings and extreme thoughts.

Offered in this book are many other PMAs beyond collage-making. You can find a list below of where to find more PMAs. In most cases they are briefly examined. Consider doing some research on your own about these marvelous methods. They all help to focus your mind and body in the here and now, to help you to stay in the present, especially when coupled with Acceptance. They support letting go of the need to control, avoiding overthinking and imagining the worst, which can ignite anxiety and suffering.

WHERE YOU CAN FIND SOME PRESENT MOMENT ACTIVITIES IN THE BOOK:

- **Deep Breathing** - page 21
- **Somatic Experience** - page 226
- **Contemplation** - page 226
- **Reflection** - page 7
- **Meditation** - page 226
- **Calming Music** - page 21
- **Half Smile** - page 117
- **Grounding Exercise-Experience** - page 125
- **CALM Exercise-Experience** - page 131

CONTENT ROUND UP to REVIEW—RECALL—REMEMBER

- Acceptance is a tool to modulate distress and other potent emotions and thoughts when working to resolve a challenge or a "something".

- A key to pacing potent emotions connected with a "something" is to stay in the here-and-now. This is accomplished by using Acceptance plus Present Moment Activities (PMAs).

- Using Acceptance and PMAs to pace emotions and thoughts can help to halt the chance of an emotional "snowball" effect where they expand and grow in intensity.

- Collage-making is profoundly effective as a PMA and it aids in Acceptance.

Jack Ravi, *YOU CAN*, Analog Collage Starter Kit, Doug + Laurie Kanyer Art Collection

GUIDED COLLAGE EXPERIENCE–MAKE A COLLAGE

1. **GATHER** materials, glue, magazines, books and a substrate (the paper you make your collage upon). Plan to use a big substrate, or make smaller elements to fit on a smaller substrate. Orient the substrate vertically. Cut a small, triangle-shaped element from your source material. Place it anywhere on the substrate to provide a personal symbol of power and strength. Doing this will offer a comforting and familiar ritual to begin this experience.

2. **LOCATE** two (2) pages in your source material that have a great deal of pattern. Tear them out. You will be making five unique shapes as symbols to represent:

   A. Resisting Acceptance.

   B. Using Acceptance and PMAs while resolving a challenge to care for emotions, feelings and thoughts.

   C. The wholeness, ease and reduction of suffering that can come from using Acceptance and PMAs.

   D. Change and new opportunities that come about when having resolved a challenge.

   E. A new frame for life that emerges when a challenge is resolved.

3. **CHOOSE** one of the pages and make a square shape. Fold the square in half and cut out a heart shape. Set the heart shape aside. Open up the remaining square and cut it in half. Put the straight edges together and glue them down on the bottom of the substrate. This symbolizes "A" from above; the tension one experiences when resisting the use of Acceptance.

4. **CUT** the heart shape in half from the top to the bottom of the heart. Locate two (2) examples of the letter "A" in your source material. Cut them out and glue them onto the front of one of the halves, they symbolize Acceptance and Acknowledgment. Locate the letters "P", "M", and "A", in your source material. Cut them out and glue them to the other heart half, to represent Present Moment Activities. The two heart shapes symbolize step "B" from above; using Acceptance/Acknowledgment and PMAs when resolving a challenge as a way to tend to feelings and thoughts.

5. **PLACE** the two heart shapes together to restore the original shape, with the letters showing. Glue them on the substrate above the first element you placed. These symbolize "C" from above; the wholeness, ease and reduction of suffering that can come from using Acceptance and PMAs. The heart is a universal symbol of love and unconditional acceptance.

6. **MAKE** a butterfly shape. Cut another square the same size as the first. Fold in half, and cut out a heart shape. Cut the heart in half. Place the separated heart with the bottom points touching and the upper parts fanned out, similar to the wings of a butterfly. MAKE another square, half the size of the last one. Fold in half and cut a smaller heart shape. Cut the heart shape in half. Place the separated smaller heart tips near the other larger heart tips to complete the wings of a butterfly.

   Glue them in the shape of a butterfly above the last element. This will symbolize "D" from above; the change and new opportunities that comes about when having resolved a challenging "something". A butterfly is a universal symbol for change and new opportunities.

7. **CHOOSE** one of the squares that remain from making the hearts. Open it up and see that it is like a frame with an open-heart shape in the middle. Glue this to the top of the substrate. This will symbolize "E" from above; a new frame for life that emerges when a challenge is resolved. Cut out from the source material elements to symbolize anything you wish to recall or remember about the use of Acceptance and PMAs. Glue these elements inside the open heart.

8. **WRITE** or use collage elements to create a supportive thought to encapsulate this experience. Put this anywhere on your collage. For example: "I can accept the effect of a "something" that needs to be solved, and use PMAs to help."

9. **PLACE** a triangle-shaped element anywhere on the substrate to symbolize your personal strength and to offer a comforting and familiar ritual.

10. **EXTEND** your transformation by completing the TAKEAWAY ACTION TOOLS (page 225).

11. **RETURN** here after completing the Takeaway Action Tools to read the ending quote below.

"Sometimes letting things go (accepting and acknowledging) is an act of far greater power than defending or hanging on."

— Eckhart Tolle

Laurie Kanyer, *Blue Tunes*, 2020, Analog Collage, Doug + Laurie Kanyer Art Collection

Ateljewjlhelm, *Sunflower Seed*, 2022, Analog Collage, Doug + Laurie Kanyer Art Collection

RESOLVING A CHALLENGE - SEGMENT FOUR

**A collage-making exercise-experience to implement a plan,
hold a celebration and evaluate outcomes.**

"Problems (challenges) are nothing but wake-up calls for creativity." — Gerhard Gschwandtner

INFORMATION TO THINK ABOUT AND CONSIDER

In this exercise-experience you will find the concluding segments; Segment Four - Generating Ideas, Seeking Support, Choosing a Direction, Implementing a Plan, Celebration and Evaluation.

Once you have moved through the first three Segments of resolving a challenge you enter into the place of finding ideas and preparing to make a plan to resolve the challenge. These ideas and preparations are featured in Segment Four. Most systems designed to resolve challenges start here. Our system meshes the previously discussed Segments with other important aspects, namely emotions and feelings.

Having completed the first three Segments, you have now accomplished the following:

Confirmed the Challenge is Yours to Be Involved in Resolving in Segment One: Before you moved ahead, you've confirmed without a doubt that this is your challenge to solve or one in which you need to be involved. You've inquired of yourself, "Is this really my challenge, or is it someone else's"?

Moved from Denial-Disbelief to Empowerment in Segment One: You have emotionally and mentally moved from denying the existence of a challenge to claiming your "call" to actively resolve it.

Observed and Investigated the Challenging "Something" in Segment Two: You have taken time and invested energy to thoroughly consider the who, what, where, when and why of the challenge. You know how it compromises your values, beliefs and impacts your life. You have considered how it came about and the known consequences of the "something".

Named and Defined the Challenge in Segment Two: You have given the challenge a specific name and defined it. This allows you now to clearly ask for suggestions and get help from others. This helps to decrease confusion and keeps you focused.

Tended to Your Feelings Along the Way in Segment Two: You have continued to identify, validate and consider your feelings about the challenge and other things in your life.

Accepted Yourself, Your Emotions, Your Feelings and Your Thoughts In Segment Three: You have accepted where you are in the challenge and see yourself as whole and capable of resolving the challenge. You recognize that feelings accompany challenges and you are working to accept them as just so.

Set Realistic Timelines in Segment Three: You recognize that there could be an timeline of undetermined length to resolve the challenge and have adjusted your expectations to reduce pressures.

Used PMAs to Stay in the Here and Now and to Care for Emotions and Feelings in Segment Three: To modulate, regulate and pace the predictable emotional tone that develops with challenges you use PMAs to stay present and reduce frustration and behavioral outbursts. It is understood that such outbursts could complicate matters. Continue to use PMAs as you proceed.

Introduction to Segment Four - Generating Ideas, Seeking Support, Choosing a Direction, Implementing a Plan, Celebration and Evaluation

You may find it unusual that Segment Four, unlike the other Segments, is offered in a to-the-point, list-like format. Segment Four on the other hand is action-oriented and direct in nature. It is almost like a checklist of activities to accomplish. In many ways it is a distinct, clear and regimented pathway toward resolution. That being said, there are a few important things to consider.

Focus on Your Strengths and Past Accomplishments

To endure your present challenge it can be very beneficial to invest time to recall and remember that you have successfully resolved challenges in the past. Whether large or small, great or minute, you have overcome previous challenges. You have skills, strengths and capabilities. The collage-making exercise-experience to follow will support your recollection of the times you resolved challenges and prove you are a challenge-resolver. Doing so will add to your confidence and provide an added dose of encouragement as you cope with any new challenge.

Extend Grace - Try to Avoid Additional Drama

As you are going through this process you may have mentioned to others what you are experiencing. This is a tender time for all. Extend grace to yourself and also to others. See the exercise-experience Avoiding Drama - Turning Toward Empowerment on page 213 to minimize the chance of adding to the problem and to embrace Empowerment with others.

Three Day Rule

There is often an optimal time to engage in the implementation of a plan toward resolving a challenge. In non-emergency challenges one can use the gift of time to your advantage. Consider adopting the skill of using the Three Day Rule. With the Three Day Rule you actively "pause" and return to it three days after you have determined a plan. You do not immediately go to work on it. You wait three days.

The Three Day Rule allows for time to pass in order to see if the challenge will further develop or possibly resolve. Doing so will allow one to avoid making decisions or taking action before the time is optimal.

This pause helps to develop your character and strengthen your ability to endure strain. This practice will help you in the future. It forms pathways in the brain to avoid reacting in a non-emergency challenge. While it may be uncomfortable, it is valid to know that moving too soon can make a "something" more complicated.

Three Day Rule Miracle

It is truly miraculous how challenges resolve or dissipate, in three days, without effort. Such resolutions may occur even when someone has a plan in place. I have frequently witnessed where a challenge resolves just before one intends to move to implement a plan. It is indeed a curious phenomenon, but I have personally and professionally experienced numerous real-life examples.

Use The Three Day Rule to Combat Fatigue

Use the Three Day Rule if you are fatigued or feeling emotionally charged. Stop, pause, and resist moving forward on decisions or actions when in these states. You are likely to make errors and make the challenge worse, or you may lose sight of the desired outcome.

Find a PMA to nourish yourself and refer to Give Yourself a Hand on page 115 to invest and track your emotional well-being. By using the Three Day Rule you can regroup and restore your energy if exhaustion has set in. The Three Day Rule offers a chance for the "something" to resolve on its own, and offers you a pause to tend to both fatigue and your emotional tone.

Avoid Comparison and Competition

When you seek support from others they will likely share their own experiences, to include both setbacks and accomplishments. Their insight and wisdom can be helpful. However, it is important to guard yourself from comparisons or expectations of similar experience. Avoid comparison and competition.

Work to see a challenge as uniquely yours, as it offers an opportunity to gain your own skills, abilities and outcomes. Use others' stories as path makers, not a prescription for how things will go for you. Stay focused on your process, using others' journeys as tips or hints to maneuver challenges. While challenges may appear similar, there are many individual aspects that are beyond comparison.

If you choose to access the wisdom, stories and experiences of others you can utilize the exercise-experience titled Asking for Help on page 193 and Suggestion Circle on page 199. Both invite support, but in a direct way that keeps things in a more businesslike path rather than a more casual one. Many people benefit from hearing others' stories as it helps to know one is not alone and decreases isolation. Knowing that others have had similar circumstances lets you know that, while this is unique to you, it is not unique to all.

Resist Taking on New Projects and Commitments

Until the challenge is resolved, practice saying "No" to other projects. Put off anything that is not needed to be done immediately. Restructure unimportant social obligations in lieu of rest and restoration. One should not re-carpet the house or throw a surprise party when one is in the middle of a big challenge. These "events" can add an additional layer of stress.

Implementing Segment Four: Building a Plan to Resolve a Challenge

Start by reminding yourself of the name and the definition of the challenge and review the facts you have gathered in Segment Two during your time of observation and investigation. Check your level of empowerment from Segment One and acceptance from Segment Three. Continue to use PMAs, especially Visualization (see page 226 for more).

The Steps of Segment Four

Note: All of the following steps will be actualized in the process of the collage-making exercise-experience to follow.

Identify Possible Solutions - Think of as many possible solutions to resolve the challenge as you are able. Make sure they are QUALITY solutions.

Ask Others for Help and Suggestions - Many challenges are resolved with teamwork and support from others. Think of who you can trust to offer assistance and quality suggestions. Formulate a temporary support team for these specific challenges. Find others who have the skills, knowledge, ability and time to help. Make sure they are wise, experienced, loyal, non-judgmental and will agree to remain confidential.

You might need some physical help or merely quality suggestions. Ponder this before asking. Others could be enlisted to check in with you about how you are doing emotionally. If this challenge is extremely complex it may be wise to get professional help (see the exercise-experience titled Asking for Help on page 193 and Suggestion Circle Tool on pages 199).

Choose a Viable Solution - Select one of the solutions you want to try first. Take time to analyze and anticipate the possible outcome of the solution you selected.

Outline All the Steps - Once you have chosen a solution, document all of the steps in writing or use the collage-making exercise to follow. List the equipment, people and other resources needed to carry out the solution.

Implement a Solution - Choose a date and time to carry out and act upon your chosen course of action. Remember to use the Three Day Rule.

Track and Collect Information - If new information comes forth, document it and consider if it has an impact on the plan. If you are working with others, share any new information.

Verify the Completion of Steps - If the plan and solution involves multiple steps, note the completion of each.

Continue to Tend to Emotions, Feelings, Thoughts and Your Overall Well-Being - Continue to monitor your well-being by referring to the Give Yourself a Hand on page 115 and the Feelings Stepping Stones Pathway on page 61.

Allow for Time and Space - Resolutions to challenges take time. Keep in mind that the challenge likely developed over a great deal of time. Accordingly, it will take time to resolve.

Monitor Timeline Expectations - Most challenges take longer than one imagines to resolve. One rule of thumb is to triple the amount of time you expect it to take. This helps avoid the burnout and frustration that can come with unrealistic time expectations.

Monitor Your Progress - Document Both Celebrations and Concerns - Take notes and document the process. Report to others any gains or setbacks. Compare this to a sporting event, where at halftime you recount what took place and make plans to move forward.

Make Adjustments and Select Other Solutions if Needed - When new information arises, or if the first solution did not work, move on to other solutions and repeat the process.

Celebration and Evaluation

When you have resolved a challenge it now becomes a victory. It is beneficial to commemorate the victory with a celebration. Celebrate and report the outcome to the support team who helped you to solve the challenge. Or hold a private celebration. Do this after some time has elapsed to offer some perspective and to rest. Thank all for their help and contributions (see page 238 in the Appendix for the Components of a Meaningful Celebration).

Take time to evaluate and review the entire process. Document what took place to recall later or to share with others who might be facing a similar situation. Consider using this documentation process to wrap up this challenge and to remember for a similar one in the future. List Things to Start, Things to Stop, Things to Keep and Things to Change. Some use a "See Me" file where they save this information if a similar challenge develops in their future. This will prevent the loss of the resolution and saves anything to remember for the future.

CONTENT ROUND UP to REVIEW—RECALL—REMEMBER

- It is an excellent practice to reflect on the times one has resolved past challenges. This reflection allows one to tap into one's strength and abilities.

- Taking time to analyze the steps of resolving a challenge will provide a helpful framework to proceed.

- Challenges usually take time to develop. They also often take time to solve. Recalling this will help decrease strain.

- Breaking down challenges into doable steps will reduce strong emotions and increase effectiveness.

GUIDED COLLAGE EXPERIENCE–MAKE A COLLAGE

Collage-Making Number One: Remembering Problems You Solved in the Past - Seeing Your Strengths

1. **GATHER** materials (glue, magazines, books and a substrate to make your collage on). Cut a small, triangle-shaped element from your source material. Place it anywhere on the substrate to provide a personal symbol of power and strength and to offer a comforting, familiar ritual to begin.

2. **THINK** of a challenge you solved in the past. This collage-making exercise-experience will demonstrate your challenge-resolution skills from times before. You will be able to bring this power to a current challenge. Search for element(s) to symbolize a challenge you solved in the past, cut the elements out, and glue them to the top of the collage.

3. **LOOK** for elements to symbolize all of the segments and steps listed above that you used to solve the challenge. Cut them out and glue them in any order you wish. Turn back to your source material and find the word: "Challenge Resolved" or find letters for the words "Challenge Resolved", and glue them anywhere on the collage. Or find an element to symbolize that the challenge was resolved.

4. **COMPLETE** this collage-making experience by cutting a small, triangle-shaped element from your source material. Place it anywhere on the substrate to show and symbolize the personal power and strength you used here. Doing this will offer a comforting and familiar ritual to end this exercise-experience.

5. **CONTINUE** or pause. If you choose to continue, TURN to page 225 and complete the TAKEAWAY ACTION TOOLS to extend and deepen your transformation. Then come back here to take part in collage-making experience Number Two to follow.

   If you choose to pause, come back to use the collage-making exercise-experience Number Two on a day when you are ready to move forward.

 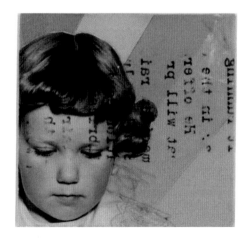

Millie Bartlett, *The Ordinary Infinite*, 2020, Mini Collage, Doug + Laurie Kanyer Art Collection

GUIDED COLLAGE EXPERIENCE–MAKE A COLLAGE

Collage-Making Number Two: Let's Solve a Current Challenge

1. **GATHER** materials, glue, magazines, books and a substrate (the paper you make your collage upon). Cut a small, triangle-shaped element from your source material. Place it anywhere on the substrate to provide a personal symbol of power and strength. Doing this will offer a comforting and familiar ritual to begin this experience. Note: You will need a large substrate for this exercise; feel free to return to the substrate to add more elements as needed, to track and document the process of resolving a challenge.

2. **LOCATE**, cut out and glue element(s) to symbolize a challenge you are currently experiencing. Glue them on the top of the substrate. Find elements to symbolize the completion of the first three Segments (1. Observation and Awareness, 2. Empowerment - Naming the Challenge/ Definition, and 3. Acceptance). Cut them out and glue them below the challenge, in a line across the substrate left to right.

3. **CHOOSE** small collage elements to symbolize all of the steps of Segment Four. Use as many collage elements as you need for all the steps. Glue the elements vertically on the left-hand side of the substrate. Take your time with this exercise. Feel free to step away and return later from the college-making exercise-experience to allow your mind to rest.

   - **Identify** Possible Solutions

   - **Ask** for Assistance and Suggestions from Others

   - **Choose** a Viable Idea to Use

   - **Outline** all of the Individual Steps as well as any related Equipment or Persons

   - **Choose** When to Implement a Solution (Remember the Three Day Rule)

   - **Track**, Collect and Document Information Along the Way

   - **Verify** the Completion of Steps

   - **Allow** for Reasonable Time and Space Expectations

   - **Continue** to Tend to Emotions, Feelings, Thoughts and Overall Well-Being

   - **Monitor** Your Progress - Document Both Celebrations and Concerns

   - **Make** Adjustments and Select Other Solutions if Needed

4. **DOCUMENT** that the challenge has been resolved by locating the words "Challenge" and "Resolved" in your source material. Or create the word from letters in your source material. Cut them out and glue them anywhere on the collage.

5. **CELEBRATE** this accomplishment in a way that feels just right for you. Choose an element(s) to symbolize your celebration, cut it out and glue it anywhere on the collage.

6. **EVALUATE** the completion of the process by choosing elements to symbolize the following categories: Things to Stop, Things to Start, Things to Keep, Things to Remember, or Things to Change. Cut them out and glue them at the bottom of the collage.

7. **WRITE** or use collage elements to create a supportive thought to encapsulate this experience. Put this anywhere on your collage. An example: "I was able to determine ideas to resolve a challenge and I made a plan that I followed through on."

8. **PLACE** a triangle-shaped element anywhere on the substrate to symbolize your personal strength and to offer a comforting and familiar ritual.

9. **EXTEND** your transformation by completing the TAKEAWAY ACTION TOOLS (page 225).

10. **RETURN** here after completing the Takeaway Action Tools to read the ending quote below.

"Rather than denying problems (challenges), focus inventively, intentionally on what solutions might look or feel like. Our mind is meant to generate ideas that help us escape circumstantial traps -- if we trust it to do so. Naturally, not all hunches are useful. But then you only need a single good idea to solve a problem (challenge)."

— Marsha Sinetar

Ateljewjlhelm, *Aura*, 2022, Analog Collage, Doug + Laurie Kanyer Art Collection

CP Harrison, *She Loves the Sounds of Sirens*, 2019, Analog Collage, Doug + Laurie Kanyer Art Collection

ASKING FOR HELP OR ASSISTANCE

A collage-making exercise-experience to practice asking for help or assistance from others.

"Don't be afraid to ask for help when you need it. I do it every day. Asking for help isn't a sign of weakness, it's a sign of strength. It shows you have the courage to admit you don't know something, and to learn something new." — Barack Obama

INFORMATION TO THINK ABOUT AND CONSIDER

Contrary to what you may believe, asking for help is a sophisticated life skill. Living in a community with others offers one the opportunity to practice the art of interdependence. Interdependence can be neatly summarized with the following statement: sometimes you are asking for help, and other times you are offering it. It is the understanding that there can be a healthy reliance on others to benefit both them and you. Interdependence helps to insure the well-being of all.

The key is to strike a balance. The value of knowing when you need help and asking for it cannot be overstated. In adulthood, finding ways to be interdependent builds the well-being of each individual and the community at large. Conversely, offering help to others in ways that fit for you helps them and you too.

There are a number of reasons one can have a difficult time asking for help.

Cultural Influences

In many cultures the notion of "rugged individualism" is highly prized. There have been times in most societies when the infrastructure to support people was lacking. People essentially had to rely upon their own initiative to survive. In such times there was no one to ask for help.

An historically recent example of this is the frontier era in the United States, when people moved to remote areas where basic community infrastructure was lacking. It was especially promoted by American President Herbert Hoover during the Great Depression when people were encouraged to rely on themselves, rather than support from the community or government programs. While this political approach may have been useful for its time, for some it has had negative effects. Know that these negative effects can be successfully challenged.

A Silly Slogan that Marginalized Asking for Help

One common slogan that enforced this thought is "Pull yourself up by your bootstraps". The notion conveyed by this statement is that one needs to be self-reliant and achieve success without help from others. There is some question as to whether this slogan has its origins in America or in Germany. Notwithstanding, it is literally impossible to achieve anything while pulling up one's bootstraps.

Consider the absurdity of this slogan. If you are attempting to move forward in life while holding onto the straps of your boots you would be hunched over, practically immobile. You would furthermore be looking downward, not up, and likely to hurt yourself by running into or tripping over something. This slogan originally meant that someone was pulling themselves out of a bog by their own hair. Again, an absurd thought. In its earlier meaning it was meant to mock someone who told tall tales of their own impossible accomplishments.

As it happens, the saying shifted over time to mean one needs to become a success all by one's own efforts and without asking for help. If this statement has been said to you, consider and understand that it is a silly, untrue ideal.

Misunderstanding from Earlier in Life

Many have gotten the impression, based on earlier childhood experiences, that not asking for help and doing it all oneself was an important character trait. During one's growing up years, caregivers may have desired and encouraged you to be independent and to be able to take care of yourselves. Things like getting dressed on your own is one example. That and many other examples may have produced a sense of personal accomplishment. This, however, may also have produced the false impression that you have to manage all life situations by yourself. You may have come to believe asking for help is a sign of immaturity and harkens back to your earlier dependency as a young child. It is important to reframe that earlier impression and to ask for help.

Not Wanting the Be a Burden to Others

Some individuals see asking for help as being a burden on others. This perception was likely based on earlier experiences from childhood. It may have come from being cared for by overwhelmed parents, teachers or other caregivers, who in their natural exasperation may have caused you to think your needs were burdensome for them. You may have avoided asking for help to decrease their stress, and in a sense take care of them. In reality, your impressions may have been formed at a potent and difficult time in the life of your caregiver, and you can revise it to see yourself as not a burden.

True Lack of Help

You may have come from a family or community where there were very few people available to help or care for you. Perhaps resources were limited or adults had too many responsibilities and lacked help themselves. Those whose job it was to care for you either neglected their roles, were ill, or ironically expected or even needed you to take care of them. In such scenarios the thought of asking for help is something far off from your past life experiences. You can learn, as an adult in the present, the value of asking for help. In doing so one helps heal the wounds from earlier in life.

Fear of Being Turned Down

You may have decided not to ask for help because you feared being turned down. The key is to keep asking for help from more than one person and seeing the process like a puzzle. Take satisfaction in the discovery of the right fit for the concern, rather than doing it yourself and worsening the problem. Remember that someone's ability or inability to help you does not indicate whether they like or dislike you. Their "No" may just mean they do not have the ability, resources, time or knowledge to support the solution right now. Try not to discard the person who said no to your request; just ask them again later when a different challenge occurs.

Being Resourceful

The truth of the matter is that we are to be dependent at times and independent at other times. One way to look at asking for help is that you are actually being resourceful. It shows you have the ability to find solutions to problems by seeking those with more knowledge or skills. Says Joan Rosenberg Ph.D., "Being resourceful and asking for help is an aspect of emotional strength. To know one's limitations and to be comfortable with oneself, and then recognizing when you are in need, is a sign of courage, vulnerability and self-insight (Rosenberg, n.d.)."

Asking Helps Others and Builds Skills

When you ask for help you are actually aiding the process of building relationships and contributing to the community. Humans are created to be helpful at times and assist others, as well as ask for and receive help. Helping is a way for social contacts to take place and elevates people's sense of self-esteem. It decreases isolation and loneliness. It builds a cooperative tone in a group and offers people a chance to practice and build skills. Says Ric Ocasek, "Refusing to ask for help when you need it is refusing someone the chance to be helpful."

The Skill of Asking for Help

In the book *Growing Up Again*, by Connie Dawson and Jean Clarke, you can find an exceptional script to ask for help in a direct, clear way that provides others with a chance to say no in a caring and respectful way too. The script goes like this:

You say, "I need some help or assistance from you (insert the thing you need help with here). Are you available on (insert when you need help)."

Continue to ask, "Can you help (assist) me or shall I ask someone else?"

In using this approach, you are being clear about what you need help with and when you need the help. In addition, you are letting the person know they can say, "No" if it is not convenient or they do not have the skills or resources to assist. They do not have to fret that your need won't get met, as you state that you are going to keep asking for help from someone else.

An important word here. Most "somethings" in life take time to develop into what one would define as a significant challenge. It may take some time to identify a solution and helpers. In the meantime, your effort here in collage-making is in fact movement toward a solution. You are consciously and actively making an effort to practice the skill of asking for help AND finding helpers. These are key aspects of resolving challenges.

CONTENT ROUND UP to REVIEW—RECALL—REMEMBER

- Asking for help is a sign of strength.

- Community and relationships are built when people ask for help and give assistance to others.

- Keep asking for help or assistance until you identify someone who is capable of assisting.

- Just because someone is not able to help at a certain time, it does not mean they will not be able to help later, nor does it mean they do not care for you.

- People can learn ways to ask for help in clear and direct ways.

Edina Picco, *Telltale*, 2022, Digital Collage, Doug + Laurie Kanyer Art Collection

GUIDED COLLAGE EXPERIENCE–MAKE A COLLAGE

1. **GATHER** materials (glue, magazines, books and a substrate to make your collage on). Cut a small, triangle-shaped element from your source material. Place it anywhere on the substrate to provide a personal symbol of power and strength and to offer a comforting, familiar ritual to begin.

2. **SELECT** elements to symbolize a "something" you need help with. Cut it out and glue it on the top of the substrate. If it is difficult to ask for help take a minute and consider your feelings and your internal conversation about asking for help. Select an element to symbolize changing your mind about asking for help, and glue this new element somewhere near the element symbolizing the problem at the top of the substrate.

3. **FIND** element(s) in your source material to symbolize which aspects of the challenge you know how to manage and solve yourself. Cut it out and glue it right in the middle of the substrate. This shows your skill, strength and ability to be coupled with help from others. Draw a circle around this element, large enough to glue additional symbolic elements within the circle.

4. **FIND** in your source material an element to symbolize how you feel about needing help solving a problem, acknowledging what you don't know how to do. Glue this element at the top of the substrate with the previously placed elements there. Now get up and walk around a bit, step outside if you can, and take a number of deep breaths.

5. **THINK** about who you know who has the skills to help solve the challenge. Or consider who you know who could point you in the right direction to help solve the problem. Anyone who comes to mind who is a possible fit to assist you. Go to your source material and find elements to symbolize each person who can help. Cut the elements out, and glue them down in order, placing the first person at twelve o' clock (12:00), and from there move around the clock face, placing each element that symbolizes your potential helpers.

6. **CHOOSE** one of the people on the collage circle to ask for help. Before you reach out to that person, get your substrate and, inserting the person's name, write the following: "(Person), I need some help (or assistance) from you today with (insert the project or situation you need help with here). Are you available on (insert when you need help)?" Finish by writing, "Can you help me or shall I ask someone else?" If the person is willing to help address the concern, terrific, go on to work to solve the challenge. If this person says, "No, I cannot help you today", say "Thank you for your consideration." Rest until the next day when you can choose to connect with the next person on the collage. Give yourself the gift of time for all of this to come together.

7. **NOTICE** if you find feelings of rejection due to someone saying "No". If you do, go to your source material and find an element which symbolizes your feelings. Glue it to the collage somewhere. Return to your source material and find an element that will remind you that someone saying "No" does not mean they do not like you, or they do not love you, or that they are unwilling to help you later in a different circumstance. Take some time to carefully look at the element(s) showing you that you are liked or loved, even when asking for help and someone is not able. Consider and know that their inability to help now has nothing to do with you or their feelings about you. Give yourself a day or more to let this new notion soak in.

8. **ONCE** you are ready, move on to finding a helper by going back to your collage and ask the next person on the circle to help you. Keep going until you find someone to assist you.

9. **CELEBRATE** when you find someone to help with your concern. Locate an element to symbolize this celebration and glue it wherever you desire on the substrate. Continue to ask for help if you find other concerns developing.

10. **WRITE** or use collage elements to create a supportive thought to encapsulate this experience. Put this anywhere on your collage. Example: "I can practice asking for help and accepting help, and I know that when someone can't help they still care for me."

11. **PLACE** a triangle-shaped element anywhere on the substrate to symbolize your personal strength and to offer a comforting and familiar ritual.

12. **EXTEND** your transformation by completing the TAKEAWAY ACTION TOOLS (page 225).

13. **RETURN** here after completing the Takeaway Action Tools to read the ending quotes below.

"I get by with a little help from my friends."

— John Lennon

Anthony Grant, *Path Marks*, 2022, Analog Collage, Doug + Laurie Kanyer Art Collection

Liliana Lalanne, *PRAYER*, 2020, Digital Collage, Doug + Laurie Kanyer Art Collection

SUGGESTION CIRCLE

**A collage-making exercise-experience to learn a method to
gather suggestions from others to resolve a challenge.**

*"Asking for advice is an act of humility. The act alone says, "I need you." The decision maker
and the adviser are pushed (invited) into a closer relationship."* — Dennis Bakke

INFORMATION TO THINK ABOUT AND CONSIDER

There are times when you need quality ideas or suggestions to resolve a challenge. Author Jean Illsley Clarke, whom sadly passed away in 2021, designed a clear and thoughtful process for asking for suggestions from others. Clarke titled the process "Suggestion Circle". It was originally designed for use in parenting education classes and facilitated work groups. I used it for decades, with great effectiveness, with the groups I worked with. It provides for an efficient, emotionally safe, and effective way to gather information to resolve challenges.

Suggestion Circle requires a few simple but extremely helpful steps. For our use in this book, Suggestion Circle has been adapted to an email format, rather than in its original form, which was used in a facilitated group setting.

It is recommended that you have completed Segments One, Two, Three, and Four prior to doing a Suggestion Circle.

What is a Suggestion Circle?

Suggestion Circle is a method used to gather information, ideas and suggestions to resolve a specific challenge.

The person with the challenge contacts other people via email, asking them to offer high-quality, action-focused suggestions and ideas.

The person with the challenge states their challenge in a clear, concise way, using three specific, well-thought-out sentences. The sentences must describe the challenge and what areas require suggestions.

The person who in reply offers suggestions and ideas does so in one or two action-focused sentences. They are encouraged to say not what they would do themselves, but rather to tell the one with the challenge what to try.

There is no discussion on the challenge between those involved, and all communication is kept confidential.

All people who are asked for suggestions are thanked for their contributions, even if they do not have an idea or suggestion for the specific challenge.

The person with the challenge collects all the suggestions and avoids initially evaluating them. They think, choose and use the suggestion(s) that works best for them.

Benefits of Suggestion Circle (Clarke, 1984):

Honors the person with a challenge.

Provides a way to get support in a direct, to-the-point, adult-like manner.

Provides high-quality, action-focused suggestions.

Encourages clear and concise thinking.

Develops an information base for present and future use.

Shares information quickly without long, belabored discussions.

Proves there are more than one or two possible resolutions to challenges.

Accepts ideas in a non-judgmental, non-degrading manner, without critique.

Provides a way for people to ask for help without shame, blame or embarrassment.

Reduces the tension of a challenge by swiftly collecting solutions, without undue drama.

Encourages people to take responsibility for the resolution of a challenge.

Encourages people to think about ways to resolve a challenge and reduces tension during potentially emotional circumstances.

Offers empathy and compassion, rather than pity, to the person with a concern, while aiming to help them.

Develops intimacy between people.

Allows for introverts, or others who may be hesitant to speak in a group, to offer solutions.

Provides a way for people to be honored for their kindness and contributions.

Increases the strength of a community by people coming together to assist one in need.

Appreciates people for being willing to help, even if they do not have suggestions to offer. Everyone who takes part is thanked.

Keeps one from selecting an idea based solely on the person who offers the idea, and one's relationship to that person.

Avoids the common emotional games people play, such as discounting, blaming, shaming and victimizing. Suggestion Circle keeps people from uttering these kinds of limiting statements: "Yes, but your ideas won't help me," or "Poor Me," or "What If…" or "If it weren't for them," or "This is a huge challenge that can't be resolved" or "I have tried that and it did not work."

Suggestion Circle is Different than Brainstorming

Suggestion Circle differs from brainstorming in that brainstorming typically involves people engaging in a process of generating creative, horizon-expanding options, often in a random format. The goal of brainstorming is to certainly find resolutions, but the process is not limited to ideas that have in the past proven to work. When brainstorming, people in a group generate ideas in a spontaneous fashion and any idea is accepted, with the hope that they land on a solution. There is no guarantee in using brainstorming that a solution will be discovered. Suggestion Circle asks for high-quality, action-focused suggestions.

Suggestion Circle Compared to Discussions

Says Clarke, "The disadvantage of discussions is that they take an indeterminate amount of time and they sometimes become competitive, rather than helpful. People may play "win-lose", as in 'If you don't like my idea, I'm not helpful or needed.' They sometimes make comparisons such as "Her suggestion is better than his." They may play "right-wrong", exemplified by the statement "It isn't fair for you to consider our ideas equally; mine is right and yours is wrong." Occasionally a discussion can lead to a game people play called, "King of the Hill," as in "My idea is the only one that counts or is the best."

All of these competitive interactions, often used in discussions, tend to draw attention away from the ideas to the people and block the free flow of ideas. During a discussion, the person with the most helpful ideas may not share them, because of their comfort, their temperament (introvert) and the established culture of the group (Clarke, 1984)."

A Checklist - Prior to Doing a Suggestion Circle

To prepare oneself for a Suggestion Circle, one should inquire of oneself.... have you:

Determined this is your challenge to resolve and not someone else's (see page 163)?

Become empowered to resolve the challenge. Are you willing to do the work to resolve the challenge (see page 163)?

Collected some data, facts and investigated the challenge (see page 169)?

Accepted yourself and others in the middle of this challenge (see page 117)?

Attended to your emotions and feelings (see pages 117)?

Use the Word "Challenge" Rather than "Problem"

A recommendation here on how you might express this to yourself or others. Consider describing the "something" as a thing you are experiencing as a challenge, not a "problem". Say, "I am experiencing this challenge (name the challenge)", rather than "I have this problem". The word problem has so many negative connotations. To say you "have a problem" indicates ownership. The definition of the word "have" is to possess, own, or hold. When one says, "I have a problem" it can indicate to others that you possess the problem. It literally means that you "own" or "hold" on to it. The truth is you are a person who is going through an experience brought on by a "something". You don't want to own, hold or possess a problem. Additionally, ownership can also denote a person's character traits, as if this "something" describes you (see the benefits of using the word challenge on page 236).

Steps to Conducting an Email Suggestion Circle

Notes and disclaimers: Read all the steps below first. Do the collage-making exercise-experience below prior to sending out any emails. Avoid asking for suggestions on social media, as this confuses the streams of interpersonal communication. Social media denotes a casual tone and one cannot ensure confidentiality.

On to the Steps:

Step 1. Create a list of people to ask for suggestions, who you know are wise, experienced, loyal, capable of being non-judgmental, and who will agree to remain confidential.

Step 2. Send an introductory email to inquire if they are willing and able to take part in offering suggestions. It is appropriate, and a sign of respect, to send an introductory email first to ask others for their permission to include them in your Suggestion Circle. Before you include your challenge send the following email. Avoid a cold call or an email with the challenge enclosed; ask for permission first and set down your expectations. This will give others a chance to decline if they are not available, or not willing to extend themselves at this time. It also avoids the challenge of being out in the world without having asked for people to be in their most adult-like mentality.

In the email write:

"I am experiencing a challenge. In order to resolve the challenge I am gathering quality suggestions from others.

I am using a tool called Suggestion Circle, which is designed to gather quality, action-focused ideas. It is a quick and efficient method to gather viable ideas towards a resolution.

I am asking you because you are a wise, discreet, experienced, loyal person. I know you are able to offer support in a non-judgmental manner. I also know you are able to agree to keep this confidential.

This process will take you under ten minutes to complete. There is no pressure at all if you are not able to take part at this time.

I am extending this inquiry to a number of people. The purpose is to ask for assistance in the resolution of this challenge by offering me ideas and suggestions. I thank you for your consideration and ask you to keep this inquiry confidential.

Are you willing to offer quality ideas?

If you are willing, please send me a response, saying, "I can assist at this time". I will send you more information in the next day or so.

If you are unable to take part at this time, please return the email receipt by saying, "I am unable at this time to take part."

If they decline, write a short email saying, "Thank you for your consideration. Can I ask you for suggestions in the future?" If they say you can ask them at a later date, keep their name on your list and thank them.

Note: It is valuable to respect a person's "No" boundary if they decline to assist. Avoid taking their "No" personally. People will have many reasons that likely have nothing to do with you when declining. Remember, just because they decline now doesn't mean they will not help in the future.

Step 3. Write an email to those who are willing to take part. In the email, define the challenge in three distinct and specific sentences, no more.

Sentence One: Describe what the challenge is exactly.

Examples:

"I have been having a difficult time staying asleep at night."

 Or

"I am having a hard time with managing getting needed repairs done around the house."

Sentence Two: Give some detail about the challenge.

Examples:

"I have been awakened at 3:00 am for a month, three nights a week and cannot get back to sleep."

Or

"I am working full-time. The shed needs a new roof by winter. It appears it will potentially leak."

Sentence Three: Say exactly what information you need from the other person.

Examples:

"I need some ideas and suggestions to fall back asleep when I wake in the night."

"I need some ideas and suggestions to accomplish getting a new roof on the shed."

Step 4. Send the email with the three-sentence challenge included. In the subject line write your name and the words "Suggestion Circle, time sensitive".

In the email write,

Hello (insert their name),

I am asking for quality suggestions to resolve the following challenge. Below you will find the challenge in a few brief sentences with information about it. If you do not have a suggestion, simply respond in a return email saying, "I don't have a solution for you at this time".

The Challenge (featuring all three sentences combined)

"I have been awakened at 3:00 am for a month, three nights a week. I need ideas to fall back asleep when I wake in the night."

It would be helpful for me if you would kindly offer solutions as briefly as possible. To keep the process moving forward please use the action-forward format (examples below). This will allow me the chance to compile solutions quickly. Please offer as many quality suggestions as you have.

For example:

"Try to (fill in the blank)."

"Read this book (fill in the blank)."

"Research this article (fill in the blank)."

"Get this product (fill in the blank)."

"Call this professional (fill in the blank)."

Please return your suggestion(s) by (insert the date).

At this time I am simply gathering ideas. Because the nature of most challenges can take time to resolve, I will be focusing on the process of resolution and will not be making follow-up progress reports at this time.

Thank you for your suggestion,

(Insert your name)

Step 5. When they respond, simply reply with this email. Avoid evaluating any of the suggestions, simply acknowledge receipt.

"Thank you very much for your suggestion(s). I will add it (or them) to the list to think about and consider. I appreciate the time you offered to help generate ideas to resolve this challenge. Please keep this correspondence confidential and between us."

Note: You are not making any promise for a follow-up conversation. This prevents undue strain on the relationship and potential magnification of the challenge. It keeps things straight forward, action-focused and adult-like.

Step 6. Copy, from each of the emails, every suggestion and compile them for your consideration. Keep ALL of the suggestions, as it has been found that a solution that may not seem to be viable immediately might be helpful later. Think, Choose and Use the one that best fits for you.

CONTENT ROUND UP to REVIEW—RECALL—REMEMBER

- Suggestion Circle offers a quick and efficient way to gather quality, action-focused ideas and information for the purpose of resolving challenges.

- Suggestion Circle honors people who have challenges with suggestions, and also honors those who offer the suggestions.

- Suggestion Circle helps to decrease the emotional strain of a challenge by helping people take responsibility and providing resources.

- Suggestion Circle strengthens the bonds between people by providing a confidential, structured method of offering help and assistance with proven, action-focused information.

Sarah Best, *North Star*, 2022, 3-D Analog Collage, Courtesy of the Artist

GUIDED COLLAGE EXPERIENCE—MAKE A COLLAGE

1. **GATHER** materials (glue, magazines, books and a substrate to make your collage on). Cut a small, triangle-shaped element from your source material. Place it anywhere on the substrate to provide a personal symbol of power and strength and to offer a comforting, familiar ritual to begin.

2. **PREPARE** to initiate a Suggestion Circle by finding elements to represent the following:

   A) The definition of the challenge that needs to be resolved.

   B) The documentation of some simple facts and evidence on the challenge.

   C) The task of asking for the information and the suggestions you need.

   Cut the elements out and glue them in the order above. Glue them down at the top of the substrate.

3. **GATHER** a list of people you know who are wise, experienced, loyal, able to be non-judgmental and who will agree to remain confidential. Cut elements out to symbolize each person and glue them down on the left-hand side of the substrate from top to bottom. Use the email format provided in this chapter to exemplify these people.

4. **CHOOSE** elements for each suggestion offered. Cut them out and place them next to the element representing the person who offered each suggestion. If they were unable to take part, choose an element(s) to show that you will ensure asking them next time.

5. **CONSIDER** the suggestions offered. Choose one to use. Find an element to symbolize the suggestion you chose. Cut it out and glue it down next to the suggestion.

6. **CHOOSE** an element to represent saying "Thank You" to those who offered suggestions. Cut it out and glue it anywhere on the collage.

7. **WRITE** or use collage elements to create a supportive thought to encapsulate this experience. Put this anywhere on your collage. For example: "I can ask people for suggestions in an organized and systematic manner."

8. **PLACE** a triangle-shaped element anywhere on the substrate to symbolize your personal strength and to offer a comforting and familiar ritual.

9. **EXTEND** your transformation by completing the TAKEAWAY ACTION TOOLS (page 225).

10. **RETURN** here after completing the Takeaway Action Tools to read the ending quote below.

"Advice (suggestions) is like snow, the softer it falls the deeper it goes."

— Jeremiah Seed

Jack Felice, *BLUR*, 2019, Analog Collage, Doug + Laurie Kanyer Art Collection

PART 5
Exercise-Experiences to Assist in Resolving Interpersonal Challenges

"Successful long-term relationships are created
through small words, small gestures,
and small acts."

— John M. Gottman

Laurie Kanyer, *I am Sure*, 2019, Analog Collage, Permanent Collection of MERZ Gallery, Sanguhar, Scotland

ESTABLISHING BOUNDARIES

A collage-making exercise-experience to learn the steps of how to set boundaries with others to maintain emotional well-being.

"No is a complete sentence." — Anne Lamont

INFORMATION TO THINK ABOUT AND CONSIDER

Humans come with the ability to set boundaries. By two-and-a-half years of age, it is hard-wired into the brain and into social experiences. Almost like clockwork, a young child begins to say the word "No". They even say "No" to things they like. My grandson, at two-and-a-half, loved the outdoors and going for walks. When he turned two-and-a-half I would ask, "Would you like to go for a walk?" He would reply, "No," and then go find his coat.

Saying "No" as a Child Sets the Stage for Later

Being able to say the word "No" to those in your closest circle, such as your family or other caregivers, gives children practice for saying "No" to those outside your closest circle later in life. And by later on, I mean when you reach the age of fifteen, or twenty-five, or forty-five, or even ninety-five. Sadly, our "Nos" at two-and-a-half devolve into "maybe," and then "sure," then eventually to "why not," and finally to "OK". This originates in early childhood, when a child gets labeled for being difficult or bossy or uncooperative. They get the message that knowing what they know and saying, "No" is not socially acceptable.

Accepting a Child's "No" is Vital

When caregivers fail to accept "No" for an answer, children begin to doubt their preferences and boundaries. They begin to adopt a "be pleasing" way of life. This "be pleasing" approach leads to a multitude of problems later in life, from being isolated from knowing one's preferences, to allowing others to dictate terms, to following the group into dangerous choices, to becoming passive-aggressive and manipulative. This, all in order to belong to the group and to feel accepted. One ultimately discovers that they have been taken advantage of by others.

Practicing Again in Adulthood

In order to have a healthy emotional life as an adult you can learn to set boundaries and choose to be with people who accept your "No" for an answer. Says, Psychologist Joaquín Selva: "A boundary is a limit or space between you and the other person; a clear place where you begin, and the other person ends. The purpose of setting a healthy boundary is, of course, to protect and take good care of you." The need to say "No" and set boundaries helps one to avoid doing more than they can humanly accomplish. Saying "No" helps one avoid burnout, and also helps one avoid the anger of being taken advantage of by others. It is a protective armor to keep one from being abused or hurt. A skill can be acquired which allows one to move from saying "Sure, come on over anytime, I am here for you" to "Please call before you come". Or from "maybe" to "No, I will not take part in that activity".

Suggested Steps in Setting a Boundary with Someone

Step One: Listen to your emotions and feelings as you have a conversation or an experience with someone with whom you need to set a boundary.

Step Two: State clearly the boundary you need to set.

Step Three: Be prepared to say "No".

Step Four: Focus on your needs, and see yourself as able to enforce the boundary.

Step Five: Have in your mind the consequences for the person if they overstep your boundary. Be prepared to enforce the consequences.

CONTENT ROUND UP to REVIEW—RECALL—REMEMBER

- Children come with boundaries instilled in them. Consider the "No" of a two-year-old.

- Over time, people can be persuaded into releasing one's boundary.

- People can restore their natural ability to set boundaries and practice this skill.

Zoë Heath, *Found (Sergeant Petals)*, 2021, Doug + Laurie Kanyer Art Collection

GUIDED COLLAGE EXPERIENCE—MAKE A COLLAGE

1. **GATHER** materials (glue, magazines, books and a substrate to make your collage on). Cut a small, triangle-shaped element from your source material. Place it anywhere on the substrate to provide a personal symbol of power and strength and to offer a comforting, familiar ritual to begin.

2. **CHOOSE** an element to symbolize someone with whom you need to set a boundary. Cut it out and glue it wherever you want on the substrate.

3. **IMAGINE** talking to the person about the boundary and what you will say to them. This is step two of boundary setting, where one states the boundary. Search in your source material and find a gate to symbolize setting a boundary. If you can't locate a gate, choose any element to symbolize a gate. Cut it out and glue it wherever you want on the substrate.

4. **FIND** elements to form the word "No". Glue as many "Nos" wherever you want on your substrate. This is step three of boundary setting, being prepared to say "No".

5. **FIND** a large element(s) you really love to symbolize you "knowing what you know" and setting a clear boundary. Glue it wherever you wish on your substrate. This is step four of boundary setting, where you keep the focus on your needs and see yourself as able to enforce the boundary. You are your own best caretaker, to be depended upon to set boundaries to keep you safe and healthy. You are showing up and taking care of yourself!

6. **FIND** an element(s) to symbolize the consequences for a person if they overstep your boundary and glue it anywhere you desire on the collage. In the case of a family member, for example, who frequently wants to talk about hurt old times, the consequence could be a reduction in time spent with them if the boundary is broken. This is step five of boundary setting, knowing the consequences and being willing to enforce the boundary with those who behave distrustfully.

7. **MAKE** a photo with your camera or phone of the collage, to keep with you for when you need a reminder of how to set a boundary. Place the collage in a place in your home that you can see often. Consider making a photo copy and place it with you at work.

8. **CONTINUE** to practice the steps. If you find your "No" not being respected or boundaries overlooked, return to these steps and use them.

9. **WRITE** or use collage elements to create a supportive thought to encapsulate this experience. Put this anywhere on your collage. For example: "I can set boundaries and work to find people who will honor my boundaries when I need to say "No".

10. **PLACE** a triangle-shaped element anywhere on the substrate to symbolize your personal strength and to offer a comforting and familiar ritual.

11. **EXTEND** your transformation by completing the TAKEAWAY ACTION TOOLS (page 225).

12. **RETURN** here after completing the Takeaway Action Tools to read the ending quote below.

"We can say what we need to say. We can gently, but assertively, speak our mind.
We do not need to be judgmental, tactless, blaming or cruel
when we speak our truths.

— Melody Beattie

Susan Lerner, *Flamingo Road*, 2018, Analog Collage, Doug + Laurie Kanyer Art Collection

AVOIDING DRAMA - TURNING TOWARD EMPOWERMENT

**A collage-making exercise-experience to practice combatting drama
and triangulation that leads to emotional pain.**

*"So many people prefer to live in drama because it is comfortable. It's like someone staying
in a bad marriage or relationship; it's actually easier to stay because they know what to
expect every day, versus leaving and not knowing what to expect."* — Ellen DeGeneres

INFORMATION TO THINK ABOUT AND CONSIDER

The Need for Recognition to Stay Emotionally Balanced

One of the contributing factors to "drama" is the natural human need to be seen and valued by others. It is a driving force. In order to stay alive, especially on an emotional level, one needs to interact with others. There is a near-constant challenge about how to receive the units of recognition to keep one feeling alive and of value. If you do not get positive recognition from others, you may choose alternatives, which are often negative units of recognition, like drama. Consider that no one wants to be a zero, to not matter or to be nothing to others. If one does not have an established pattern or natural flow of healthy human interaction, one can be tempted to start or take part in drama.

As a reference point consider the movie *Cast Away*, featuring actor Tom Hanks. Hanks' character is alone on a deserted island. His mental status is eroding due to lack of human contact or recognition from another soul. One day he has an accident on the island. His hand was badly injured. He grabs a volleyball that has washed ashore, and the blood from his hand makes an imprinted pattern on the ball that resembles a human face. The blood dries and the shape of the face remains. From that point on he has a running conversation with the ball, which he names Wilson. The reflective relationship between Hanks and Wilson kept him literally alive, functioning mentally and emotionally.

Wilson was essentially giving him units of recognition—the connection he needed. A pivotal scene is the heartbreak of Hanks' character when Wilson, his best friend, is lost at sea. He needed the imprinted face on the surface of the volleyball to provide him a reflection of who he was, to keep him emotionally alive.

Models Explaining and Illustrating Drama Patterns

There are three social behavioral models that use the triangle to depict ways people aim to get units of recognition. Two of them, "Drama Triangle" and "Triangulation", usually end in emotional pain and human suffering. The third, called the "The Empowerment Triangle", offers positive recognition leading to well-being and constructive problem solving. I maintain that in many cases the pain that comes from interpersonal drama can be avoided. Knowing about these models may help you to turn from the pain caused by engaging in drama.

Drama Triangle

Dr. Steven Karpman designed the model called the Drama Triangle (Karpman, 2020). The Drama Triangle illustrates how some of the human communication patterns used to receive units of recognition can cause pain and suffering. The Drama Triangle uses the three points of the triangle to demonstrate unhelpful patterns of communication. Karpman chose the term "Drama" as a metaphor to show the roles people use—like actors in a play—that can cause pain and hardship for one another. The three roles are Victim (poor me), Rescuer (let me help you), and Persecutor (it's your fault).

Occasionally, whether inside or outside of their conscious awareness, people may step onto the Drama Triangle to get their need for recognition met. Their hope is netting an outcome of belonging and attention. People often do this because they are operating from a prescribed role projected upon them by others. It might be a role connected to their birth order, gender, or labels from others. One may adopt a role prescribed by others in order to meet their need for recognition, either positive or negative.

Karpman believes the Drama Triangle begins when someone plays the role of victim or persecutor. Eventually, another person is invited to join in the conflict and drama, and that person assumes the role of a rescuer. The actors in the Drama Triangle move and change positions, navigating between the roles as the drama unfolds. It is as if they are playing a dangerous interpersonal game to gain recognition, power and control. The result is pain, and the pattern of interpersonal interaction results in suffering.

Triangulation

Murray Bowen invented a related social behavioral theory in 1966 for the purpose of explaining the actions of people. He called this theory Triangulation. This concept infers that when two people are experiencing some upset or strain between them, in order to manage the conflict and in an attempt to decrease the intensity, they will invite another person to get involved. The process of getting people to join onto the triangle is called Triangulation, and it is a form of manipulation (Jones, 2020).

What Triangulation does is it moves the focus away from the two original people who have the challenge. Triangulation spreads out the depth and weight of stress between the original two and attempts to involve another. While the third person had no role initially, they are invited into the tension so that the stress can be deferred onto them.

Unfortunately, the one invited into the conflict can become entangled with the others, and drama can increase for all. The original problem between the two often does not get amended when Triangulation is used. It is a no-win situation, resulting in confusion and chaos.

A Challenge and Opportunity

My purpose in sharing these models is to describe negative ways to get units of recognition. I aim to highlight these trends so that you can be aware when you or others are tempted to use them during human interaction. The reason we ask you to make a triangle is to highlight noble human traits and their use in every exercise-experience. This is to remind you to work toward higher living, gathering units of recognition from positive social interactions. You can choose to practice using the honorable historical meanings of the Triangle to avoid painful drama and triangulation.

An Alternative: The Empowerment Triangle

There is a wonderful alternative to the Drama Triangle and Triangulation, and it's called The Empowerment Triangle. The Drama Triangle and Triangulation can be described as an anxiety driven, problem focused, and disabling way to function. In contrast, The Empowerment Triangle was developed in 1990 by Acey Choy and invites people to take on healthy roles that lead to solving challenges. It taps into strengths, talents and passions. This is a positive-solutions, strengths-based social model of human interaction (Choy, 1990).

In The Empowerment Triangle, the Victim (from the Drama Triangle) becomes the Creator, a person who is taking responsibility for the situation in which they find themselves. They actively seek answers and choose to be vulnerable with others about the areas of growth they need related to a concern or problem. This offers victims the new role of challenge-solver and to become a creator of a new possibility, one who addresses issues proactively and positively.

The Persecutor (from the Drama Triangle) becomes the Challenger, a person who is offering an assertive, constructive, direct, yet kind, challenge to the Creator. The Challenger moves from the harsh and critical stance of the Persecutor to a person who is firm about the significance of the behavior or situation, while at the same time seeing the issue(s) as an opportunity to grow and solve challenges. This leads to greater productivity and also tends to meet the needs of the Creator. In this role, challenges are addressed constructively and with balance, rather than aggression and lack of kindness. They seek to bring light to the consequences of actions in order to motivate the Creator.

The Rescuer (from the Drama Triangle) becomes the Coach, a person who is offering support through listening and asking clarifying questions. The Coach offers solutions and information to the Creator in an effort to expand everyone's self-awareness. The Coach holds the belief that the Creator can solve challenges, can make a plan with new information, and can make positive choices to improve their life. The Coach will offer thoughtful instruction, helpful information, and encouragement.

In summary, The Empowerment Triangle expects people to function in healthy ways to uplift and build on strengths. Conversely, the Drama Triangle tends to produce actions that seek recognition and attention through negative exchanges and hurtful intentions.

Authority to Choose Empowerment

When facing an invitation to enter into drama, you have the power to choose to rise above and invest in a higher level of functioning by using The Empowerment Triangle. In doing so you will impose upon yourself an alternative to drama, and you will be able to adopt and operate with higher character traits. In doing so you will have the power and strength to oppose any invitation to jump onto the Drama Triangle that others unfortunately may decide to join.

The exercise-experience to follow will help you to be able to see with greater acuity the games people play to get units of recognition. You will be able to observe how drama and triangulation unfolds. You will be able to choose to send out the transformational energy of love, respect and honor toward them, rather than enter into Triangulation or jump onto the Drama Triangle. You will gain and have possession of deeper wisdom, to avoid conflict in the present day and transform your emotions and life experiences from the past.

CONTENT ROUND UP to REVIEW—RECALL—REMEMBER

- The Drama Triangle is a pattern of human interaction where people play the roles of Victim (poor me), Rescuer (let me help you), and Persecutor (it's your fault) in order to get their needs met.

- The Drama Triangle is a certain recipe for emotional pain and suffering among people.

- People use Triangulation to decrease upset or strain between them by inviting another person to get involved in their drama.

- An alternative to drama and triangulation is The Empowerment Triangle.

- The Empowerment Triangle invites people to take on healthy roles that lead to solving problems. It taps into strengths, talents and passions. This is a positive-solutions, strengths-based social model of human interaction

GUIDED COLLAGE EXPERIENCE–MAKE A COLLAGE

1. **GATHER** materials (glue, magazines, books and a substrate to make your collage on). Cut a small, triangle-shaped element from your source material. Place it anywhere on the substrate to provide a personal symbol of power and strength and to offer a comforting, familiar ritual to begin.

2. **CUT** from your source material two triangles that are the same size and are large enough to nearly fill the substrate. Glue one of the triangles on to the substrate with the point oriented toward the top of the page. Glue the other triangle onto the substrate with a point oriented toward the bottom of the page. Find a letter E and glue it on the top of the top triangle, directly in the middle. Find a letter D and glue it on the top of the bottom triangle, directly in the middle. Notice the top triangle is facing upward. This symbolizes the positive, higher-living principles of the Empowerment Triangle. Notice that the bottom triangle is pointing downward. This symbolizes the negative, destructive process of the Drama Triangle.

3. **FIND** elements to symbolize each of the persons as described below. Place and glue each element in the following spots.

   A) **Creator** - Top triangle, near the top point

   B) **Coach** - Top triangle, near the right-side point

   C) **Challenger** - Top triangle, near the left-side point

   D) **Victim** - Bottom triangle, near the bottom point

   E) **Rescuer** - Bottom triangle, near the right-side point

   F) **Persecutor** - Bottom triangle, near the left-side point

4. **FIND** elements to symbolize the script or driving statement of each person listed below. Cut out and place the elements next to them.

   A) **Creator** - Top triangle, near the top point - "I can do it!" (I have skills, I can express a need for help and can solve problems.)

   B) **Coach** - Top triangle, near the right-side point – "How will you do it?" (What skills can I teach you or information do you need from me?)

   C) **Challenger** - Top triangle, near the left-side point – "You can do it!" (Call for the person to move to action and take responsibility.)

   D) **Victim** - Bottom triangle, near the bottom point - "Poor me!" (I have no power.)

   E) **Rescuer** - Bottom triangle, near the right-side point - "Poor you!" (I hope you need me to take care of you or relieve your discomfort, so I can feel important.)

   F) **Persecutor** - Bottom triangle near the left-side point - "Shame on you." (Aims to tear the person down and blame.)

5. **SELECT** three elements to symbolize the three people. Using them like players in a board game, come up with a scenario from your past involving the three people. Place the element(s) on the Drama Triangle first. To yourself say what you imagine each person might say to one another in this scenario. Once completed, move the elements to The Empowerment Triangle, and using your scenario say to yourself what you imagine each person might say to one another. Notice the difference. Challenge yourself to take this new learning into your world. When faced with a temptation to start a Drama Triangle yourself or when others invite you into a drama, pause and review this material to avoid getting negative units of recognition.

6. **WRITE** or use collage elements to create a supportive thought to encapsulate this experience. Put this anywhere on your collage. Example: "I can practice becoming aware of the use of the Drama Triangle and seek to move to use The Empowerment Triangle."

7. **PLACE** a triangle-shaped element anywhere on the substrate to symbolize your personal strength and to offer a comforting and familiar ritual.

8. **EXTEND** your transformation by completing the TAKEAWAY ACTION TOOLS (page 225).

9. **RETURN** here after completing the Takeaway Action Tools to read the ending quote below.

"You can free yourself from emotional drama by uncovering the lies you believe in."

— Miguel Angel Ruiz

Celia Crane, *Every Cloud Has A Silver Lining For A Clever Tailor*, 2022, Analog Collage, Doug + Laurie Kanyer Art Collection

Julie Liger-Belair, *Untitled*, 2023, Analog Collage, Doug + Laurie Kanyer Art Collection

APOLOGIZING - ASKING FOR FORGIVENESS

A collage-making exercise-experience to learn the process of making an apology.

"An apology is the superglue of life! It can repair just about anything!!"
— Lynn Johnston

"Never ruin an apology with an excuse."
— Benjamin Franklin

INFORMATION TO THINK ABOUT AND CONSIDER

Have you ever made an error or a mistake? Have you hurt someone or done something you regret? Join the crowd. Ask yourself, did anyone teach you the appropriate steps to apologize? Would it not be great to have an amend-making pattern to follow when you need to ask forgiveness?

Harriett Lerner Ph.D. wrote a groundbreaking book titled *Dance of Anger* that has sold over 3 million copies. She has studied forgiveness and apologizing. She has created a sound, balanced, step-by-step pattern you can use when you need to say you are sorry.

Dr. Lerner's accomplishments and contributions are significant. Her most recent work on apologizing and forgiveness is compelling and is entitled *Why Won't You Apologize?* I endorse it enthusiastically. For this exercise-experience I summarize her steps and thoughts in a very basic way. She has discovered and invented a phenomenal method to help people on the topic of forgiveness and the art of apologizing.

An Apology Needs to Be Heartfelt

In order for forgiveness to take place the person making the apology must do so with a heartfelt approach. The relationship between the parties must be one in which it is safe to make apologies, and in doing so it is understood to be a function of personal growth and gaining skills in life. Says Lerner, "It is understood that people being human will make mistakes and that people will get hurt and will hurt one another (Lerner, 2017)."

I Am Sorry

Part of being in a relationship involves using the phrase "I am sorry" in a heartfelt manner. For an apology to be accepted it needs to be delivered in a thoughtful and powerful way. A poor apology will cause compromise in the relationship and may cause the relationship to deteriorate (Lerner, 2017).

Apologies are Gifts and Can Enhance Relationships

Lerner shares, "A quality apology is a gift to the offended party, as it releases the person from the tendency toward obsessiveness over the hurt. It allows them to feel safe in the relationship, and that the person who apologized cares about their feelings and emotional safety. It validates the hurt party's sense of reality (Lerner, 2017)."

Lerner stresses that, for the person who is apologizing, "It is a gift to them as well, as they no longer have to control what happened. It does expose them to criticism and it takes away their 'edge', shows they are not perfect, however, thus increases one's maturity and self-worth!" It is a gift to a relationship by healing the disconnection and offers a chance for further conversations (Lerner, 2017).

Essential Steps to Making an Apology

Lerner has developed 9 Essential Ingredients to make a heartfelt apology. They can be found in her book (Lerner, 2017). Please get a copy of *Why Won't You Apologize?* for a deeper investigation on this critical life skill. The ingredients are remarkable, profound and are summarized here:

- **Step One:** A true apology does not include the word BUT added to the apology. One must not say "I am sorry but, I was under great stress" or "I am sorry, but you were being a jerk." Add no justifications or excuses for your mistake. The "but" will cancel out the apology. If you call out the other person's behavior, it is not an apology.

- **Step Two:** A true apology keeps the focus on your actions and not the other person's response and feelings. Do not formulate a defense or excuse in your apology. Be clear what you said or did.

- **Step Three:** A true apology makes an offer of restitution that fits the situation. Replacement of an accidentally broken item for example.

- **Step Four:** A true apology does not "over-do" or "under-do" itself. One type of excessive apology is to feel guilty and responsible about everything, which disrupts the flow of conversations. The other type is where one is so full of one's own pain that you over-apologize to a degree others now feel bad. In this example you are hijacking the attention. Do not "over-do" it as it shifts the focus to you. This is no longer an apology, rather it is now an invitation to take care of your pain.

- **Step Five:** A true apology does not get caught up with who is more in the wrong or who started the discourse. You apologize first for your part of the problem, even if the person can't see their part and regardless of what "percent" you were responsible. It is a recipe for relationship failure to wait for the other person to apologize first. We are trying to learn in relationships about practicing being your best self.

- **Step Six:** A true apology works hard to avoid repeating the same offense over and over. It nullifies the apology if you don't change.

- **Step Seven:** Do not silence the person who has been offended. They may bring the offense up and it is important to just listen. Do not use the apology to silence a person or to get out of a situation. Just because you apologized does not mean they are not still hurt.

- **Step Eight:** A true apology should not be offered to make you feel better if it risks making the hurt party feel worse. Not all apologies are welcomed. It is not an apology if it simply soothes or reduces your guilt quotient. If someone says no contact, that means no contact.

- **Step Nine:** A true apology does not ask the hurt party to do anything for you, not even to forgive. It is not a tool to get things done in the relationship, to get back to normal for example.

CONTENT ROUND UP to REVIEW—RECALL—REMEMBER

- There are appropriate and researched steps to making an apology.

- Apologies are gifts and opportunities to help relationships.

Laurie Kanyer, *A Pit Stop in Joshua Tree*, 2022, Analog Collage, Doug + Laurie Kanyer Art Collection

GUIDED COLLAGE EXPERIENCE–MAKE A COLLAGE

1. **GATHER** materials (glue, magazines, books and a substrate to make your collage on). Cut a small, triangle-shaped element from your source material. Place it anywhere on the substrate to provide a personal symbol of power and strength and to offer a comforting, familiar ritual to begin.

2. **THINK** about an apology you need to make to someone with whom you have a relationship, someone you care about. Find an element in your source materials to represent your error or mistake. Cut it out and glue it on your substrate.

3. **RETURN** to your source material and find the word BUT. Cut it out and glue it somewhere on your substrate. Take your markers and mark the word BUT out, or cover it with a triangle or other element. Keep in mind that making an apology and then using the word BUT to explain why you acted a certain way is not a true apology.

4. **FIND** elements to show each of the actions you need to apologize for. Cut them out and glue them on the substrate. Remember that a true apology keeps the focus on your actions and not the other person's response and feelings. Do not formulate your defense or use an excuse in your apology. Be clear what you said or did.

5. **FIND** elements to show what you can do to make restitution for the mistake you made. Cut them out and glue them on your substrate.

6. **FIND** an element to remind you to make the apology without going on excessively, to not overdo it thereby shifting the attention to you. Glue this down on the substrate.

7. **FIND** an element to remind you to apologize first. You know what you did that needs to be apologized for, so focus on your part. Consider finding the word FIRST or ME, and once you find the element, glue it down on the substrate.

8. **FIND** an element(s) to remind you to avoid making this mistake again. Cut it out and place it on the substrate.

9. **FIND** an element to remind you that the person you hurt does not have to do anything for you, that this is not about making you feel better. Cut it out and glue it down on the substrate. Remember that, while this may be difficult, the person is not required to even forgive you.

   In the event that the person you need to apologize to is unwilling to hear your apology, you must avoid the impulse to vigorously push it, as it may evolve into your need to get something off your chest. The unwillingness may mean that they do not want to work on the relationship at this time. Remember, not all apologies are welcome, and they are certainly not offered just to make you feel better. If the person to whom you want to apologize has blocked you or does not want to see you in person, you must accept this and respect the boundary. If this is the circumstance, go to your source material and find an element to remind you to NOT try to apologize, cut it out and glue it on the substrate.

10. **PLAN** to make this apology. On the back of the substrate write your apology. Start by writing down what you are sorry for (fill in the blank for the offending action), and say "I would like to make restitution for (fill in the blank)". Further write a statement about whether it would be acceptable or is there another way to make restitution? Then pause, stop there, and be prepared to listen. As Lerner says, "Listen with the same passion we want to be heard."

11. **WRITE** or use collage elements to create a supportive thought to encapsulate this experience. Put this anywhere on your collage. For example: "I make an apology in a productive way to support my relationships".

12. **PLACE** a triangle-shaped element anywhere on the substrate to symbolize your personal strength and to offer a comforting and familiar ritual.

13. **EXTEND** your transformation by completing the TAKEAWAY ACTION TOOLS (page 225).

14. **RETURN** here after completing the Takeaway Action Tools to read the ending quotes below.

"If an apology is followed by an excuse or a reason, it means they are going to commit the same mistake again they just apologized for."

— Amit Kalantri

"Apologizing does not always mean you're wrong and the other person is right. It just means you value your relationship more than your ego."

— Mark Matthews

Marcus Dawson, *A Field of His Dreams*, 2022, Analog Collage, Courtesy of the Artist

Torea Frey, *You Can*, 2022, Analog Collage, Doug + Laurie Kanyer Art Collection

TAKEAWAY ACTION TOOLS

Once you have finished each exercise-experience you will be directed here to use these Takeaway Action Tools. The Tools will deepen and expand the benefits of the collage-making exercise-experience you just completed. As with all of this material, choose the Tools that fit best for you.

Consider experimenting, exploring, using all of the Tools, or just a few. The Tools can be useful in a multitude of life situations, including those that are well beyond the specific topic being addressed in the exercise-experience.

When coupled with the information and exercise-experience you have just read and finished, the Tools will offer you a way to further pace your emotions and feelings. Using the Tools can open channels for clarity in thinking about the topics. They will deepen your understanding and widen your mental horizons. I used these Tools with my students and clients for decades. After completing each Tool, continue on by adding elements to your collage to symbolize what you've experienced.

Some Takeaway Action Tools are Present Moment Activities

Many of the Tools listed below are Present Moment Activities (PMAs). A PMA is an activity that helps to ground and balance you in the "here and now" when faced with challenges or the demands of life. The collage-making process in itself is a PMA. PMAs help you to stay in the present moment rather than moving toward rumination, future-tripping or anxiety. By definition, future-tripping is worrying about something that has not yet happened, or of which there is no evidence it will ever happen.

PMAs can reduce extreme emotions, feelings and thoughts by offering one perspective and additional insight. They provide a way to focus the mind, and in the process provide space and perspective. In this space one is able to have a new awareness or moments of calm to consider a "something". They are identified in the list below with (PMA) next to each Tool that is a Present Moment Activity.

TAKEAWAY ACTION TOOLS to Practice and Use Following an Exercise-Experience

▶ **REFLECT and PONDER** (PMA) - Take as much time as you need to reflect upon your collage and the exercise-experience. Let the collage you created be a mirror to any new learnings, transformations or inspirations. You may also have identified areas of growth to explore in the future. Allow the collage image to magnify any new awareness and understanding you are now experiencing. Remember to 'reflect' rather than 'ruminate' (see page 7 for more on the benefits of reflection versus rumination). Add collage element(s) to symbolize your reflection and glue it anywhere on your collage.

▶ **INQUIRE** - Ask of yourself, in a gentle, kind, and respectful manner, the following questions. The questions offered here give you a way to have a deeper conversation with yourself. They have a way of clarifying and challenging your thoughts, feelings, and beliefs. They will contribute to new choices and decisions you have made while doing the exercise-experience. Answer them all, or choose just a few:

> ***What are you feeling?*** What new and important feelings have you noticed? Were there shifts or changes in how you feel? If so, how?

> ***What are you thinking or what did you learn?*** What new ideas or thoughts do you have? What new information do you want to remember? What other information might you need to research?

> ***What are you deciding?*** Did you change your mind about something? Do you have new and revised impressions? If so, what are they?

What is missing? As you inquire of yourself, are there things you left off your collage? If so, why? Feel free to add them now or in the future.

What are you celebrating? What excites you and causes you to feel joy (or other pleasurable feelings) about this material? What are you proud of and how have you grown?

Is there a new promise you would like to make? Are there any new promises you would like to begin to make to yourself, to the best of your ability? What things do you want to adjust?

Add collage element(s) to symbolize your answers and glue them anywhere that fits for you.

▶ **MEDITATE** (PMA) **and/or Use a Somatic Experience** (PMA): Read the following Options, with their inherent instructions, and then proceed. This tool offers you a guided self-meditation with some calming, somatic physical exercises. The intent is to engage your mind, body and heart. It is offered so you can absorb the exercise-experience mentally and physically, with transformation and additional self-knowledge. Add element(s) to your collage to symbolize your time of meditation and using a Somatic Experience.

Option One
Choose an inspirational word. Place your right hand on your left shoulder and your left hand on your right shoulder. Close your eyes, if you wish. Take a few deep breaths, in through the nose then out through the mouth. Continue by breathing normally, repeating the inspirational word to yourself. Tap your shoulders gently with your fingertips and continue to repeat your inspirational word(s) to yourself. Notice your energy shifting. Continue for a period of time, perhaps three to five minutes. Open your eyes when ready (Levine, 2005).

Option Two
Choose an inspirational word. Place your right hand in the middle of your left armpit. Place your left hand on your right shoulder. Close your eyes, if you wish. Take a few deep breaths, in through the nose then out through the mouth. Continue by breathing normally, repeating your inspirational word to yourself. Notice your energy shifting. Continue for a period of time, perhaps three to five minutes. Open your eyes when ready (Levine, 2005).

▶ **VISUALIZE** (PMA) - This Tool uses the proven power of positive visualization to crystallize in your mind the exercise-experience and your related transformation. Think of positive visualization as a "mental rehearsal" for the future carried out in the mind. Close your eyes and see, in your mind's eye, you coming closer to knowing and embracing your True Self. See yourself implementing any new skill, information or awareness you learned in the exercise-experience. See yourself achieving your hopes after completing this exercise-experience. Add an element(s) to your collage to symbolize your visualization.

▶ **READ ALOUD** the Supportive Thought you wrote in the exercise-experience (PMA). Using this Tool offers you the opportunity to actually hear your new thoughts audibly. Hearing the Supportive Thought read out loud will engage your mind in a different way than with your eyes. This will help to amplify and magnify your new life impressions with an original supportive thought created by you, for you. Add element(s) to your collage to symbolize your supportive thought having been read aloud and heard.

▶ **CONTEMPLATE** (PMA) the acknowledgment of surprises and miracles you experienced in the exercise-experience. Contemplation offers a chance for your mind to wander and then refocus on an expansive awareness. This helps one crystallize thoughts and have new ideas. As you contemplate, focus on any miracles, surprises or deepening of your spirit and spirituality that came forth. When you contemplate you very often interact with the divine and are able to have awareness that there is more than can be seen on the surface. You may be able to recognize there are things going on behind the scenes that are advocating for goodness and transformation in your life. Add element(s) to your collage to symbolize your time of contemplation.

▶ **THANK and ACKNOWLEDGE YOURSELF** and all of the parts of yourself for the compassion, curiosity, calmness, clarity, creativity, courage, confidence and connectedness you brought to this exercise-experience (Schwartz, 2020). By using this Tool of thanking yourself, you are acknowledging and honoring your effort and hard work. This is a respectful and kind act of deep and intentional appreciation. People too often emphasize the acknowledgments of others and miss the chance to truly appreciate one's own efforts. It is of great value to note your own personal accomplishments, aside from what others notice or don't. It is your opinion of yourself that really matters, and thanking yourself is a way to form a noteworthy opinion of oneself. Add element(s) to your collage to symbolize thanking yourself.

▶ **COMMIT to TRANSFORMATION OVER TIME** by making a personal invitation to yourself to provide space to transform and grow in the future. Choose a collage element to signal this invitation and to note any time you witness new transformations. Add an element(s) to your collage to symbolize this invitation.

▶ **COMMIT to SELF-CARE** as a way to show love and tender consideration to yourself. Taking care of oneself by tending to your body, mind and soul assures you are fit and able to perform the task of daily life. Miraculously, as you do so you will be able to witness yourself caring for yourself. The act of tending to oneself and witnessing it allows for one to in some ways psychologically parent oneself. This is an astonishing fact. Tending to yourself in the mirror allows you to witness and see yourself, to love and appreciate your very being. Witnessing yourself doing an exercise-experience shows that you care about your emotional well-being. Add an element(s) to your collage to symbolize this commitment to caring for your mind, body and soul.

▶ **NAME and DEFINE** this entire experience for yourself in your own words. I gave this exercise-experience a unique title; now it is your opportunity to name and define it for yourself. Design and choose a name for this entire experience. This is a special designation and new memory imprint of your very own. Add an element(s) to your collage to symbolize the name or label you choose.

▶ **SHARE with OTHERS** your experience and collage, in your own timing and your own space. Doing so will deepen your awareness and transformation. It will also strengthen bonds with others, and offer them an opportunity to grow and learn. When you see others hearing your story and viewing your collage it helps you to decrease isolation. As others are offered the opportunity to witness your experience, they will have an opportunity to express compassion, empathy and encouragement to you. They may also have a chance to share a similar story, and you will get to know them better. Add element(s) to your collage to symbolize having shared with someone.

▶ **COMPLETE by RETURNING** to the exercise-experience you were working on and read the ending quote. You have now come to the completion of this exercise-experience and you have a record of this journey on your collage.

Laurie Kanyer, *Finding Peace*, 2022, Collage, Doug + Laurie Kanyer Art Collection

EPILOGUE

As long as there have been humans, there have been emotions. People have been confused and confounded by emotions for that long. Thankfully, today we are at a place in our evolution where we have more insight, information and knowledge of the processes of emotions.

Having read this book not only have you gained key information on emotions, but used collage as a way to experience new information on feelings. You now have keen insight as to how using paper, pieced together in a collage, will assist in expanding your knowledge, transforming your emotions, understanding yourself and others better.

What you have read in *Collage Care: The Method* is information I shared about emotions in my counseling practice and in the classroom. Information and collage was used to expand their knowledge and improve their well-being.

I hope you will continue to use collage as a tool to sort out your emotional experiences and life events. I know if you use it as a regular life practice you will gain deeper understanding of yourself and others.

If you discover additional ways collage helps please let me know. This will contribute to the budding research on the value of collage as a somatic tool.

"Given the vagaries of memory, life itself is a collage.
Perhaps that is part of the reason why putting
disparate images together and making
something new of them can be
so involving, meaningful
and therapeutic."

—Dr. Rachel Morris

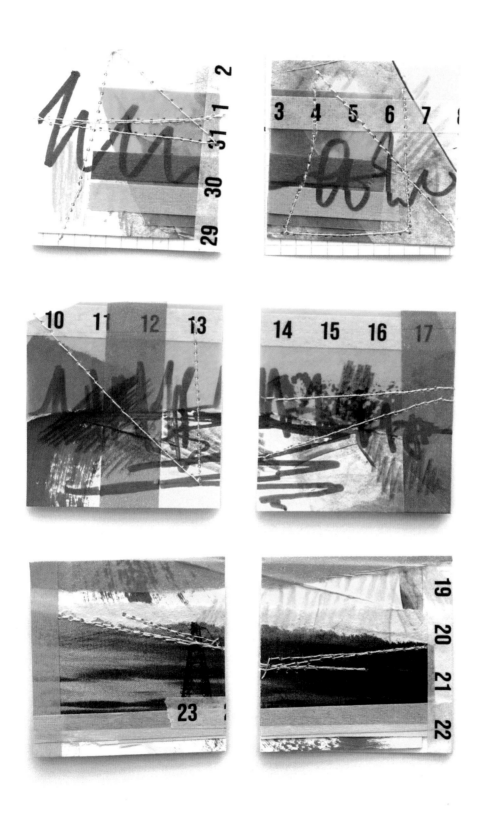

Eve Baldry, *Fleeting Moments*, 2020, Mini Collage, Doug + Laurie Kanyer Art Collection

APPENDIX

Vocabulary of Feeling Words

abandoned	cheerless	done for	hatred	miffed	shaky
abhor	cheery	doubtful	heartbroken	miserable	shocked
abused	comforted	doubting	helpful	misunderstood	sickened
accepted	compassionate	down	helpless	moved	silly
adored	competent	downcast	hesitant	mystified	skeptical
affectionate	concerned	downhearted	hindered	needed	slandered
affronted	confident	downtrodden	hopeless	negative	sleepy
afraid	conflicted	dread	horrible	neglected	slighted
aggravated	confused	dreadful	humble	nervous	snubbed
aghast	constrained	drowsy	humiliated	numb	spiteful
agitated	contented	ecstatic	hurt	obsessive	startled
alarmed	covetous	edgy	hypocritical	obsolete	stifled
alienated	craving	elevated	ignored	offended	surprised
alone	critical	embarrassed	ill at ease	on cloud nine	suspicious
amazed	criticized	empty	impaired	on edge	swamped
amused	cross	enraged	impatient	oppressed	tearful
angry	crushed	enthusiastic	impotent	optimistic	tense
anguish	cunning	envious	imprisoned	ostracized	terrified
annoyed	cynical	euphoric	in the dumps	outraged	threatened
anxious	debased	excited	inadequate	overlooked	thrilled
appreciated	defeated	excluded	incapable	overwhelmed	tired
apprehensive	deficient	exhausted	incensed	panicky	tormented
ardent	deflated	exhilarated	incompetent	passionate	transcendent
ashamed	dejected	exposed	ineffective	perplexed	triumphant
aspire	delirious	exultant	inept	pleased	troubled
astonished	demoralized	fantastic	inferior	powerless	trusting
at ease	depreciated	fearful	inflamed	pressured	uncertain
awful	depressed	fervent	infuriated	proud	uncomfortable
awkward	deserted	fine	insecure	put down	uncooperative
baffled	desolate	fit	insignificant	puzzled	underrated
battered	despair	fond of	intimidated	reborn	understood
beat	desperate	foolish	irritated	rebuked	uneasy
befuddled	despised	forlorn	jazzed	regret	unhappy
belittled	despondent	forsaken	jealous	rejected	unimportant
belligerent	disappointed	frantic	jilted	rejuvenated	unloved
below par	disbelieving	friendless	jittery	relaxed	unnoticed
bemused	disconcerted	friendly	jovial	relieved	unqualified
bewildered	discontent	frightened	joyful	repulsed	unsatisfied
bitter	discouraged	frustrated	jumpy	resented	unsure
blamed	discredited	fuming	laughed at	resentful	upset
blissful	disenchanted	furious	left out	restless	uptight
blue	disgraced	futile	liable	revengeful	want
bored	disheartened	glad	liked	ridiculed	wanted
bothered	disinterested	gloomy	loathe	ridiculous	warmhearted
bottled up	disliked	glorious	lonely	rotten	warped
branded	dismal	good	lonesome	run down	wary
broken	disparate	grand	longing	sad	whipped
bushed	dispassionate	grateful	lost	saddened	worn-out
calm	displeased	gratified	lousy	satisfied	worried
capable	disregarded	great	loved	scared	worshipped
cared for	dissatisfied	grieved	loving	self-conscious	worthless
cast off	distressed	guilty	low	selfish	worthy
cheapened	distrustful	happy	mad	sensual	wounded
cheerful	disturbed	hated	maligned	serene	zoned

APPENDIX

Collage Care GEMS: How Collage-Making Helps, Heals and Transforms

The following list contains over 125 ways, called Gems, that document how collage helps, heals and transforms emotions, feelings and life experiences. The Gems are empirical evidence of the value of collage-making, which I have discovered over many decades. I have used collage-making with my clients and students in clinical settings and also in the classroom.

My first book on this topic, *Collage Care: Transforming Emotions and Life Experiences with Collage*, documents the Gems with deeper, more detailed, explanations. For our purposes here, we offer a simplified version of each of the Gems, in a list format, for quick reference.

For a more complete explanation of each Gem you can purchase the E-Book version of *Collage Care: Transforming Emotions and Life Experiences with Collage* at www.KanyerArtCollection.com, or you may purchase the hard copy book at amazon.com.

Here are the GEMS:

Collage-making is nearly free and is available to everyone.

Collage-making eases expression by offering ready-made images to use as symbols of life experiences.

Collage-making offers permission to feel and express emotions.

Collage-making allows you to be present for yourself.

Collage-making helps to pace stress hormones through the use of small muscles.

Collage-making counsels and advises.

Collage-making familiarizes you with your internal dialogue.

Collage-making accesses the subconscious—reveals your hidden language.

Collage-making communicates feelings quickly and accurately.

Collage-making removes interpretation.

Collage-making offers access to your True self.

Collage-making is a form of meditation.

Collage-making helps to illustrate the song in your heart.

Collage-making facilitates the process of transforming feelings.

Collage-making helps work through mental blocks and emotional loops.

Collage-making confronts and shields one from shame.

Collage-making allows observation of the physical sensations connected to emotions.

Collage-making allows for the substrate to be a container to hold one's emotions so one does not have to hold them.

Collage-making decreases physical pain.

Collage-making expands one's vocabulary of feeling words.

Collage-making validates and acknowledges feelings.

Collage-making offers visual cues on emotions, feelings, memories, and beliefs.

Collage-making confirms and affirms intuition.

Collage-making promotes letting go.

Collage-making safely releases angry feelings.

Collage-making offers a focal point.

Collage-making allows for dramatic expression.

Collage-making offers distance from one's emotions.

Collage-making reveals the exact problem needing to be addressed.

Collage-making affirms your ability to solve problems.

Collage-making inspires new ideas and offers miraculous, endless possibilities.

Collage-making shows the complexity of a problem.

Collage-making expands options and motivates one to keep looking for solutions.

Collage-making can tackle a number of challenges at the same time.

Collage-making helps one to make decisions and commit.

Collage-making supports the Three Day Rule.

Collage-making allows for mess-making.

Collage-making practices the art-of-flow to ease stress.

Collage-making shows what is under the surface.

Collage-making exercises the various areas of the brain.

Collage-making releases positive emotional hormones.

Collage-making releases pressure by emptying your brain.

Collage-making calms the body.

Collage-making offers a needed escape.

Collage-making investigates the harmful effects of advertising.

Collage-making uses humor to release emotional tensions.

Collage-making uses potent words with some distance.

Collage-making invites a playful spirit.

Collage-making keeps one from feeling overwhelmed.

Collage-making encourages change and life improvement.

Collage-making deepens self-awareness.

Collage-making considers inherited stories.

Collage-making dissolves one's defenses.

Collage-making reduces the potency of strong personality traits.

Collage-making shows one's unique genius.

Collage-making helps to examine and confront self-talk.

Collage-making discovers and documents one's true value.

Collage-making confronts social conditioning, peer pressure, and social media.

Collage-making documents a miracle.

Collage-making offers profound bliss.

Collage-making uses one's preferred color to get a point across.

Collage-making explores relationships with materials and connections to things.

Collage-making magnifies a promise and a commitment.

Collage-making shows renewal.

Collage-making builds a legacy.

Collage-making shows one's history.

Collage-making can be a private diary.

Collage-making marks important milestones.

Collage-making decreases helplessness.

Collage-making inspires hope.

Collage-making demonstrates self-efficacy and mastery.

Collage-making highlights the value of gluing and repairing.

Collage-making allows you to be your own Superhero.

Collage-making improves self-esteem.

Collage-making offers a chance to evaluate life.

Collage-making addresses and minimizes drama.

Collage-making creates opportunities for leadership.

Collage-making offers a way to plan to reconfigure life.

Collage-making gives one something-to-do when you feel like nothing can be done.

Collage-making helps you to learn and practice skills.

Collage-making shows the value of small steps.

Collage-making explores memories and identity.

Collage-making allows for mindful reflection of memories.

Collage-making offers insight to decades past.

Collage-making records a dream.

Collage-making discovers personal truths.

Collage-making illustrates bonds.

Collage-making evaluates relationships.

Collage-making sets boundaries.

Collage-making challenges mind-reading.

Collage-making challenges all-or-nothing thinking.

Collage-making highlights the value of layers.

Collage-making exposes what is behind-the-scenes.

Collage-making addresses thoughts of persecution.

Collage-making depicts a cumulative effect of life.

Collage-making confirms what is true.

Collage-making helps one to confront bullies and oppressors.

Collage-making uses one's first language, the language of sight.

Collage-making uses sight to ensure accurate understanding.

Collage-making fosters a universally understood language.

Collage-making plans for important conversations.

Collage-making clarifies beliefs.

Collage-making shows one's point of view.

Collage-making reframes and considers others' points of view.

Collage-making allows for a Do-Over.

Collage-making offers a way to plan to make apologies.

Collage-making can document a protest.

Collage-making evokes sublime awe and wonder.

Collage-making inspires beauty.

Collage-making shows the mystery of happenstance.

Collage-making inspires wonder.

Collage-making creates the sacred.

Collage-making shows curious connections in life.

Collage-making liberates and offers beneficial spontaneity.

Collage-making illustrates what is too difficult to speak.

Collage-making illustrates disaster or loss.

Collage-making illustrates pain, which helps others to understand.

Collage-making is confidential.

Collage-making shows you can put things back together.

Collage-making illustrates wholeness and restoration.

Collage-making helps with the impact of grief.

Collage-making proves you are alive when there has been a significant loss.

Collage-making supports the expression of grief.

Collage-making mirrors the experience of loss and grief.

Collage-making helps tell harmful secrets without words.

Collage-making helps one to grow in interdependence and cooperation.

Collage-making humbles you.

Collage-making builds belonging through sharing a project.

Collage-making remembers someone you love.

Collage-making expresses gratitude.

Collage-making offers a way to practice giving.

Collage-making takes part in a cause and makes contributions.

Collage-making tracks one's life dreams and inspires hope to achieve them.

Collage-making visually reminds you of your heart's desires.

Collage-making assists in project planning and goal actualization.

Collage-making decreases isolation.

APPENDIX

Using the word "Challenge" versus the word "Problem"

There are real benefits to using the word "challenge", rather than the word "problem", when faced with a "something" in life (Sheppard, 2022).

A "something", by definition, is a person, place, event, circumstance, or situation that is currently taking place, or took place at some time in the past. The "something" causes one's Emotional Response System (ERS) to be activated and calls for resolution. To resolve a "something" one will need information, skills and tools to resolve.

I advocate avoiding the word "problem" when describing the "something" (the thing you are experiencing as a challenge). The word "problem" has so many negative connotations. To say you "have a problem" indicates ownership, and could implicate one as the source or cause of the "something". In truth many "somethings" are endured and not caused by the person who is experiencing them. Consider that a "something" like a natural disaster, a car accident caused by another, new laws enforced by the government, or the death of a loved one, are all "somethings" that are not initiated by you. All of these "somethings" could be a challenge to you and affect your life.

The definition of the word "have" is to possess, own, or hold. When one says, "I have a problem" it can indicate to yourself and to others that you possess the problem. It literally means that you "own" or "hold" on to it.

The truth is that you are a person who is going through an experience brought on by a "something". You don't want to own, hold or possess a problem. Suggesting you have a problem can also denote a person's character traits, as if this "something" describes you. Far too often, when saying one has a problem, one could over-identify with it; it could in essence become part of you, like a Visigoth invading your being.

"Challenges" on the other hand have qualities to them, as described below, that once resolved enhance one's character and expand one's mastery of life. You might adopt the habit of saying "I am experiencing this challenge (name the challenge)", rather than "I have this problem".

The Benefits of Defining a "Something" as a Challenge versus a Problem (Sheppard, 2022)

Challenges are like a conquest to be engaged in (rather than a problem full of shame and blame).

Challenges provide a way to discover and demonstrate your personal power.

Challenges are something that stand outside of you. They are something that you experience. Problems can become part of your identity, and others can see you as your problem.

Challenges instill a mindset of looking forward as opposed to the deficit mindset associated with problems, which discourage the language of "poor me" or "it's not fair".

Challenges have the sporting parlance of a game or match to be won.

Challenges require getting support and often enlisting a team of others.

Challenges allow for others to give encouragement.

Challenges engage the mind to use creativity.

Challenges require one to use skills.

Challenges require one to gain and practice new skills.

Challenges require a forward mental focus.

Challenges encourage building bridges to get from where one is towards an end point.

Challenges build character and demonstrate integrity.

Challenges have endpoints.

Challenges involve working hard for a sustained time, but it is assumed one will pause and take breaks. Think of a sporting game with quarters and half-times.

Challenges use rules and have expected conduct and behaviors.

Challenges use tools to help resolve them, like using a boat and oars to cross a lake.

Challenges offer you the will to get to the other side. It may not be pretty, but you will come through it.

When a challenge is resolved, one's character is enhanced, wisdom is gained and one possesses new mastery.

One gains in strength having accomplished a challenge.

One gains in status after accomplishing a challenge.

Challenges may bring pain, suffering and hardship, but the effort extended fortifies one rather than defeats. Think of the pressure a diamond goes through.

Challenges invite encouraging self-talk.

Even if one experiences feelings of defeat during a challenge, there is understanding and empathy from others.

Challenges come with an anticipated time of rest once resolution is completed.

When facing challenges, progress is tracked and seen as something one endured and moved through. "Look how far you have come."

Challenges elicit awe and wonder once endured and survived.

Challenges expect one to pivot and be flexible.

Challenges acknowledge the possibility of mystery and the influence of luck.

Challenges can be broken into phases, stages, segments, and parts.

Challenges assume you have strengths.

Challenges seem to make one a better person.

Challenges invite one to adopt an "overcomer" mentality, where one has found one's way through an arduous situation and emerges victorious on the other side.

Challenges are seen as obstacles to overcome.

Challenges invite one to make a plan and make strategies, but allow for and expect revisions.

Challenges do not require one to have all the answers.

Challenges allow and expect one to ask for help.

Challenges offer a chance to exhibit and exert courage.

APPENDIX

Components of a Meaningful Celebration to Mark the Resolution of a Challenge

Whether you resolve a challenge on your own or with others, it is important to pause and make time to celebrate the accomplishment. All over the globe, in a vast array of cultures, there are some typical and meaningful components people use to mark important events.

If you are celebrating a singular accomplishment choose to invite a special someone to take part in a celebration. You don't have to go overboard. Instead choose to have a simple, but meaningful time to celebrate. The value emotionally is remarkable.

Consider using a three-part structure and flow as you celebrate the resolution of a challenge; a beginning middle and an ending. For each part select reflective words that portray honor, recall memories and note accomplishments. Assign roles ahead of time of who will start the event off with a welcoming opening, speak midway, and close the event with significant words. The opening could be a blessing, a poem, a bell being rung, a note or two on the piano or a toast. The middle could consist of songs, sharing of food, and the giving of tokens of appreciation. Midway through there can be a time where people are offered a chance to speak about their experience. When the ending time approaches, gather everyone together for a few closing words of thanks, appreciation for the time spent together and a successful resolution to the challenge.

Choose a special, significant time to gather. If extending an invitation, state the beginning and ending time.

Select meaningful music.

Locate and use special lighting such as lighted candles.

Use unique aromas such as essential oils or a scented candle. Keep in mind some might be allergic, so do inquire first.

Encourage people to wear special clothes. Ask people to dress up for the celebration.

Decorate with simple but special symbols, such as flowers, banners or balloons.

Offer special foods. You might wish to prepare and offer foods traditional to your culture.

Give a small gift for people to come away with to anchor to the experience, something visual to remind them of the time spent overcoming the challenge.

APPENDIX

24-Hour National Hotlines

PHONE

Suicide Prevention Lifeline: 1-800-273-TALK (8255) or contact the Crisis Text Line by texting TALK to 741-741.

Spanish Lifeline: 800-273-TALK (8255) and Press 2 or 888-628-9454.

National Substance Use and Disorder Issues Referral and Treatment Hotline: 1-800-662-HELP (4357)

TEXT OR INSTANT MESSAGING (IM)

Crisis Text Line/Peer Support: Free, 24/7, Confidential. Text the word "HOME" or START" to 741741.(Text "Steve" if you are a student of color and you will be prioritized for getting a counselor who is a POC; some culturally Deaf counselors are available, so if you prefer one, ask if any are available.

Lifeline Crisis Chat: (IM, also 1-800-273-TALK).

Online PEER Support Chat: (LGBTQ, IM, also 1-888-843-4564).

Veterans Crisis Line

Veteran's Live Chat: 1-800-273-TALK (8255) and Press 1 or text to 838255 (global access for American vets).

LGBTQ Youth

The Trevor Lifeline:1-866-488-7386, national 24-hour, confidential suicide hotline.

Trans Lifeline (For Trans people and staffed by Trans people): US 877-565-8860; Canada: 877-330-6366. If you have medical/police/EMT trauma, they do not call 911 without consent. translifeline.org

Domestic Violence Sexual Assault

National Sexual Assault Hotline: 1-800-656-HOPE (1-800-656-4673).

Love is Respect: (National Dating Abuse Helpline) 1-866-331-9474, Text: LOVEIS to 22522.

National Domestic Violence Hotline: (24/7) 800-799-SAFE (7233), Text: START to 88788 FAINN Online Hotline (sexual assault, global access): 800-656-HOPE (4673)

NOTES

Achor, S. (2018). The happiness advantage: how a positive brain fuels success in work and life. Currency.

Ackerman, C. (2021). What are positive and negative emotions? Why we need both? Positive Psychology.com, https://positivepsychology.com/positive-negative-emotions/

Berne, E. (1961). Transactional analysis and psychotherapy. Grove Press.

Bourg Carter, S. (2012). Emotions are contagious—Choose your company wisely. Psychology Today, https://www.psychologytoday.com/us/blog/high-octane-women/201210/emotions-are-contagious-choose-your-company-wisely

Bowen, M. (n.d). Triangles. The Bowen Center for the Study of the Family, Family https://www.thebowencenter.org/triangles

Brackett, M. (2020). Permission to feel. Celadon Books.

Brown, B. (n.d.). https://www.youtube.com/watch?v=TdtabNt4S7E

Burns, D. (1999). The feeling good handbook. Plume.

Cherry, K. (2020, May 15). What is memory, Very Well Mind. https://www.verywellmind.com/what-is-memory-2795006

Choy, A. (1990). The winner's triangle. Transactional Analysis Journal, https://journals.sagepub.com/doi/10.1177/036215379002000105

Clarke, J.I. (1984). We newsletter, volume 5, number 6, Plymouth, MN.

Clarke, J.I. (1995). Personal conversation.

Dahl, S. (2020, Feb. 3). If you can say it you can feel it. Some scents belief we have infinite emotions as long as we can feel them. The Cut, https://www.thecut.com/2020/02/new-theory-of-complex-emotions.html

Dahlhauser, K. (2022, December). Personal conversation.

Dawson, C. (2016). Life beyond shame: rewriting the rules. Balboa Press.

Dorbin, A. (2013, July 16). Your memory isn't what you think. Psychology Today. https://www.psychologytoday.com/us/blog/am-i-right/201307/your-memory-isnt-what-you-think-it-is

Eagleman, D. (2020). Livewired: The inside story of the ever-changing brain. Pantheon.

Eissinger, S. (2019). What is a sterb and why should you care? Sagebrush Coaching Blog, http://www.sagebrushcoaching.com/what-is-a-sterb-and-why-should-you-care/

Future Talent Learning, (October 2, 2020). Nutshell: how to escape the drama triangle. Changeboard, https://www.changeboard.com/article-details/17186/nutshell-how-to-escape-the-drama-triangle/

Gordon, T. (1994). Parent effectiveness training (p.e.t.): the proven program for raising responsible children. Peter H. Wyden, Inc.

Graham, L. (n.d). The triangle of victim, recuser, persecutor—what it is and how to get out. Linda Graham, MFT, https://lindagraham-mft.net/triangle-victim-rescuer-persecutor-get/

Hanaford, C. (2007). Smart moves: why learning is not all in your head. Great River Books.

Hudson, R, Riso, D. R. (1999). The wisdom of the enneagram: The complete guide to psychological and spiritual growth for the nine types. Bantam.

Johnston, K. (1984). Hemingway and freud: The tip of the iceberg. The Journal of Narrative Theory, pages 68-73.

Jones, D. (2020). The difference between triangles and triangulation: Family systems theory for church leaders. The Presbyterian Outlook, https://pres-outlook.org/2020/02/the-difference-between-triangles-and-triangulation-family-systems-theory-for-church-leaders/

NOTES

Kanyer, L. (2018). Collage saves. Kolaj Magazine, Issue #24, pages 20 - 24.

Kanyer, L. (2004). Twenty-five things to do when grandpa passes away, mom and dad get divorced or the dog dies. Chicago Review Press.

Karpman, S. (2020). A game of life: the definitive book on the drama triangle and compassion triangle by the originate and author, the new transactional analysis of intimacy, openness, and happiness. Drama Triangle Publications.

Kennedy. T. (n.d.). Why negative emotions aren't that bad (and how to handle them). Lifehack, https://www.lifehack. org/articles/communication/how-handle-negative-emotions.html

Knights, C. (2020). Personal conversation.

Lerner, H. (2017). Why won't you apologize?: healing big betrayals and everyday hurts. Gallery Books.

Levine, P. A. (2005). Healing trauma, a pioneering program for restoring the wisdom of your body. Sounds True.

Linehan, M M. (2015). DBT skills training manual. The Guilford Press.

Menakem, R. (2017). My grandmother's hands: radicalized trauma and the pathway to mending our hearts and bodies. Central Recovery Press.

Miller, G. (2010). How our brains make memories, surprising new research about the act of remembering may help people with post-traumatic stress disorder. Smithsonian Magazine. https://www.smithsonianmag.com/science-nature/how-our-brains-make-memories-14466850/

Naiman, L. (ND). https://www.creativityatwork.com/about/linda-naiman/

Nestor, J. (2020). Breathe: The new science of a lost art. Riverhead Books.

NICABM, National Institute for the Clinical Application of Behavioral Medicine. (2017). Infographic how trauma impacts four different types of memory. https://www.nicabm.com/trauma-how-trauma-can-impact-4-types-of-memory-infographic/

Oppong, T. (2022). Allan watts on the read secret of life, 'now' is the greatest time of all. The Medium Blog, https://medium.com/personal-growth/allan-watts-on-the-real-secret-of-life-f0649d7d29f9

Putnam, R. (2019). The symbolism of a triangle: what is the spiritual meaning?, Crystal Clear Intuition Blog, Retrieved from: https://crystalclearintuition.com/symbolism-of-a-triangle/

Rosenberg, J. (n.d.). Podcast, https://drjoanrosenberg.com/asking-for-help/

Royzman, E Rozin, P. (2001). Negativity bias, negativity dominance, and contagion. Personality and Social Psychology Review, 5(4), 296-320.

Schwartz, R. (2021). No bad parts: healing trauma and restoring wholeness with the internal family systems model. Sounds True.

Schwartz. R, (n.d.). https://ifs-institute.com/resources/articles/evolution-internal-family-systems-model-dr-richard-schwartz-ph-d. about 8cs

Sheppard, N. (2022, August). Personal conversation.

Tomlingson, I. (2010). Why all our emotions are important. Manchester Psychotherapy, https://manchesterpsychotherapy.co.uk/emotions/

ORDERING INFORMATION

Hardcopies: Books by Kanyer Publishing, including *Collage Care, Transforming Emotions and Life Experiences with Collage, Black Collagist: The Book* and *Collage Care: The Method,* are available on Amazon.

Ebooks: The books and other materials published by Kanyer Publishing can be found at www.KanyerArtCollection.com.

FORTHCOMING MATERIALS

For Professionals: *Collage Care, Transforming Emotions and Life Experiences with Collage,* has been used in numerous professional settings. It is our intention to develop additional materials especially geared for professionals. In the near future you will find resources for professionals at www.KanyerArtCollection.com.

Individual Exercise-Experiences: In the near future you will find all of the exercise-experiences that appear in this book, and more over time, available for purchase individually at a modest price. You will be able to locate individual exercise-experiences on a specific topic for your personal use or use as a professional and download it immediately. All the exercise-experiences will be available in printable formatted at www.KanyerArtCollection.com.

ACKNOWLEDGEMENTS

It is with great honor and sincere appreciation that I acknowledge the help of the following individuals.

The first person to see the power of this book was artist CP Harrison. I announced this project on social media and CP related to the theme. CP tested all 100 of the original exercise-experiences. He spent countless hours in his studio examining the truths you read within these pages.

My husband Doug Kanyer offered to edit this book. He knows my voice and overall intent better than anyone. He also funded these efforts, patiently listened to me, and provided rock-like encouragement. His generosity and handiwork made this book possible. It is very special for a husband and wife to work on a book project. We have been doing writing projects since 1994.

Thank you to JuSt Design, the designers of this book. To work face-to-face with the lead Nela Sheppard has been a dream come true. Her professionalism, enthusiasm, and attention to detail helped to support this book. To Jed Gibbs and Dawn Kugler, the husband-and-wife team who laid this book out and proofread it, you two are gifts!

Thank you Wyatt Kanyer, my son, who is a social worker and a yogi. At a critical point he offered key insight and information that shaped the content. His knowledge on the models of Somatic Experiencing and Internal Family Systems was necessary. His words helped this project to turn a vital corner.

Kirsten Dahlhauser, my daughter, who is a nutritionist and a yogi, I thank you for offering quintessential information on the power of acceptance and non-attachment as a way to decrease suffering.

Thank you to Sarah Best and Celia Crane, both of whom worked hard on *Collage Care: Transforming Emotions and Life Exercises with Collage*, and now this book. They offered hours of strong critique, profound insight, and support. Not to mention keen editing insight.

Miranda Millward and Sonia Boué read a good part of the content in the early stages and looked over all the drafts. They offered eagle-eye insight from both personal and professional experience. They especially helped to guide the layout to make this material helpful for neuro-divergent people.

When *Collage Care, Transforming Emotions and Life Experiences with Collage* came out I had the privilege of meeting Les Jones. Les is the publisher of Contemporary Collage Magazine. He kindly offered to feature some of the Gems from the book in the magazine. Thank you Les for seeing the importance of this material and including it in your magazine each month.

When the book was nearly completed it became clear that some additional research was needed to confirm certain theoretical aspects. One way to accomplish this was by testing a newly added exercise. I am deeply grateful to Michelle L. Miller, Rosita Schandy, Donna Stiller, Kathy Why, Lori Stambler-Dunsmore and Daphna Epstein who generously offered hours of insight to evaluate the material. Their words and evaluation helped to provide deep structural shifts.

To the reviewers of this book, thank you. Christina McCarthy, who helped on my first book in 1995, stepped in at a critical point to help with this volume. Les Jones, Andrea Burgay, Jane Chipp, Emily Shoemaker, Hollie Chastain, Julie Liger-Belair, Juliette Pestel, Catherine Rogers, Meikel Church, Miranda Millward, Petra Zehner, Kim Hamburg, Scott Gordon, Millie Bartlett, Miss.Printed aka Angela Gibbons and Dr. Freya Gowrley, all read the book and offered support and encouragement.

ABOUT THE AUTHOR

Laurie Kanyer, MA

Laurie Kanyer, MA is an author, publisher, counselor, artist and organizational consultant. She has worked with individuals, families and organizations since 1983. Kanyer holds a Masters degree in Human Development focusing on Infant Mental Health, Childhood Grief and Loss and Organizational Development from Saint Mary's University of Minnesota.

She has recently published *Collage Care: Transforming Emotions and Life Experiences with Collage* (2021), and *Collage Care: The Method* (2023). Kanyer has used collage as a therapeutic tool with her clients and students for decades.

She founded Passport to Parenting in 1990, a program associated with Yakima Valley Memorial Hospital and was acknowledged by the United Nations for Inspiring Warmheartedness for this program. She founded Growing Capable Parents in 1999, a program focusing on the needs of pregnant and parenting women experiencing poverty.

She founded Yakima Light Project in 2007, the first non-profit gallery in the downtown core of Yakima Washington. At the time this was one of the most poverty-stricken areas in the State of Washington, with limited access to the visual arts. In 2015 she received the Washington Museum Association Award of Individual Excellence for this project.

She and her husband Doug have been art collectors since 1978. In 2016 the Kanyers dedicated their efforts to collage exclusively. They are one of very few private art collector in the world focusing solely on collage (see www.KanyerArtCollection.com). They met in college in 1977 and have been married since 1981. They have three grown children, two sons-in-law and and two grandchildren. They live in the high desert region of Central Washington State, USA.

Laurie Kanyer, *Abundance*, 2020, Analog Collage, Doug + Laurie Kanyer Art Collection

ISBN 9798379343347

Written by Laurie Kanyer, MA
Co-created by CP Harrison
Edited by Doug Kanyer
Design by JuSt Design
Content curated by Sarah Best and Celia Crane
Cover art by Laurie Kanyer

Title: *Collage Care: The Method*

Subjects: Psychology, Art, Collage, Personal Transformation, Relationships, Self-Help, Art History

Website: KanyerArtCollection.com
Instagram: @KanyerArtCollection

Disclaimer: This publication is meant to be a source of valuable information for the reader. While using these ideas may help you on your wellness journey, this is not designed to replace mental health care or any form of health care treatment. This is a collection of ways that describe how collage helps people, but it is not art therapy nor is it designed to replace getting professional mental health care. It can, however, complement therapy and deepen conversations with people and professionals. It can provide insight while nurturing higher self-esteem and self-appreciation. We further disclaim any liability to any party for any perceived loss, damage or disruption caused by errors or omissions, whether such errors or omissions result from negligence, accident or any other cause. Again, this book is not meant as a substitute for direct expert assistance. If such level of assistance is required, the services of a competent professional should be sought. The author has checked with sources believed to be reliable in her efforts to provide information that is complete and generally in accord with the standards that are accepted at the time of publication. However, in view of the possibility of human error or changes in the care of emotional well-being, the author, nor the editor and the publisher, nor any party who had been involved in the preparation or publication of this work warrants that the information contained herein is in every respect accurate or complete, and they are not responsible for any error or omission or the result obtained from the use of this book. Readers are encouraged to confirm the information contained in this book with other sources.

Made in the USA
Middletown, DE
02 November 2023

41830024R00150